# My Lord,
# What a Morning

# MUSIC IN AMERICAN LIFE

*A list of books in the series
appears at the end of this book.*

# My Lord, What a Morning

AN AUTOBIOGRAPHY

## MARIAN ANDERSON

*Foreword by James Anderson DePreist*

UNIVERSITY OF ILLINOIS PRESS

*Urbana and Chicago*

Library of Congress Cataloging-in-Publication Data
Anderson, Marian, 1897–1993.
My Lord, what a morning : an autobiography / Marian Anderson ;
foreword by James Anderson DePreist.
p. cm. — (Music in American life)
Originally published: New York : Viking Press, 1956.
Includes index.
ISBN 0-252-07053-4 (pbk. : alk. paper)
1. Anderson, Marian, 1897–1993. 2. Contraltos—United States—
Biography. I. Title. II. Series.
ML420.A6A3      2002
782.1'092—dc21      2001040980
[B]

To My Mother

# Contents

*Illustrations follow page 150*

# Foreword

## James Anderson DePreist

Marian Anderson was my mother's sister, my grandmother's oldest daughter, and my aunt. Ours was a very close family in which faith played a major role. My grandmother, Anna D. Anderson, a member of the Tindley Temple Methodist Church, viewed with a certain bemused and puzzled good nature her daughters' becoming Baptists. By the time 762–64 South Martin Street had become the family home, the Union Baptist Church was diagonally across from us at the corner of Fitzwater and Martin Streets, close enough to fill our house each summer Sunday with the unforgettably touching strains of the congregation singing the familiar hymns and spirituals. Clearly, one did not have to be in the church to hear and feel its song. Aunt Marian's voice joined this song, and Union Baptist nurtured her glorious gift. But, undoubtedly, the strongest influence on my aunt was her mother. My grandmother's force of character was grounded in faith. Having been a teacher, she possessed a teacher's penchant for precise and elegant language. Hers was a decorous and quiet demeanor that conveyed immense compassion, humility, and authority. Propriety, modesty, and gratitude were her watchwords, and they became my aunt's as well. It is staggering to see how powerful apparent self-effacement can be when combined with commanding presence. Though she was diminutive and unassuming, I can remember no more towering moral force than my grandmother, seated.

When I think of those qualities most often associated with Marian Anderson, humility first comes to mind, humility anchored in faith and gratitude for her gifts. Arrogance was inconceivable. My aunt never felt that her successes were hers alone, rather they were primarily God's doing. "My part in it is very small indeed," she would say.

She was also ever mindful of the difficult life her mother had experienced in Philadelphia, and the letters between them show the depth of my aunt's concern for my grandmother's well-being. After she began touring more extensively, Aunt Marian would write to urge my grandmother not to try to shovel coal into the furnace, to make certain that she had enough warm blankets, and to be sure to get enough rest. Anna's letters to Marian tended to be positive and reassuring, allowing her daughter to concentrate on her performances. These touching letters always conveyed thanks for God's blessings and an acknowledgment of the fragility of good fortune. My grandmother had a saying, "Don't let it get good to you," which served as a reminder to avoid becoming accustomed to good fortune. Consequently, no successes were ever taken for granted.

My aunt's devotion to her mother manifested itself in countless ways, but two gestures capture for me the spirit of my aunt's love. My grandmother worked at the famous John Wanamaker store in Philadelphia, cleaning bathrooms among other menial jobs. This pained my aunt tremendously, so one can imagine the sheer joy of being able to call Anna's supervisor to tell her that Mrs. Anderson would not be coming to work on that or any other day. Despite having honors and extraordinary international fame, my aunt always considered this phone call one of the single most gratifying moments of her life. The second manifestation of my aunt's devotion was a joy to behold, a simple joy that fascinated me and remains vivid in my memory. Dr. Carpinelli, a podiatrist, came to Martin Street regularly to care for my grandmother's feet in the most gentle way one could imagine. Immaculately dressed and with a waxed moustache, he was a most dapper visitor. My grandmother would sit comfortably in her favorite chair in the living room, while Dr. Carpinelli anointed her feet with lotions and ointments that were both soothing and salubrious. He revered my aunt Marian and could not have held her mother's feet more gently had they been those of *his* mother. The comfort these visits brought to my grandmother was clear with every step she took. It was the kind of pampering she never dreamed possible, and, of course, she was so grateful to God and to "dear Marian."

The wonder of Marian Anderson was her remarkable ability to both draw and project strength from her humility and her faith. On stage she was the consummate professional: assured, charismatic, regal, undeniably a "star." No one ever forgot seeing and hearing Marian Anderson. Her ability to move her audiences was extraordinary.

Wherever I travel, someone recalling the unforgettable experience of attending their first Marian Anderson recital approaches me. The common thread in all of these recollections is the listener's personal experience of being moved by singing that seemed to come from *their* emotional center.

My aunt frequently appeared on radio's Bell Telephone Hour. When I was a young boy, the magic of radio only heightened the magic of this "Marian Anderson" the announcer kept mentioning. Marian Anderson was singing from New York on the radio and ten minutes after the program Aunt Marian would call to talk with my mother about the musical aspects of her performance and then chat with my grandmother and me for a bit. In my youth I never knew "Marian Anderson," only Aunt Marian, who cooked, cleaned, shopped for groceries, and doted on her mother—a very normal aunt who happened to travel a lot, singing. The "two Marians" took some understanding.

As her career began, she became the provider for the family. My father died in 1942, when I was six years old. My aunt Marian toured, and my mother maintained the household for her sister, Alyce, her mother, and me. My aunt Alyce was active in Democratic politics, was the first African American presidential elector, and served as executive secretary for the Marian Anderson Scholarship Fund. She not only processed the hundreds of applications that would come to the house each year but also supervised the auditions to determine the winner. Thus we each had our role in the family. My job was a simple one, namely, to do well in school and to become a lawyer. But, for some reason, the birthday gifts I received from my aunt were always study scores of Beethoven symphonies and recordings of orchestral masterpieces. She must have known something that I didn't. Today, each time I conduct one of these works I think of her and of the subliminal influence of these wonderful presents of music.

When my aunt Marian's home became Mill Plain, Connecticut, near Danbury, the family would leave the comfortable urban confines of Martin Street each summer for the gracious rural expanse of Marianna Farm. What an incredible treat! Here we saw Marian in the garden or riding her horse or shopping for groceries or swimming. Removed from her hectic concert schedule, she could truly relax for a bit. But music was never far away. Her accompanist, Franz Rupp, would come for a working visit, and together they would choose and prepare the programs for the coming season. To us, Franz was practically a member of the family.

By nature my aunt was exceedingly private, and the thought of an autobiography would never have originated with her; therefore, *My Lord, What a Morning* is often an objective narrative of personal experiences and should be read as a broad outline of an extraordinary woman who viewed herself simply as someone blessed with a voice and a burning desire to sing.

Practically every interviewer wanted her to describe the 1939 Constitution Hall/D.A.R. cause célèbre. After all, this was a singular moment in American history involving demonstrable discrimination by what had been, until then, a respected organization, the pointed resignation from that group by the wife of the president of the United States, and the government's offering of the Lincoln Memorial for the concert which was attended by more than seventy-five thousand people; slightly important, one might say.

But my aunt Marian never brought up the D.A.R. incident and never gloated over it. In her view, so much had already been said and written about the incident that further comment by her would be superfluous. She was pleased that things had changed. She saw herself neither as victim nor heroine, simply as an artist who happened to be crossing an intersection of United States history when racism collided with conscience.

When I made my debut with the National Symphony in 1969, it was the orchestra's final season in its home, Constitution Hall. I parked my car, walked in the stage door, and shortly thereafter began rehearsing. All was normal and uneventful, as it should have been. After rehearsal, from my dressing room

I called Aunt Marian to tell her how extraordinarily inconceivable it was that she had been denied the right to do what for me had been so very easy. "Well, dear heart, I'm just delighted that some things have changed," was her response. That day brought home to me, perhaps more vividly than for anyone else, the level of pervasive racial stupidity my aunt and every other African American had to deal with.

It must have required all of Marian Anderson's religious faith and secular stoicism to cope with the daily indignities encountered in the pursuit of her career in the United States during the '30s, '40s, and '50s. Limitations on freedom of choice were everywhere. Travel, accommodations, restaurants, and most other services were segregated; an informal network of private homes in African American communities made touring possible. When she could stay in hotels, she was often required to use the service elevator. To be of a mind to sing beautifully in the midst of such oppressive ugliness required a strength of uncommon resiliency.

The Negro spirituals that closed her recitals were not novelties but rather profound evocations of a people's past pains that, unfortunately, had persistent and contemporary echoes. As late as 1955, when at last Marian Anderson made her debut with the Metropolitan Opera, we learn from Rudolf Bing, the Met's general manager at the time, that his invitation to even so celebrated an artist was not necessarily greeted by some on his board with anything remotely resembling enthusiasm. To them, it was not Marian Anderson's voice but her race that was at issue.

At the other extreme of her experiences was celebrity and admiration that bordered on adoration. Toscanini praised her, universities honored her, presidents invited her to sing for their inaugurals, kings decorated her, *Time* put her on its cover, "Person to Person" interviewed her, and Ed Murrow made a documentary called "The Lady from Philadelphia." All these trappings of fame she handled with grace, modesty, and considerable gratitude.

Hers was such a fascinating life that even the most casual account of it conveys the outlines of a remarkable odyssey. For *My Lord, What a Morning,* my aunt relied heavily upon her exceptional memory of events and people. A subsequent biographer, Allan Keiler, researched her life with meticulous care and understanding. His definitive biography, *Marian Anderson, A Singer's Journey,* also serves as an annotating companion to *My Lord, What a Morning,* providing a treasure of detail, new information, and completion to the story of Marian Anderson.

Although my aunt's career was ending as mine was beginning, I did have the rare privilege of conducting for two of her farewell concerts, in Philadelphia and Chicago. She spent the last nine months of her life in our home in Portland, Oregon, where my wife, Ginette, had replicated her Connecticut bedroom. She was always surprised to observe that people still recognized her, and I know she would have been stunned to see her obituary on the front page of the *New York Times,* above the fold.

We had a memorial service for my aunt Marian in a packed Carnegie Hall, at which the only singing heard and the only spirit felt was that of Marian Anderson. As her recorded voice filled the hall, it all seemed so very natural, her voice in that hallowed place, and, as usual, her singing seemed to come from the emotional center of each of us.

My Lord,
What a Morning

# Philadelphia Childhood

LIFE with Mother and Father, while he lived, was a thing of great joy, as I remember it now. It is easy to look back self-indulgently, feeling pleasantly sorry for oneself and saying I didn't have this and I didn't have that. But that is only the grown woman regretting the hardships of a little girl who never thought they were hardships at all. Certainly there were a lot of things she did not have, but she never missed them, because she didn't really need them. She had the things that really mattered.

I remember John Anderson, my father, very clearly. We do not have any photograph of him, but I have a picture in my mind of a man, dark, handsome, tall, and neither too stout nor too thin. I cannot say how tall, but he was well over six feet and stood very erect. Mother is a tiny woman; when she and I stand side by side, her head does not reach quite up to my shoulder. I remember once when she was helping Father put on his tie and she was reaching up on tiptoe. He laughed heartily and told her to get a newspaper to stand on to make herself a little taller.

I don't know all the things my father did to earn a living. As a child I was not concerned. But I do know that for many years he was employed by day at the Reading Terminal Market, in the refrigerator room, and we looked forward to his homecoming every evening. At the end of the week—not every week, of course—he would bring home a long, golden bar of pound cake, and my appetite for all other food would vanish. I am told that he sold coal and ice, and he had other jobs. I know he worked hard and looked after his family well. During his life my mother stayed home to take care of us—my younger sisters, Alyce, Ethel, and me. Mother attended to everything in the home, and occasionally when the family needed something special, she did not hesitate to do some outside work, such as cleaning or laundering.

A Virginian by birth, Mother came to Philadelphia from Lynchburg, where she was a schoolteacher. She might have been able to teach eventually in Philadelphia, but while she was having her children and Father was alive she did not try. Her interest lay in her home and family.

Father's people lived in South Philadelphia. His mother was a large woman, used to being the boss of her own house and the people in it, as we learned later when we lived with her for a time.

I was born on Webster Street in South Philadelphia in a room my parents had rented when they were married. I was about two years old when we first moved to my grandmother's. She had a big house, and there was going to be more room for the three of us and the new baby. My earliest recollection is of the third-story room my parents occupied in that house. Somehow I was in the room—I had crawled under the bed when the doctor had arrived and perhaps had fallen asleep there. I heard a cry. It was the first cry of my new sister, Alyce. I peeked out. There was the doctor and there was his black bag. Long after I should have known better, I believed that Alyce had been fetched in that black bag.

As the family increased, so did the need for larger quarters, and we moved again. This time we rented a house all to ourselves on Colorado Street, not too far from Grandmother's. It was a small house, but big enough for our purposes. The living room contained a minimum of furniture. Behind it was a little dining room, and behind that a shed kitchen. Upstairs there was a front bedroom and a back bedroom, the latter for my sisters—Ethel came not too long after Alyce—and me. This house did not have a real bathroom, but Mother was undaunted. We were lathered and rinsed at least once a day, and on Saturday a huge wooden tub was set in the center of the kitchen floor. After sufficiently warm water was poured in, we were lifted inside. Mother would kneel and give us a good scrubbing with Ivory soap. Then we were put to bed.

Mother spent a lot of time in the kitchen. Because I was the eldest I was soon allowed to remain with her when my sisters were tucked into bed. Sometimes I would try to help with little things, though I don't know how much use I really was to Mother. I could carry dishes from the table to the dishpan, and with my very own carpet sweeper I made a big thing of cleaning up. Most often, though, I sat at the table or on a little bench, beating out some sort of rhythm with my hands and feet and la-la-la-ing a vocal accompaniment. It meant nothing to anyone else, I know.

Some people might say that these were the first signs of music in me. I would only say that I felt cozy and happy.

Apparently I was a happy child. I remember that I was once sitting in a little chair in the dining room and Mother came in from the kitchen to find out what I was laughing about. I had been looking at a border around the wall not far from the ceiling. It was a gaily decorated border, filled with flowers—I realized later that they were flowers. At that moment the wall was alive with the faces of people, small persons and adults. Some were leaning out of windows and chatting with neighbors, and some were waving at me. It seemed to me like a little town where a lot of people were having a grand time.

Mother was busy most of the time, and my sisters and I had to amuse ourselves. We had toys, mostly dolls, and we did the things and played the games common to all children. I remember that Mother seemed to me very smart; indeed, now I know that she was. My sisters and I, like other children, did things that were wrong, and Mother scolded us. She probably spared the rod when others might have used it, though I would not say that she was too lenient with us.

Our big outing each year was a trip to the Barnum and Bailey Circus. To us it was like a great journey away from home. We prepared for the day long in advance; it was the next biggest day to Christmas. Father would buy us something new to wear. A basket or two was prepared, and off we went, taking a trolley car for what seemed like an endless ride. We had wonderful lunches and afternoon snacks. Our eyes were big with delight, trying to follow all the acts going on at the same time under the big tent. Then

[6]

we trudged wearily to the trolley and took the long ride home. By then we were so tired that our parents must have had a bad time getting us ready for bed.

Easter was another big day. Father made it a point to provide us with new bonnets, and he would go to a shop and select them himself. When we were very young he would bring each of us one of the sailor hats then in fashion, with a gay ribbon trailing down the back. Later on he chose different bonnets for each of us, and he always insisted that they be trimmed with flowers. He would wait in the store while a brightly colored bloom was sewed to each hat. When he got home, carrying his gifts in a paper bag, he would take them out happily and present them to us, making sure that they fit.

Father took pride in his work at the Union Baptist Church. He was a special officer there, and among other things had charge of the ushers. He received no pay for his service; it was something that a person did out of love for his religion and duty to his church. He loved this job and never missed a Sunday at church.

Even before I was six I was taken along to church every Sunday, partly, I suppose, to alleviate my mother's burden of taking care of three children. I would take part in the Sunday school and then sit through the main service. After my sixth birthday I was enrolled in the junior choir of the church.

I looked forward to choir every Sunday. I got to know other little boys and girls. One of these girls, who lived across the street from our house, was Viola Johnson, whom I liked especially. We became playmates, and a year or two later she and I were entrusted with a duet.

[7]

The man who led the junior choir was Alexander Robinson. He was not a voice teacher or professional musician, but another person who, out of sheer love for the church and out of a spirit of service, gave his time freely to help others. It gave him pleasure to work with those young voices, and since he loved music and understood enough to communicate his feeling to us, he was able to do something with us. It was not long before the group was singing so well that it was invited to appear before the older children's Sunday school, which convened in the afternoon.

I remember the day when Mr. Robinson gave me a piece of music to take home, and another copy to Viola Johnson. It was a hymn, "Dear to the Heart of the Shepherd." Viola and I were to look it over, and then we would sing it together, she the upper and I the lower part. Mr. Robinson played the melody over for us, and after I had heard it enough I could remember it. Viola and I rehearsed it carefully and seriously. Then came the Sunday morning when we sang it in church—my first public appearance.

Mother was not there. It was not such a great event, and in any case she had my sisters to look after at home. On the way home from church, Father stopped at Grandmother's house, which was on the direct route from the church to our house, and he chatted for a while. By the time we got home Mr. Robinson had been there and gone. He had left word with Mother that he would like Viola and me to be in church earlier the next Sunday because he wanted us to rehearse the duet again, for the main service this time. And I remember that Father, in his pride, declared firmly, "I'm not going to have them singing my child to death."

That made me feel terribly important for a moment. If

Father had asked me and I had stopped to think about it, I would have said that I liked singing. I liked to hear singing. My parents did not consider themselves singers, but when they sang it pleased me. I remember Father's singing while he dressed, bits of "Asleep in the Deep," never finishing it. I don't recall feeling that there was anything special about his voice, but maybe there was and I was too young to know. Mother liked to sing at home, and as a youngster she had sung in church choirs. On rainy evenings, when we could not go out to sit on the steps and visit with our neighbors, Mother and my sisters and I might sing for our own amusement—old American songs, hymns, and spirituals.

Mother saw to it that we were in earnest about our schooling. She has always had a way of saying things that I feel are things to live by. About school tasks at home, she said, "If it takes you half an hour to do your lessons and it takes someone else fifteen minutes, take the half-hour and do them right." It took me some time to realize the value of this advice and what it implied. If we can't do a thing as quickly as someone else, then take the necessary time and do a good job.

I could have used Mother's good advice often, particularly once in grammar school when I was called on by the teacher to give a summary of a book I was supposed to have read. I had not taken the time to read the book at all thoroughly. I rattled off a story out of my head around the few facts I had gathered in my very quick reading. And to this day I can feel some of the embarrassment of that moment.

Every day when children sang in an adjoining room

—it was where classes went to sing—I did not hear a word my teacher spoke. I was as completely in that other room as one could be while one's body was elsewhere. When the day came for our class to go there for singing, I was the happiest child in the school. I knew every song— at least I thought I did. I remember that when my favorite song was passed out to the children I just put back my head and sang as loudly as I could. The teacher came down the aisle and tapped me on the shoulder.

"Marian, what are you singing?" she asked.

"Sleep, Polly, sleep," I told her proudly.

"Look at the words," she said.

I looked. They were "Peacefully sleep." Through the wall they had sounded like "Sleep, Polly, sleep."

When I was about eight years old Father got us a piano. He bought it from his brother, who had had it in his home, where no one used it. When it arrived at our house what excitement and joy! We ran our fingers over it, listening delightedly to the notes of the scale. Father, I remember, permitted me to sit on his knee. I tried playing a scale with five fingers, slipping the thumb under the hand to get all eight notes without a break, the way I had seen people play in school and church. When Father put his hand on the piano, I tried to guide his fingers to play a scale. Because he was understanding, he hit two notes with one finger, and his scale did not come out as well as mine.

I did not have music lessons; there was not enough money for a teacher. However, we did acquire from some-where a card, marked with the notes, that one could set up directly back of the keys. With the help of this, we learned some simple melodies. But it did not occur to me that I might be able to learn to play the piano properly. I was walking along the street one day, carrying a basket of laundry that I was delivering for my mother, when I heard the sound of a piano. I set down my basket, went up the steps, and looked into the window. I knew it was wrong to peep, but I could not resist the temptation. I saw a woman seated at a piano, playing ever so beautifully. Her skin was dark, like mine. I realized that if she could, I could.

As Mother has said so often, "Remember, wherever you are and whatever you do, someone always sees you." I remembered that woman, who never knew the effect she had on me, when I tried years later to study the piano. I loved music, but I had been taking it for granted that it must be for others.

I was too young to concentrate on any one phase of music. Suddenly I discovered the violin. I had heard someone play it, I no longer remember who—probably it was in church—and I thought it would be a fine thing to play that instrument.

At this time I was beginning to earn some money. My first job was scrubbing the steps of our neighbors' houses. If you scrubbed a whole set of steps you could earn as much as five cents. I worked hard at it, making sure the steps I scrubbed were cleaner than the steps the other kids were scrubbing. At first I used the pennies for candy when we were allowed to have it, and for tiny contributions in Sunday school. Then I began to save. I also ran errands. We had a lot of company at our house, and sometimes a visitor gave me a nickel or a dime. After a while I had four dollars. It was time to buy a violin.

I had seen one hanging in the window of a pawnshop, but was not allowed to go in. An older cousin was sent along with me to help with the purchase. The pawnbroker had a violin for three dollars and ninety-eight cents. I remember asking him several times whether it was a real good one, and he assured me that it was just short of being a Stradivarius.

We carried the violin home proudly. Of course there was still no money for a teacher. A friend of the family taught me how to tune it and I tried going up and down the scale, not knowing where to shift from one string to another. The poor instrument got extraordinary treatment. First one string gave out, then another, and then the bridge fell down. A grown-up who knew a little about it straightened the bridge and fixed new strings. But the strings continued to give out, one after another, and over and over again, and the violin was finally a wreck. Thus ended the career of another would-be violinist.

I continued to scrub steps, run errands, and save small sums. Then, for the first time, I went to a store—Blum Brothers in Philadelphia—and bought a dress. It was a blue-striped affair with a long waist, and a little black trim around the hipline and the short sleeves. I picked it out myself; that made it important. It cost forty-nine cents, and when a dress like it was advertised in the Philadelphia *Inquirer* by one of the larger stores at much more money, I felt like a shrewd shopper. No one can know the joy I derived from that forty-nine-cent dress.

Mother was also teaching us to sew. As children we were given scraps of material, and it was an accomplishment to make a little underskirt, dress, or hat for the doll. Later, when I had sewing classes in school, I was commended by the teacher for the neatness of my work. The big thrill came when I finally made something for myself. I remember that Mother bought a piece of white and orchid checked material for me. I bought a pattern for fifteen cents, and Mother showed me how to use it. When the dress was finished, it needed no alterations. And it was a proud day when I wore that dress.

All this time I kept on singing in the junior choir at church, mostly alto. The music we had to sing was not very high, and I could just as well have sung the soprano part, but there were always more sopranos than altos, and I thought I would like to be where I was needed most. As time went on Mr. Robinson gave me a little more to do. After the duet with Viola, I took part in a quartet of little girls, singing the lowest part.

My aunt—my father's sister—was active in the Union Baptist Church and sang in the senior choir. Several times we did duets together, she taking the soprano and I the alto part. I remember that one of our numbers was "Sing me to sleep, the shadows fall."

Being an energetic woman, my aunt found time to interest herself in the music of other churches. Among the people she knew was a Mr. Newby, who was starting as a preacher in a storefront church. His hope was that eventually his congregation might become large enough to warrant his having a real church. My aunt, realizing how he was struggling, tried to help him and arranged a concert for the building fund. She told me that I was to sing in it. I agreed, and thought no more of it.

One day when I was on my way to the grocery to buy

something for my mother, my eyes caught sight of a small handbill lying on the street. Even from a distance it looked vaguely familiar. I picked it up, and there in a corner was my picture with my name under it. "Come and hear the baby contralto, ten years old," it said. I was actually eight. What excitement! Clutching the paper in my hand, I hurried to the grocer's. When I got home I discovered that I had bought potatoes instead of the bread Mother had sent me for. Before I could explain what had possessed me, Mother had turned me around and hurried me back to the store. I trotted away again, still holding fast to the handbill that proclaimed my fame. I have a far more vivid memory of the handbill than of the actual singing at the concert.

There were sad things to come the year that I was ten. Father received an accidental blow on the head while at work and fell gravely ill. The doctor discovered later that he had a tumor. As Christmas approached he lay helpless in his bed.

A woman who lived in our neighborhood met me on the street a few days before Christmas and asked me what I wanted to find under the tree. She was married, had no children, and was very well off. Perhaps I hoped she could help with our Christmas, although I had not thought much about the fact that Father's illness would affect our celebration of the holiday. In any event, I told her what I wanted from Santa Claus and she replied, "Well, you're not going to get it. I'm ashamed of you, a girl as old as you who doesn't know there is no Santa Claus." I was old enough to know, of course, but I had been told at home that there was a Santa Claus and that was it for me. My eyes filled with tears. I could not speak about it to Mother. We did get some gifts at Christmas time, but they were things that Mother knew we needed, and the woman's thoughtlessness clung to me and spoiled that Christmas.

And then, a short time later, Father died in our home on Colorado Street. My sisters and I did not put it into so many words that we were orphans. But we knew that tragedy had moved into our home, and we knew, too, that our lives would change.

# CHAPTER 2

# Life at Grandmother's

AFTER the funeral my aunt gathered us up and took us to live again with our grandparents on Fitzwater Street. Grandmother was an impressive woman, tall, rather stout, and good-looking. She liked to remind people that she was part Indian. Grandpa was a quiet man; whether he was so by nature or whether through the years he had found it necessary to adopt this attitude to maintain peace and harmony in his home I do not know. True enough, he was dominated, though he was not weak. His endurance had a breaking-point, and Grandma knew that borderline better than anyone else and had some respect for it.

This handsome, fine-featured man of medium build and height was dearly beloved. He worked every day, and Grandmother always had some extra change in her pocket. Grandfather's religion was of tremendous importance to him. He was not a member of the Baptist Church. In his religion he observed Saturday as his Sabbath, spent the whole day at the Temple, and referred to himself as a Black Jew. The words "Passover" and "unleavened bread" I heard first from his lips.

Life was different at Grandmother's. My aunt ran the house, and Mother contributed our share by working. Grandmother was home all day and found lots to do. What she said was law. Everyone knew she was the boss, and if she wanted any of us at any time we came flying.

I remember her with her sewing basket always at her side. It was a daily ritual, the bringing of the basket downstairs each morning, where it remained within easy reach all day, whether she used it or not. In the evening one of us carried it back to her room.

There was an old-fashioned organ in Grandmother's parlor, and I remember that she occasionally played it, her body swaying to the rhythmic pressure of her feet on the pedals. We would sit and listen quietly, knowing better than to disturb her.

Grandmother loved children and always had scads of them living in her house. There were five of us Anderson girls, including our cousins, Queenie and Grace. Then there were two, sometimes as many as three, other children in the house at one time or another. Their mothers had to work, and Grandmother was paid a little something for taking care of them. She enjoyed having them and gave them her love. I remember that the mother of one child was able to come and visit her only once a week. How sorry we felt that she could not have her mother all the time!

The house had three stories, and although it was shallow and a little too small for us we all had comfortable places to sleep. It was not long, however, before we moved into a much larger house on Christian Street, where the living room was twice the size of the one in the old house. Here we spread out considerably. There was always a lot of activity, for Grandmother saw to it that we each had our little jobs to do and that life was not all play. It may sound like a crowded, noisy place, with all the children around, and there may have been times when we were too much for Grandmother, but generally she knew how to keep us under control. And there were useful things for us to learn, living all together. For one thing, we learned how to share a home with others, how to understand their ways and respect their rights and privileges.

When it came to my singing in church, Grandmother was sympathetic. As far as I know she had always attended Union Baptist Church and in the days when I had gone with Father she was usually there by the time we arrived. In those days I had been allowed to sit with her while he carried out his duties as special officer.

Mother worked hard to support us—how hard we did not know then and can scarcely realize today. She went out to work by the day and occasionally she took in laundry. Whatever Mother did, she did conscientiously and well.

My sister Alyce and I would sometimes deliver the laundry. We took the trolley car to the home of a lady who lived near the University of Pennsylvania. I remember that she had an old-fashioned clothesrack with a long mirror in the entrance hall, and one day I noticed four different hats on it, each one more elegant than the next. "If I could only have one hat like that someday, I'd be just delighted," I thought.

One delivery I have never forgotten. We were in need of money, and Mother had hurried through this batch of laundry so that it could be delivered and we could be paid before the week end. I took the bundle of clothes to a small apartment in a private house, entered, and called out. No one answered. I called out again and again; then I went into the next room, part of which was cut off by a screen. I peeped around the screen and caught a glimpse of the young woman whose laundry I was delivering. She was sitting as quietly as a mouse, a book in her hands. I suspect she knew who was calling, and I can only guess that she did not answer because she did not have the money to pay. I could not bring myself to let her know that I knew she was there. I left the laundry and went home without the money. Mother did not scold me; somehow she managed that week end.

Mother never complained then or at any other time that things were too hard. She did not grumble that the weather was too hot or too cold for her, that it was wearying when a day's work was done to wait at corners for streetcars. I am sure that she labored to the limits of her capacities—and beyond.

At the end of the day's work she would collect her pay, stop at the corner store, pick up some groceries, and come home. Then she would proceed to cook and serve our dinner. Mother was meticulous about taking care of her own children.

In the mornings she might have to go off before we had our breakfasts, and Grandmother took care of us. Grandma was a firm believer in hot cereals; she insisted that they built strong bones. She was especially fond of oatmeal. One of the little boys she took care of could not bear oatmeal, but Grandma stood over him and made sure he ate his portion. He was no more than eight, and the business of the oatmeal became a trial to him. I remember once that he took a large mouthful, and his eyes seemed to get larger and larger by the second. Finally he began to cry. "When I get to be a man," he blubbered, "I won't make my children eat oatmeal if they don't want to."

Mother had a special set of canisters for us. They contained tea, coffee, sugar, flour, and cookies. These supplies were not exclusively for us; they were available for anyone in the household who might need them, but the important thing was that they were the only supplies we could help ourselves to freely. Mother did not want us going into Grandmother's or my aunt's things.

Mother was scrupulous about shouldering her share of the household's burdens. She made regular payments toward the rent and upkeep of the house. On Sundays or holidays, when she was home, she often cooked for everybody. What it cost her to work as she did and look after her children I did not find out until later. She had been a qualified schoolteacher in Virginia, but since it would have taken too long to obtain a teaching license in Philadelphia, she worked at whatever legitimate job she could find. She had opportunities to remarry, but she chose the way that seemed right to her. Distant relatives and neighbors would say to her, "Marian is a big girl now, let her go out and work." I was a big girl; people thought I was sixteen before I was even fourteen. There were others who told her to place all three of us in a home; she was still young and had a right to a life of her own. Mother listened to all the advice, smiled quietly, and went her own way.

Even if I had been old enough to work, I know now,

Mother would have discouraged it. She believed in education. When I completed grammar school I went on to high school. The first I attended was William Penn High School, where I started with the idea of taking a commercial course. I knew deep in my heart by this time that what I wanted most was to study music, but I also knew that I had to prepare myself to get a job as soon as possible—both to help Mother and to have some money for music studies. A friend of the family had told us that if I learned to type and take dictation her husband would place me in a job.

Unhappily, I did not get along too well in the shorthand classes and I found myself in deeper waters with the bookkeeping course. My heart was not in these studies, and I was happiest when we had our music period once a week. Our music teacher was a fine person who saw to it that people with any aptitude got special opportunities. As a result, I not only sang in the school chorus but also had occasional small solos.

I once sang some solos at an assembly attended by visitors. Afterward I was summoned to the principal's office. I have forgotten the principal's name, but I remember the name of the stranger in the office, Dr. Rohrer, who had gone to the principal's office to speak of me. When I entered the room he turned to the principal and said, "I don't understand why this girl is taking shorthand and typewriting. She should have a straight college preparatory course and do as much as possible in music."

I transferred to South Philadelphia High School. The principal there was Dr. Lucy Wilson, who took a personal interest in me. It was her custom to arrange interesting

assemblies, inviting prominent people to talk to or perform for the students, and she also had members of the
student body appear on the platform to play and sing. I
remember once that I sang when there was a young woman
visitor named Lisa Roma. She was a friend of Dr. Wilson's
and proved very helpful, as I shall relate later.

We had another house by this time, and the piano was
standard equipment. I enjoyed sitting at it and trying out
new tunes. Even when I was much smaller, I had tried
picking out tunes by ear without knowing what fingers to
use for what note and without being able to read music at
all. I would hear a song, learn it by singing it repeatedly,
and then try to play the melody on the piano. Somehow we
came into possession of one of those cards you prop up behind the keys, and I learned to associate a C on a sheet of
music with the C on the piano. This helped immeasurably,
and I could do things at the piano much more easily.

I liked the key of E flat for bright songs, and I was attracted to the key of D flat because it was so flattering to
a low voice like mine. D flat made me think of velvet. I
would take my courage in my hands and try to play in
those keys, regardless of the roadblocks of the flats, but
it was a mad scramble to land on the proper notes at the
right time.

When I began to make my first appearances in public
I had to play my own accompaniments, which had to be
simple. As soon as I could afford it I tried taking piano
lessons. One of my teachers was an active performer, and
he was often away from home. Moreover, I did not always
have the money for lessons. As a result, they were not
regular, but some progress was made. After hearing me

play, Franz Rupp, my present accompanist, remarked teasingly, "When it doesn't go any more as now, then you'll play and I'll sing."

The extent of my preoccupation with music in school or at home was not great during this period. On Sundays we usually had company in to dinner, and my aunt liked to set a good table. As Grandmother used to say, there was no money in the Anderson family because we ate all the profit. I enjoyed these Sunday afternoons, for often we sat around and sang.

The church played a very important part in my life, socially as well as musically. I was fond of the spelling bees; I remember winning several first prizes, one of which was a sea shell I still own. As I grew older I became a member of the B. Y. P. U. (Baptist Young People's Union). Now I could go to the church unaccompanied by an adult and could join the boys and girls of my age in the Union's activities. We had all sorts of competitions, one of which was speechmaking. I remember delivering an address on the word "Bible," which seemed to me then an impressive effort; my speech even had a Latin title. We were all young and enthusiastic, and we tried to outdo one another. Many worth-while things came out of these activities.

As I moved into my teens, singing at the church took on more importance. When I was thirteen I was invited to join the adult choir. I accepted gladly, and I continued my work with the junior choir. In fact, I sang with both groups until I was past twenty.

Singing was a serious business with me, and I had a deep sense of responsibility about my work with the choirs. Our church was large. The senior choir sang in the upper balcony at one end, and our minister was at the other end. Without knowing anything about the tricks of the trade, I sang naturally, free as a bird, with a voice of considerable size and wide range. There was no difficulty in filling the church auditorium. In my youthful exuberance I let myself go, and on several occasions it was suggested gently that my voice was a little too prominent.

I had no thought about technique or style. It may seem boastful to say so, but at that moment I did not need them. I had no difficulty with any music set before me, for I could sing any note in any of the registers. Usually I sang the alto part, but I could fill in for the soprano or tenor. If necessary, I also filled in for the baritone or bass, though in that case I would sing an octave higher. When the choir sang an anthem, if one of the soloists was absent I was given the nod. The minister would always recognize my voice and make some comment about it. That was my reward.

I became convinced that my presence in the senior and junior choirs was not only a duty but a necessity for the church and me, and I never missed a Sunday. The congregation made me feel that I was an indispensable part of what went on there. It was a stimulating experience.

*CHAPTER 3*

# Branching Out

IF IT had not been singing, it might have been medicine. At least that's what I dreamed about when I was a youngster and what I came back to whenever there were difficult and disappointing moments in connection with singing. In my doll days I kept imagining that the dolls were ill or wounded and needed to be ministered to, and thinking just how I would do this. When childhood friends were hurt—and often when they were not hurt—I found excuses to do some bandaging. I wanted to be a surgeon, to do something grand like correcting deformities.

Singing in the presence of other people seemed to me a normal activity all through the years of growing up. I loved to sing. I liked to have other people listen and was likewise glad to hear others perform. I think I am honest in saying that there was no desire to be a show-off.

I became accustomed early to appearing on a platform because there were all sorts of occasions to do so in school and church. I remember one time when I was actually part of a show at the Philadelphia Academy of Music.

Some of my people arranged a big affair with specialty acts, comedy skits, and singing and dancing numbers for which special music was written. There must have been about forty of us taking part. My assignment was to go on alone and sing a song at certain intervals in the entertainment, and these appearances served as introductions to what was to follow. Although my acting was confined to a few gestures here and there, I was immeasurably happy about the whole venture.

A little later there was a show with and for the Camp Fire Girls, of which I was a member. This time I was in the chorus line. We had a coach who told us how to move about and how to appear natural and at ease. Now singing was one thing, but dancing! Oh, the rare challenge of it. At one time I thought I would like to learn ballet dancing, and night after night I dreamed of floating away, poised on a downy cloud for support. I managed to obtain a pair of ballet slippers. They had no padding in the toes, but that did not disturb me. I would develop the muscles in my toes and manage without padding, I thought. Since I had no room with a *barre,* the back of a chair had to suffice for support. I remember how I would hurry home from school and get into the soft black shoes. After a time I could actually stand on my toes for a very short while, but soon enough it became clear to me that I was not the type for ballet. It is a wonder, however, that I did not tumble on my face and smash my teeth.

If I could not float away on my toes, as I had imagined myself doing, the chorus line of the Camp Fire Girls was the next best thing. The affair, everyone said, was a success. Again I realized that I liked being on the stage, but

I had no illusions that I was cut out to be an actress. When I was in high school I went occasionally to see a company of Negro actors and actresses, excellent by any standard, and I knew that, if I ever tried, this was how I would want acting to be, natural and convincing. When I finally reached the Metropolitan Opera and had the opportunity to act I gave a thought to those memories.

But the singing counted most in those days of girlhood. The conductor of the senior choir did not worry about absentees, even when they were his soloists. He had discovered that I liked to take home the music and that I would learn all the solo parts. Whenever anyone was away, I was ready to fill in. Some soloists seemed to be absent quite often, but not Mrs. Buford, the solo contralto. She was there every Sunday—or so it seemed to me.

The Union Baptist Church was well known and popular. People from out of town felt that they had to visit this church if they were in Philadelphia, for they would be asked about it when they got home. Our minister and our choir leader were proud of the church's reputation, and they liked to do things that were a bit unusual. This was certainly true for the music of the church.

One of the choir's show pieces was "Inflammatus," which had a series of high C's for the soprano soloist. Mr. Williams, the choir leader, liked to spring pieces on us without advance warning. One Sunday morning he motioned to me to take the seat of the absent first soprano. He handed out "Inflammatus," and we began to sing. The high C's did not daunt me at all. I was happy to have a chance to sing them, and they came out with no effort. They may not have been perfect, but they certainly were uninhibited. Later on, when I began formal training of my voice, I lost that early freedom for a while and approached those high C's with trepidation. But at thirteen, fourteen, or fifteen I did not stop to think. The music just poured forth.

The visitors who came to the Union Baptist Church were often responsible for invitations to the choir to sing elsewhere. When the distance was too great and traveling expenses were too steep for the whole choir to go, a double quartet, a quartet, or a duet might be sent. Sometimes it happened that one individual represented the church. I was frequently a member of the group that went, and eventually I was sent out as representative alone.

My first visit to New York was with a group from our senior choir. We sang at the Abyssinian Baptist Church; I believe it is the largest church in Harlem. The minister of the church is now Congressman Adam Clayton Powell, and its minister then was his father, who was a friend of our Reverend Parks.

Music meant a great deal to Reverend Parks. He saw to it that we had a big concert at the Union Baptist Church once a year, and this event drew people from all parts of the city, church people and music-lovers alike. The person most often engaged for the gala concert was Roland Hayes, the distinguished tenor, who became my inspiration. Reverend Parks had known Mr. Hayes's mother, something of her life, and also of the ambitions, struggles, and achievements of her son. All this he admired, and because among us Roland Hayes represented the best in his field Reverend Parks engaged him year after year. His appearance was the highlight of the Philadelphia concert season. Mr. Hayes sang old Italian airs, German Lieder, and French songs exquisitely. Even people with little understanding of music knew it was beautiful singing, and they were proud that Mr. Hayes was one of their own and world-famous. But after a time a few grumbled that they did not understand what he was singing. And there were some who said, "If our Marian were on the program, we would understand what *she* was singing about." So eventually I was permitted to appear on his program and sing two or three numbers.

Mr. Hayes was good enough to take an interest in me. He came to visit Grandmother, and he told her that I should start professional studies. He recommended his teacher, Mr. Arthur J. Hubbard of Boston, saying that he had spoken to Mr. Hubbard about me and that Mr. Hubbard was willing to take me as a pupil. Grandmother told Mr. Hayes that we had no money to pay for lessons, and Mr. Hayes replied that Mr. Hubbard was willing to let me earn my way by working in his home. Grandmother was not impressed. So far as she was concerned, I could sing and what was the need of lessons? There were discussions pro and con. Mother would not oppose Grandmother, and Grandmother decided that a young girl should not be sent away from home. To Boston I did not go.

Then the congregation, led by Reverend Parks, decided to do something for me. The pastor arranged to take up a collection at a service. I remember his words: "We want to do something for our Marian." The regular collection had been taken that Sunday morning, and this was an extra one. The people came up and donated what they could. The total collected, I remember so clearly, was seventeen dollars and two cents. The money was turned over to

Mother, and she was told that it was for anything I needed.

What I needed was shoes. I was hard on them. And what I wanted most for school was a pair of Buster Brown high shoes that had round, stubby toes. I also needed a dress for special occasions. When Mother and I went downtown we discovered that the shoes were more expensive than we had imagined. We must have given the salesman a bad time, for we kept trying on all sorts of shoes; but I would not take any substitute, and we left without new shoes. For the dress, Mother and I decided to go to Wanamaker's, where I saw a dress I liked. It was white silk, trimmed with rows of cording around the neck, sleeves, and hem. We were told the price, and were appalled to hear that it cost fourteen ninety-eight. We should have known that Wanamaker's would be more expensive than some other smaller stores, but we thought it was the best store, and, as Mother always said, the best is cheapest in the long run. I was frightfully naïve, and I remember saying to Mother that Mr. Wanamaker had so many dresses, and if he knew how badly I needed one he would arrange it so that we could get this one cheaper. Mother just looked at me and smiled. We left without the dress.

We decided to make a dress ourselves, using part of the collection money for materials. We bought some satin and a pattern, and Mother supervised the cutting-out. I was allowed to use her Singer sewing machine. When the sewing was finished I trimmed the dress around the square neck and the sleeves and just above the four-inch hem with a five-and-ten-cent store "gold" braid decorated with miniature blooms and leaves. This was my evening dress for quite some time, and in some ways it made me happier than the one that would have cost fourteen ninety-eight. When people complimented me on it I felt pretty good.

That dress cost less than ten dollars. What we did with the rest of the collection money I do not remember, but there were little things I needed, and I could get them. I cannot put into words how grateful I felt to those good people at the church.

I was fortunate to have so many opportunities to sing in public, and when I began to cultivate my voice seriously these appearances proved to be a useful backlog of experience. Having learned to accompany myself at the piano in a few songs, I dared to appear on my own. Some event was always taking place in one church or another, and I was often invited to sing. I would come home from school, try to scramble through my lessons and do whatever chores I was expected to attend to, and then I would run out to fill my engagements. With my aunt I would hurry from the Y. M. C. A. to the Y. W. C. A. to a Methodist or Baptist or Episcopal church. I might appear at three different places in an evening, singing the same songs and accompanying myself.

Did I receive payment? Sometimes yes and sometimes no. It did not matter; it was a pleasure to sing. If I appeared at a social arranged by some ladies' auxiliary and it was well attended, the ladies might be able to spare a dollar and would give it to me gladly. Once in a while I was paid as much as a dollar and a half or two dollars. I had no sense of being a wage-earner, but every little bit helped to ease Mother's burden a trifle.

The singing I did outside drew even more attention to

me in church. Visitors who had heard me elsewhere might send up a note to the minister or choirmaster asking for a solo by Marian Anderson, and often these requests were granted. My voice at that time never wearied. I sang the contralto aria in *The Messiah*, "He shall feed His flock like a shepherd," and the one for soprano, "Come unto Him, all ye that labor," tossing off trills and other gymnastics without the slightest vocal difficulties.

The more I did in church the more call there was for me to sing in other places. From the socials I went on, while still in high school, to bigger events. I was paid a little more for such appearances, and soon I was emboldened to establish a minimum of five dollars for an appearance. I remember that once after a service at our church some visitors approached me and asked me to come and sing at an affair they were running. One of the women said to me, perhaps a little belligerently and unbelievingly, "Somebody told me you were charging five dollars. Is that true?"

I must say that my resolution wavered, but I felt I had to go through with it and I said firmly, "Yes."

The woman shook her head as if to say, What is this world coming to? After consultation with her friends, she said, "Well, all right."

What did I do with the fee? I gave each of my sisters a dollar, two to Mother, and one I kept. In those days I was not dressed so grandly that I needed taxis to deliver me to the places where I sang. A trolley car sufficed, and the fare was my only expenditure. Mother insisted that the carfare must come out of the money I had turned over to her. And when my fees inched up beyond the five-dollar minimum she argued that I was entitled to keep a larger share for myself.

The opportunity to belong to the Philadelphia Choral Society came along and provided me with another musical outlet. The people in this Negro group sang for the love of it, as I did. With its excellent director, Alfred Hill, the society prepared major works for presentation to its large following. I remember that several years later, when I went to my second voice teacher, the members of this group raised money to help pay for my lessons.

One of the officers of the society, a Mr. Young, called on my family one day, and during the conversation he turned to Mother and told her with the air of a prophet, "Mrs. Anderson, I am going to tell you something. You mark my words, one of these days this child is going to earn fifty dollars a night. Did you hear me?" Here his voice deepened and he spoke more slowly and gravely. "I said fifty dollars a night. Now you mark my words."

We marked his words. It was several years before his prophecy came true, and I don't remember the exact occasion when it happened, but our family remembered Mr. Young's prediction, and we had a little private celebration to signalize the event. And years later, when Mr. Young's vision became a reality multiplied many times, my family talked about him and his faith in my future with affection and an appreciation of what it had meant to us at the time.

Looking back, I have no sense of having jumped by great leaps from one bracket to the next. It seemed like a gradual development. There were disillusionments along the way. Once, after singing for a hospital and receiving

my five-dollar fee (this time it was a gold piece), I had a
visit from a man who lived in our part of town. He had
heard me and had come to promise us glorious things—
it was my first encounter with a promoter. He had grand
plans for me: he would arrange a special concert for which
he would bring together all kinds of talent, and I would
sing regularly under his guidance. He did arrange an affair,
at which I wore for the first time the satin dress Mother
and I had made. He paid me seven dollars and fifty cents.
When he promised fifteen dollars for the next program
he proposed to put on, I could feel my head swimming at
the prospect of a real fee. I appeared on that program, and
he did not pay me at all. I could not bring myself to hound
him for the money, but I kept waiting for him to make
payment. Years passed before I could screw up enough
courage to go after him. It was much too late.

Thanks to the kindness of friends, I began to get modest
fees for engagements out of town, not too far from Philadelphia. Roland Hayes often recommended me to people
who were arranging these programs. I would travel short
distances to Negro colleges and churches that presented
young talent and gave it a start on the road to success.
These dates amounted to small tours, which kept me away
from home for several days at a time, and I would return
to my classes in high school, wondering whether I would
manage to get passing grades. I have never been able to
explain how it happened that when I did not miss school
days went by when I seemed not to learn an earthly thing;
but just let me stay away a couple of days, and the class
had gone wild learning new things. My teachers were
understanding. When I returned after an absence of some

days, they would assign extra lessons and then give me make-up examinations.

All this time I was singing from nature, so to speak, without any thought of *how*. My heart was filled when I sang, and I wanted to share what I felt. It slowly dawned on me that I had to have some training.

It was through a family acquaintance, John Thomas Butler, who gave public readings in his spare time and who had invited me to appear on his programs, that I met my first vocal teacher. He called on us and asked whether he could take me to sing for a friend of his. The lady he took me to see was Mary Saunders Patterson, a Negro who lived not too far from our house. She had a magnificent soprano voice, and she had studied uptown, as we called it, with a real vocal teacher. After listening to me, she told me that she would like to teach me what she knew. She charged a dollar a lesson, which Mr. Butler knew, and he had decided in his generosity that he would pay for the instruction out of his own pocket.

Mrs. Patterson waited until he was out of the room and asked whether my family was prepared to pay for the lessons. I was compelled to tell her that we could not afford them. She said she did not believe that young people just starting on what might be long careers should have obligations or strings attached to them, no matter how unselfish or noble the offer of help might be. She offered to give me the lessons free of charge.

I stayed with Mrs. Patterson for quite a few months. It was she who first taught me that in singing you must not call on your capital, that you must use your voice so that your capital remains intact. It was she, too, who showed me first the song by Schumann, "Die Rose die Lilie, die Taube, die Sonne." It was Mrs. Patterson who presented me with my first real evening gown.

At the end of the season Mrs. Patterson, eager to show the progress of her pupils, arranged class concerts. We did more than sing individual numbers; in an operetta that employed the voices of most of her pupils we had to act a bit as well. Our families came, and there was a great deal of excitement, and we were thrilled. For the operetta she had a special dress made for me at her house. As for the evening gown she gave me, I wore it many times in succeeding months and still cherish pieces of it that I have saved through the years.

# CHAPTER 4

# Shock

IF I had it all to do over again, I would wish to study at least in part at an established school of music for the extra benefits beyond individual vocal training. A pianist, a violinist, any sort of instrumentalist must follow a prescribed course of standard studies if he is to belong. A singer starts by having his instrument as a gift of God. Nowadays most singers attend conservatories, and it is well that they do. Some do not and manage to have careers, though they must scramble and learn musicianship the hard way.

I sensed the need for a formal musical education when I was in my teens and was beginning to make my first modest tours. I decided, in fact, to see if I could not go to a music school. I did not know whether we could afford it, but I thought that I ought to find out. Mother encouraged me, and so did other friends, but I had no idea where to turn until a person who had shown some interest in my problem suggested a school.

That music school no longer exists in Philadelphia, and

its name does not matter. I went there one day at a time when enrollments were beginning, and I took my place in line. There was a young girl behind a cage who answered questions and gave out application blanks to be filled out. When my turn came she looked past me and called on the person standing behind me. This went on until there was no one else in line. Then she spoke to me, and her voice was not friendly. "What do *you* want?"

I tried to ignore her manner and replied that I had come to make inquiries regarding an application for entry to the school.

She looked at me coldly and said, "We don't take colored."

I don't think I said a word. I just looked at this girl and was shocked that such words could come from one so young. If she had been old and sour-faced I might not have been startled. I cannot say why her youth shocked me as much as her words. On second thought, I could not conceive of a person surrounded as she was with the joy that is music without having some sense of its beauty and understanding rub off on her. I did not argue with her or ask to see her superior. It was as if a cold, horrifying hand had been laid on me. I turned and walked out.

It was my first contact with the blunt, brutal words, and this school of music was the last place I expected to hear them. True enough, my skin was different, but not my feelings.

It must be remembered that we grew up in a mixed neighborhood. White and Negro lived side by side and shared joys and sorrows. At school and on the street we encountered all kinds of children. Did we live in a poor neighborhood? "Poor" is relative. Some people owned their homes in that street and considered themselves well off. We had enough to eat and we dressed decently. We were not so poor that we had nothing, and our neighbors were in the same situation.

There were times when we heard our relatives and friends talking, and we knew we might come in contact with this, that, or the other thing. In some stores we might have to stand around longer than other people until we were waited on. There were times when we stood on a street corner, waiting for a trolley car, and the motorman would pass us by. There were places in town where all people could go, and there were others where some of us could not go. There were girls we played with and others we didn't. There were parties we went to, and some we didn't. We were interested in neither the places nor the people who did not want us.

I tried to put the thought of a music school out of my mind, for I could not help thinking of other music schools and wondering whether this would be their attitude too. I would not risk rejection again, and for some years the idea was not mentioned.

Of course I came to Mother with the story of what had happened. Mother was reassuring: there would be another way to get what I wanted and needed. I don't want to give the impression that she was placid and passive, however. It is true that she was not as aggressive as my aunt was, and I did not tell my aunt about the incident. If I had, she would have gone straight to that music school, I am sure, and demanded to see someone higher up and to be told why and wherefore. Mother had her own opinions of the rights and wrongs of things, but she believed profoundly that somehow someone would be raised up who would be understanding, and that another way would be found to accomplish what might have been accomplished at the conservatory.

There were other shocks to come. Though I was prepared for them, so I thought, the contact with reality never ceased to have its disturbing impact. Mother had grown up in Virginia, and we had friends who had come from farther south, so I had heard about Jim Crow, but meeting it bit deeply into the soul.

I was still in high school when I took my first long trip to participate in a gala concert. Mother went with me. At Washington we changed trains, and this time our bags were taken to the first coach—the Jim Crow car!

The windows were badly in need of washing; inside and outside the car was not clean, and the ventilation and lighting were poor. When the air became much too stuffy and windows were raised it just might happen that you would get, along with your fresh air, smoke and soot from the train's engine. At mealtime containers of all shapes and sizes were brought down from the racks, and the train vendor had a sizable supply of soft drinks, fruit, and packaged cookies.

The night seemed interminably long as we sat through it. On arrival in Savannah we were given a warm welcome by a small group of school officials, and later at the home of the president we became acquainted first-hand with genuine Southern hospitality. Our bedroom was quite large, with a fireplace and an adjoining bath. In the morning a girl came in and lit the fire so that the room was most comfortable when we arose.

Throughout our stay in Savannah my thoughts went often to that first coach. We returned to Washington under the same conditions, a bit wiser but sadder and so ashamed. I had looked closely at my people in that train. Some seemed to be embarrassed to the core. Others appeared to accept the situation as if it were beyond repair. Of course some fitted neither of these classes. Habit, I thought, can be good if it has an elevated aim; it can be devastating if it means taking bad things for granted; and I wondered how long it would take people on both sides to see a change. I have lived long enough to see some progress and to realize something of the great work being done by so many people, sincere in their efforts, to bring about better understanding.

It was shortly after that first long trip that I had my second experience. This time I traveled with Billy King, a young man who was my accompanist, of whom I have much more to say later. Billy spoke to a porter who happened to be passing through our car, and inquired about the chances of getting some hot food in the dining car. The porter was kind enough to go to the dining room to make inquiries for us, and he returned with the message that if we appeared at a given time we would be served.

At the fixed time Billy King and I started from our coach to the dining car. We passed through a coach occupied by white people, and we noticed immediately that the accommodations, though not first class, were much better than in our car. The dining car was empty when we reached it. Nevertheless we were seated at one end of it, where curtains could be drawn. Our seats were those occupied by the waiters when they ate, and the curtains no doubt were there to be drawn if a waiter should happen to be finishing his meal when the guests began to arrive.

We had fine hot meals, and the service was excellent. The chef and the waiters, it seemed to me, put themselves out to make us comfortable; there were extra things at our table, and even extra-large portions. This was their way of saying that they were glad we had had the courage to come back and be served.

I had more opportunity to observe other things on this trip. I knew about the separate waiting rooms, but no matter how much you are prepared and steeled for them they have their effect on you. I noticed that facilities in the Negro waiting rooms were indifferent. Some might have places where you could purchase a magazine or newspaper; some might not. Probably the Negro trade in some stations was meager, for those who could afford other modes of travel used them to avoid the humiliation. But there are plenty of persons who must make journeys and have no other resort than train travel. I suppose it was naïve of me to think then, as I think now—and it has been said by many people in more eloquent ways—that if one only searched one's heart one would know that none of us is responsible for the complexion of his skin, and that we could not change it if we wished to, and many of us don't wish to, and that this fact of nature offers no clue to the character or quality of the person underneath.

In the next few years I had occasion to do much more traveling. My tours were modest, but the concerts were increasing in number, and many of these engagements were in the south. Billy King still traveled with me, and we were giving full programs. I did not have the attention that a big managerial office can provide for a performer, and it was important to have travel conditions as convenient and comfortable as possible. I tried to make my own travel arrangements, but I found that often if I presented myself at a railroad ticket window, sometimes even in Philadelphia, there would be no reservations available. At other times the agent would sell me what was called "Berth 13."

I discovered that Berth 13 was a euphemism in the trade. It meant the drawing room. Of course if the drawing room had been sold I could not get even Berth 13. In most cases, however, Berth 13 was accepted as a valid reservation by the Pullman conductor.

There was one occasion when we were sold two tickets for Berth 13. This was an overnight trip, and Billy King tried to get a berth outside. He was told that none was available. We checked, and we thought that some berths that night were empty, but we had no cooperation. If we had wanted to share Berth 13 that night it might have been a different matter. To be forced to do so—that was demeaning.

After this incident we tried to have our separate reservations in hand before we started on a trip. If we were lucky —and these things seemed to depend a lot on what ticketseller was behind a window—we got ordinary berths, as other people did, instead of Berth 13. But this might lead to other unpleasantnesses. You would naturally have to use the washroom in the morning, and you never knew what you would encounter when you entered. One woman might say "good morning" pleasantly; another might stare at you; and a third might look you up and down and then flounce out.

Lest there be any misunderstanding, I want to make it clear that I was not on a train to make a social occasion of it. I wanted smooth and comfortable traveling because it helped me to prepare for a performance. I wanted good service because I needed it, not because I wanted to be with or like the other fellow. In the Jim Crow car I was with my own people, but as individuals they were persons I had never seen before and would not see again. In the first-class car my attitude was the same. I was merely trying to make a comfortable journey from here to there.

I tried to relax on these trips, but I could not help being tense at least part of the time. I remember one incident that turned out to be rather funny, probably because I was tense. Billy King and I were on our way somewhere, and we were seated in Berth 13. The Pullman conductor came in to take up the tickets. He glanced at Billy, who is a Negro, and I don't know what he thought. Then he turned to me and said, "Are you a Negro?"

I looked at him in amazement. Somehow his putting the question so plainly robbed me of my tongue. I uttered some sounds, but they did not come out as words. The conductor looked at me for a long time, took the tickets, and went out. Apparently he decided that I could not speak English, and we never found out what he had in mind. Billy King and I were amused; my reaction had been comical, and so had the conductor's.

After a while we learned that it was wisest not to arrange for our own transportation. We began to rely on a man in Philadelphia to make as many advance arrangements as possible. He looked after the entire itinerary, and if he foresaw that some leg of a journey would not be comfortable for one reason or another, he warned us in advance, and we tried to make this part of the trip by auto. This we could afford to do only on short runs.

Many years later I happened to be on my way to appear in Hampton, Virginia. There had been a storm and the roadbed below Washington had been partly washed out. All trains were delayed, and we sat around in the Washington station through the entire night, waiting for a train to be made up and sent out. In the morning a train was finally ready, and people filled every space in every car. This was an emergency situation, and no effort was made to enforce the usual Jim Crow rules. I saw a white woman take a Negro child and hold it on her lap to give the mother a few minutes of rest. I saw other expressions of brotherhood. Negroes and whites talked to one another; they shared their newspapers and even their food. The world did not crumble.

Things are changing in our country, and I am hopeful. But I cannot suppress a private regret. I still wish that I could have gone to a music school.

# CHAPTER 5

# Learning How

W HEN I went to my first singing teacher, Mary Saunders Patterson, seeking that all-important foundation of singing style, I was in my third year of high school and had already been singing in public for a long time, if you count the early start at church. I remember that Mrs. Patterson asked me how I produced a note, and I looked at her blankly. I simply opened my mouth, and there it was with ease—a high B or C or a low D.

But how? I had never given the question a thought. Mrs. Patterson insisted that I begin thinking about how I sang a tone. She taught me to throw the voice toward a corner of the ceiling, high up where two walls joined, and she said that I must seek to direct the voice toward one point. She did not use the word "focus," which I heard a great deal about later on with other teachers.

And so I started pushing notes toward that corner at the ceiling. I would not say that I was a hundred per cent successful in projecting the voice as she wished me to do, and there was no way of being sure I was on target except for Mrs. Patterson's keen ear and her constant watchfulness of my vocal production. In the beginning it was difficult, but before long it ceased to be a problem. I went to Mrs. Patterson once a week and soon became even more aware that there were two ways of singing—the natural, unreflecting way and the thoughtful, controlled way. Whether it was good for me at that stage to stop and think about how I sang, I did not sit down to figure out. But I know it was excellent that I was made to realize that the voice could be controlled and channeled.

There was always the temptation to revert to old habits and to sing as I had in the past. Thus it was that when I was learning the first Schubert song that Mrs. Patterson gave me I was torn between just singing it and aiming each tone at the ceiling. In time I learned how to handle a complete song as Mrs. Patterson wished.

When it came to the way I breathed while I sang, Mrs. Patterson did not waste too much time. She merely checked the way I handled my breathing. She had been taught that it should be natural, and since I had no difficulty with my breathing when I aimed my tones at the target on the wall, she did not seek to change anything.

Mrs. Patterson, I know, gave me a useful foundation. She had had excellent instruction and done considerable performing herself, and was well equipped as a teacher. Much of my voice must have been well placed by nature, and what seemed difficult in the beginning was really the process of getting acquainted with a new method.

When the time came for a change of teacher it was Mrs. Patterson who urged it. I was sent to Agnes Reifsnyder, a woman who had a fine reputation as a vocal teacher in

Philadelphia. I don't remember how long I stayed with Miss Reifsnyder, but it was longer than I worked with Mrs. Patterson. My new teacher was a friend of Kathryn Meisle, a contralto who had reached the Metropolitan Opera. I never learned whether Miss Meisle had studied with Miss Reifsnyder, but something about Miss Meisle's singing persuaded my friends that Miss Reifsnyder could help me.

Miss Reifsnyder was a contralto herself, and she felt that she was better equipped to teach a contralto than a soprano. She spent a lot of time working on my medium and low tones. She was not interested in fireworks or vocal gymnastics, but she concentrated a great deal on breathing and gave me exercises further to set the voice. She introduced me to the songs of Brahms, among others, and helped me to prepare whole programs for the concerts I was beginning to give out of town. Beyond these things, I cannot remember much about my studies with Miss Reifsnyder. I was so busy with so many things in those days that other events have remained more vivid in my memory. Many years later Miss Reifsnyder was gracious enough to serve as a judge in the Marian Anderson scholarship trials.

Shortly before I left high school I was introduced to Giuseppe Boghetti, who remained my teacher for many years, with breaks here and there, until he died. Dr. Lucy Wilson, my high school principal, had arranged to have me sing for David Bispham, an outstanding American baritone. Mr. Bispham said kind things, but nothing more happened. Then Lisa Roma, a young musician and a

[ 48 ]

friend of my principal, offered to take me to Mr. Boghetti, her teacher.

I remember that Dr. Wilson and Miss Roma accompanied me to Mr. Boghetti's studio. Mr. Boghetti was short, stocky, and dynamic. He could be pleasant, but there were times when he could be stern and forbidding. At that first meeting he was severe, even gruff. He began by declaring that he had no time, that he wanted no additional pupils, and that he was giving his precious time to listen to this young person only as a favor to Miss Roma. Dr. Wilson did not look happy. I was amazed.

My song was "Deep River." I did not look at Mr. Boghetti as I sang, and my eyes were averted from him when I had finished. He came to the point quickly. "I will make room for you right away," he said firmly, "and I will need only two years with you. After that, you will be able to go anywhere and sing for anybody." Then he began to talk about his fees as if the lessons would begin at once.

They could not begin at once. There was no money for lessons. Dr. Wilson said that she would see what could be done, and I murmured something, and then we left. I might have known that my neighbors and the people at the Union Baptist Church would find a way to provide. Mrs. Ida Asbury, who lived across the street from us, and some other neighbors and friends arranged a gala concert at our church. The main presentation of the evening was "In a Persian Garden," and among the soloists was, I believe, Roland Hayes. After all expenses, about six hundred dollars were realized, and with that money Mr. Boghetti was engaged to be my teacher.

At that first audition, I should add, Mr. Boghetti had given me a scale to sing after I had finished "Deep River." Once I began to appear regularly at his studio I found out why. He had discovered unequal tones in that scale, and he set to work immediately to iron out the unevenness. It gradually dawned on me that, although I had worked with two teachers, I had not yet reached the point where I had relinquished my wholly natural and spontaneous manner of singing for a consistently controlled method.

Mr. Boghetti started by giving me exercises. First I did nothing but hum them until I could feel the vibration. Then I would attempt to place the tone exactly where I was humming. The idea was a little like Mrs. Patterson's. Looking back on all these things calmly, I can see how Mr. Boghetti's approach was more useful. In a concert hall, after all, it might be awkward to find the right kind of corner to use as a target, but if you did the focusing inside your head the chances were fair that your head would always be there with you.

The E flat was my best tone, according to Mr. Boghetti, because it was perfectly placed. He contrived vocal exercises starting from that tone, moving up and down, and he reminded me that all the other tones must be produced in the same way. His objective was to provide me with an even, unbroken vocal line from the lowest tone to the highest.

Attention was paid to breathing. Mr. Boghetti suggested holding the sides tightly and then breathing slowly to see how far I could expand the body wall. I found that I got a gratifying expansion. But when I got around to singing songs I would forget to check on ribs, body wall, and maximum expansion, and I would not pause to wonder whether or not I was breathing according to rule. So long as the breath came naturally and there was enough of it for the song I was called upon to do, I did not let it worry me.

Mr. Boghetti did not make a fetish of training any particular section of a voice. He worked with all of it—top, middle, and bottom. When I did my exercises he got me to move up to an A, then to a B, and finally to a high C. The B and C were designed to serve as extra insurance for the A, which I used constantly on stage. We spent a good deal of time striving for agility. The exercises were done rapidly and lightly, and Mr. Boghetti saw to it that I had all sorts of embellishments to practice.

One thing I did not master in his studio was a pianissimo that pleased me. As a result I have never sung in public two songs I love most dearly, the "Ave Maria" from Verdi's *Otello,* and Handel's "Care Selve."

"Do you want to be a pianissimo contralto?" Mr. Boghetti demanded.

"No," I replied with unaccustomed boldness, "but the person who sings loudest is not always the one who sings best."

He was unyielding that day. "I am the teacher and shall make the decisions," he said.

Some days later he relented and gave me exercises to develop a decent pianissimo. We worked on these exercises from time to time with occasional good results, but we did not concentrate on this problem persistently enough, and I never learned the pianissimo so as to command it securely at every tone throughout the range. The fault may have been mine. Mr. Boghetti had two sopranos as stu-

[ 51 ]

dents who had beautiful pianissimi. I don't know whether these girls had these tones before they reached our teacher or whether he taught them the secret that was so elusive to me.

I recall a curious encounter with an Italian musician some years ago. I was visiting Harry T. Burleigh, one of the finest musicians my people has produced. We were at Ricordi, the publisher, and for some reason Mr. Burleigh led me upstairs to a studio where there was a musician, an Italian who was, I think, a singing teacher. We three chatted. Then I sang for this man.

"Let's do an exercise," he said. We started together, and he took me up the scale. As we got above the staff, I murmured, "Oh, this is too high." He shouted, "You can do it, you can do it." It was as if his yells had strings that pulled my voice higher and higher. I found myself singing high C's. I had at one time sung those high C's without a second thought, but by this time I no longer ventured that high.

Mr. Burleigh smiled with delight, and the Italian musician said, "Why sure she can do Aida!" I was not convinced.

Another time, on my first trip to England, I met a young singer who insisted that she would persuade her teacher to give me five minutes of her precious lesson time. I went with her and did an exercise for her teacher, who said, "I will have you singing Aida in six months."

But I was not interested in singing Aida. The fact that you can emit a screech on high C does not give you the right to sing Aida, not by a long shot. I knew perfectly well that I was a contralto, not a soprano. Why Aida?

As it happened, there were occasions when I sang the

music of Amneris in Mr. Boghetti's studio. Mr. Boghetti was a tenor, and he joined me in singing the fourth-act scene for Rhadames and Amneris. He loved to sing, and I suppose he would have preferred singing in opera to teaching. You could see his pleasure when he proposed that we do this operatic scene together rather than the usual lesson. I might have had my mind set on trying out something else, but he was the teacher, and how could one resist the gleam in his eyes as we played at being operatic figures? Once we started I enjoyed the *Aida* scenes as much as he did. I realized then that I liked doing opera tremendously, but years were to pass before I finally did so in an opera house.

With Mr. Boghetti I learned some of the songs I still sing today: Schubert and Brahms, and later Schumann and Hugo Wolf in German; songs by Rachmaninoff and other Russians, in English; Italian arias; songs in French, and songs in English by American and British composers.

Like the best teachers, Mr. Boghetti was watchful for difficulties I might encounter in the course of certain songs. I might not be able to fit a word to a tone in just the right way, and he would concentrate on that passage. He would invent exercises not to be found in any book but especially designed to overcome the problem.

It was in Mr. Boghetti's studio, too, that I became aware of the meaning of professionalism for a public performer. There I learned that the purpose of all the exercises and labors was to give you a thoroughly reliable foundation and to make sure that you could do your job under any circumstances. There is no shortcut. You must understand the how and why of what you are doing. If you do, you can

give an acceptable performance even when you are indisposed. You cannot say, "Tonight I don't feel good and I
won't appear." You have to be prepared to carry on even
on nights when you would rather do anything else but perform.

During the years I stayed with Mr. Boghetti my tours
increased. I went through all my programs for him, and he
criticized and corrected. Toward the end of his life, by
which time I was busy and away singing most of the time,
I kept coming back to him, letting him check on what I
was doing. And he was enormously helpful in this respect,
too. It is easy to pick up bad habits in the stress of a heavy
schedule of performances, and a teacher who is objective
can notice things that have escaped your attention.

Mr. Boghetti was a strict teacher. He expected you to
do a lot of homework. I shudder to think what he would
have said if he had known how often I failed to do mine. I
was caught up in so many activities when I was young that
I could not always find time for practice. Nor, for that
matter, could I always find a place where I could practice
without becoming a nuisance to other people. However,
on days before my lessons I concentrated madly. I would
take the music to bed with me and read over the words and
study the notes far into the night. The next day I would
take the music to school and steal glances at it when I
should have been paying some mind to classwork. By the
time I reached Mr. Boghetti's studio I had soaked myself
in the music, and he would say with satisfaction, "I see
that you have really been studying this week."

He could be terrifying, as I have said. I once saw a girl
running out of his studio in tears. He minced no words; if

you did not study he told you he did not want you in his studio. "I don't take society people," he would shout, "who think it would be nice to sing." When he saw that I was serious he let me stay after my lesson and listen to other pupils who were more advanced, and this was most helpful. He had a way of singing along with you during your lessons. Sometimes it disturbed you, but you did not dare to ask him to stop.

The clock was always within view. When your thirty minutes were up someone else was always waiting. You watched anxiously as that clock ticked away the short time of the lesson that meant so much to you. There were times when Mr. Boghetti spent some of those treasured minutes talking, explaining things, and probably this was necessary, but you wished you could invent some way to hold back the clock or cut off conversation. Some days you felt like talking, and you had the feeling that Mr. Boghetti was watching the clock as anxiously as you did when he talked. If another pupil happened not to turn up Mr. Boghetti let you stay on, and those extra minutes you cherished and remembered.

Mr. Boghetti arranged recitals in his studio, and some of us were invited to sing for his guests. This man had an odd magnetic quality. He would sit in one of the front rows and fix his eyes squarely on yours when you were singing. Somehow he helped you to sing better than you thought you could. I noticed that he had this effect on me when I sang on more formal occasions in regular halls in Philadelphia. He was sure to be in a seat up front where I could see him. I knew he was watching me, and I just had to do what he expected of me.

[ 55 ]

There came a time when the money provided for the lessons by my friends and neighbors was exhausted, but Mr. Boghetti did not put me out of his studio. A friend of his offered to advance two hundred and fifty dollars toward my lessons in return for a promise that I appear in some concerts for him. I did not know where the concerts would be or under what auspices, and neither did Mr. Boghetti. I did not know people in the music business to whom I could turn for advice, and I was uneasy about the proposal and turned it down. Mr. Boghetti was not annoyed with me. Indeed, he carried me without payment of any kind for more than a year. During this period he went so far as to say that I need not pay and that he was wiping out the arrears. I am certain that he meant it, but in time I was fortunate to be able to repay him in full. I should add that there were times when I earned a little extra money by giving singing lessons, though I was still a student myself.

Philadelphia had a lot of music by famous artists in those years, and it would have been helpful to attend concerts often, if only to supplement what I was learning in the studio with the experience of hearing others sing songs I was working on. But I could not afford to go to concerts frequently. Although the concert hall was within reasonable walking distance of my home, it was not advisable to come home alone at night. It was difficult enough to spare the money for one ticket, and I could not think of spending money on two so that I could have a companion.

Nevertheless, I did manage to hear some singers. Ernestine Schumann-Heink, who was no longer young, reached me most deeply. She did some of the Schubert songs I was studying, and her low tones were impressive. I heard Sigrid Onegin, and Mr. Franz Rupp, who is now my accompanist, played for her. I did not meet either of them at that time. Onegin sang a song that intrigued me—Richard Strauss's "Schlechtes Wetter." I had not heard music like that before, and as soon as I could spare the money I bought a copy. I studied it but did not attempt it because it was then too difficult for my capacities. I still own that copy. Several years ago I got it out, thinking that now perhaps I might learn it for one of my programs. Again I set it aside.

I remember that I was also excited by the way Schumann-Heink sang Schubert's "Gretchen am Spinnrade." I realized that what she sang was pure German, something I was far from being able to do. I could recall the way Roland Hayes had sung German songs at our church concerts. When he sang things like "An die Musik" or "Adelaide" I tried to evoke a picture of what the words meant, and from the music and manner in which Mr. Hayes caressed a phrase I tried to invent a translation. Mind you, I knew no German at this time, and I found out later that some of my translations were way off the mark.

Hearing these great artists deal with foreign languages so masterfully made me aware of the fact that I had a lot to learn in this direction. I sensed what should be done, but I had neither the time nor the means. Some French I learned in high school, and Mr. Boghetti was most helpful with Italian. My German, however, was merely an approximation.

I sang a concert in those early years for a group at the University of Pennsylvania. It may have been a student affair. In any event, it was not a full program; I sang for about forty-five minutes. A young teacher of foreign languages at the university was in the audience, and he did something I shall not forget. He went to the trouble of finding out where I lived, and came to our house. There he spoke to me in the presence of my mother and told me with great earnestness that a person with a voice like mine had no business being satisfied to sing foreign languages so badly. How right he was, and how painfully this truth was driven into me some time later!

I did not do anything about this problem immediately, but what he said reinforced in me an idea that had been growing for some time—that some way, somehow, sometime I must get to Europe. Lawrence Brown, who was Roland Hayes's accompanist, had suggested several years earlier that I ought to think about studying abroad as Mr. Hayes had, and that if I ever decided to go, the best teacher for me there would be Raimund von Zur Mühlen. I would find him in England, he said, and if it was mastery of Lieder I wanted, this man had been one of their greatest interpreters and was a renowned teacher.

I filed the suggestion away in my mind. Working with Mr. Boghetti gave added impetus to my secret desire to go to Europe. He had been trained there, and so much about his musical style had a flavor that attracted me.

In the meantime, my problem was to devise some system for getting enough work done on my voice. The sensible way would have been to allot certain segments of each day for vocal exercises, for languages, for all the tasks I needed to do. I had lots of excuses for myself—and yet for others they would not have been excuses. I was sensitive about disturbing people if I worked aloud. Other people might have said, "I don't care." I just couldn't, and I was the loser.

When I was making my earliest tours I was obliged to stay in private homes. People were generous enough to be my hosts, but I was a public performer and therefore something of a curiosity. Friends and neighbors of the hosts would arrive to visit with me in all friendliness or just to look me over. I did not have the time to myself that I needed for practice. I might explain to my hostess that I needed a little time to myself, and she would reply sweetly or apologetically that these were the people she lived with and that she had to share me with them.

I arrived at one home early in the morning and got cleaned up. "Whenever you are ready," my hostess said most amiably, "you can have breakfast."

I thanked her and sat down at the table. In a few minutes the doorbell rang, and my hostess said, "Oh my, I wonder who that is." She went to the door and ushered in a woman and some children. "Come right into the dining room," she told them.

They all marched in, and they were as nice as could be. Then the visitor said to the hostess, "You know, when you called me I was so busy I didn't know how I could get over."

My hostess had meant no harm. On the contrary, I think she took pride in showing me off as her guest. Perhaps I should have had the nerve, when staying at private homes or hotels, to go ahead and practice, leaving it to others to say whether they were being disturbed. It is possible to overdo worrying about what a neighbor may think.

Some years ago I had a portable phonograph with me on my travels because there were some recordings I wanted to listen to. I started to play a Heifetz record in my hotel bedroom one morning, and it occurred to me that the music might well disturb my neighbor, so I carried the phonograph into the living room, turned it low, and closed the doors. Presently there was a knock on the locked door leading into my neighbor's quarters, and a woman's voice called, "I beg your pardon, but we'd love to hear that music. Could you turn it up louder?" I was delighted to oblige. I moved the phonograph near my neighbor's door and let it play loudly enough for her to enjoy. I never met her, but she made me realize that I could not make decisions for her.

The years with Mr. Boghetti were invaluable, and as I see them in retrospect I would not wish to have been without them. I might not have spent so much time with him if a plan projected in Chicago had worked out. I happened to be in that city during a convention of the National Association of Negro Musicians, a rather strong organization with branches in some twenty-five states. For its big program the convention had a nationally famous performer and for lesser events it invited aspiring musicians. One afternoon I sang. As soon as I had finished—indeed, while I was still in the room—someone rose to make a motion that the association should help me with my musical education. The motion was seconded. People began raising their hands and pledging certain sums. Soon there were pledges of about a thousand dollars. Various music schools were suggested, and it was agreed that I should try for the Yale School of Music. I went back to Philadelphia and filled out an application, which was then forwarded to a member of the organization who had been assigned to complete the arrangements. Yale accepted the application. Unhappily, not all the pledges were redeemed, and at the start of the school term there were not enough funds in hand to pay the tuition. Whatever was raised was turned over to Mr. Boghetti. It seemed to be ordained that I should remain with him.

*CHAPTER 6*

# Up and—Way Down

WHILE I was still studying with Mrs. Patterson and running about to sing a song here and a song there, playing my own accompaniments, my teacher said one day, "Marian, I think you will soon have to decide whom you would like to have as your accompanist."

Whom I would like to have as accompanist? A strange wave of excitement raced through me. I could hardly answer Mrs. Patterson; at that moment I could not have put my reaction into words. I had kept busy with the little chores of singing and had gladly accepted whatever payment was offered, but having an accompanist meant something quite different—a step upward.

The subject was not pursued further that day. Several lessons later Mrs. Patterson returned to it. "Speaking of accompanists," she remarked, "I think a good person for you would be Billy King."

Again I could scarcely speak. Billy King represented the ultimate in accompanists to me. I was thrilled that Mrs.

Patterson regarded my talents as worthy of him, for I felt that he was beyond my reach.

"Oh, I couldn't have Billy King," I protested. "He is Lydia's accompanist."

Billy King—or William King, to give him his formal name—was very popular among Philadelphia musicians. As a young man he was organist and choirmaster of an Episcopal church in Philadelphia and the "official" accompanist when guest artists arrived in town without their own pianists. He had even accompanied Roland Hayes at some concerts. Today he holds a position as organist in New York.

He will forgive me for saying that he could well have become one of the outstanding musicians of our time if he had worked a little harder, for he was extremely talented. He liked people, and they liked him. I remember hearing his father admonish him, "Billy, you'd better study." Another time his mother, in my presence, repeated another of his father's warnings, "Be careful, Billy. Don't let Marian pass you. She may come up to you and pass you."

When Mrs. Patterson mentioned his name I could not imagine myself competing for Billy's services with Lydia McClain. She was a beautiful girl; she looked Spanish rather than Negro. Her soprano had a strange, appealing quality that people found most attractive. She did a lot of singing in and around Philadelphia, and Billy was her pianist.

On one of those busy evenings when I was singing in several different places, I arrived at the Y. W. C. A., ready to do a few songs. I sat down at the piano and sang my first number. When I finished and looked up, there was a young man standing beside me. "May I?" he whispered, and took my place on the piano bench. It was Billy King. I don't know how I got through the next number, I was so excited that Billy King had offered to play for me. When I got home that night I was still walking on air. I didn't sleep a wink.

Billy King did not become my regular accompanist immediately. Thanks to Mrs. Patterson, a number of people played for me. I wish I could list each one. There was Marie Holland, who later became a sister in the Catholic faith; she is now Sister Mary Benigna. Marie and I were fellow students in high school, and for a time she lived with Mrs. Patterson.

After that night at the Y. W. C. A. Billy did play for me occasionally. Then came a concert in Orange, New Jersey, which changed things considerably. Lydia and I had been engaged by the ladies' group of an Orange church to give a program. We took the day coach to Orange together— Lydia and I and Billy King, who would play for both of us, and a doctor friend of Lydia's who, as far as Billy and I knew, was just going along to hear her sing. We sat facing one another, chattering gaily. When we got to our station Billy and I rose to leave, but Lydia and her friend stayed on. Billy and I could not understand why, but there was no time to discuss the situation. We assumed that Lydia and her doctor wanted to make a brief side trip and that she would turn up at the church in time to sing. But at concert time she had not arrived, and the ladies rushed back and demanded to know where she was. We said we guessed she would be along any minute. She did not turn up. We found out later that she and her doctor had gone on to New York to be married.

At nine o'clock the ladies, looking grim, came and told us we had better start. I sang the entire program. I noticed that our audience was small, which did not make me more cheerful. After the singing was over and the listeners had dispersed, we stood around and waited to be paid. My fee by then was twenty-five dollars, and out of this sum I had to pay Billy King as well as the train fare for both of us. No one came near us, and I began to look around for someone to approach for my money. Finally one of the women came up and said, "We want to see you in the study." Being invited into the pastor's study usually means trouble, and I followed her reluctantly.

There were several women in the room, and their spokesman said, "You saw for yourself that we didn't have the people tonight, and we want to know what you are going to do about it."

I looked at them in astonishment, but I decided to be reasonable and offered to contribute the six dollars it had cost to hire the piano.

The spokesman looked at me in annoyance. "Is that the best you can do?" she demanded.

I was speechless, and the ladies sat silent. They were waiting, presumably, for me to waive the fee. "So that's the best you can do," the spokesman said irritably. "You see, our mistake was that we thought you were a drawing card. Give her the money."

The treasurer made no move to hand over the money, and I stood there, angry and mortified. "All right, give her the money," the spokesman snapped. "I just thought she might want to come back here again."

There was another occasion, in Philadelphia, when a joint recital ended in unpleasantness. In this case I shared the program with a fairly well-known singer from the middle west, who was the main attraction. Since this was my home town and the people putting on the concert reckoned that I had a lot of friends, they booked me too. I suspect that the lady was not happy about this. I was scheduled for only two numbers, and I assumed I would sing them together. But the program was arranged so that I would follow her with one number at the end of the first half and with the other after her second half. I could not blame her for being irritated at this arrangement. I did not like it much myself.

She sang her first half. Then Billy King, who was at the piano for both of us, did a solo number, and I followed with my song. I don't know what the lady thought of the reaction to my singing by the home folks, but before she returned for her second half she had the manager announce that she was singing despite the fact that she had laryngitis.

That evening she was wearing a dress with the longest train I have ever seen. The only train to approach it I ever saw was one worn by Marguerite d'Alvarez at a concert in Berlin some years later. I remember that when Madame d'Alvarez left the stage her lacy train fanned out like a stupendous bridal gown. The point about the lady's spectacular train was that when she and Billy King were going offstage after the second half he inadvertently stepped on it and almost caused a major catastrophe. She accused Billy of stepping on her train deliberately, and for a few minutes there was much excitement backstage.

At about this time G. Grant Williams, one of the editors of the Philadelphia *Tribune,* came to our house and spoke to Grandmother, offering to help me in any way that he could. He suggested that he might be useful, through acquaintances on Negro papers in other towns, in having my performances covered, and he thought that he might be able to get engagements for me. Presently a contract was made with him, and I had a manager, which put my work on another level.

Mr. Williams managed my appearances for some time after Billy King came along. Then Mr. Williams became ill and had to give up this work. Billy King took over the job of managing and did it for a number of years, in addition to being my accompanist. He got up a booklet and had some fliers printed and distributed. He billed me as Marian E. Anderson; the E. was an added initial, like a grace note.

By the time I was graduated from high school we were able to think of touring on a much larger scale than we had attempted before. Having Billy King as accompanist even before he added the duties of manager was helpful, for his name on a program carried weight. When it became more or less official that he would play for me, he visited my home and met my people and I was taken to his house to meet his parents. His family lived in a house that was detached on one side, and it was possible to practice there without disturbing other people. It was deemed all right for me to go to his house, for our people knew each other.

As manager, Billy found a lot of ways to get dates for us. He had appeared with Roland Hayes as well as other performers in some towns, and he wrote to the people in these communities, telling them that he had a new singer. The singers who visited and sang in his church were another source of contact with distant towns. They would go back home and, stimulated by Billy's enthusiasm, would induce their local organizations to invite us for concerts.

Our tours were focused around Negro colleges in the South. In some places that did not have such institutions individuals got together and arranged special concerts, and in time a college might offer to arrange several other appearances in its vicinity. In return we would take a lower fee from this college, which was only fair. The more engagements we had in any neighborhood, the less would be the proportionate cost of the fare for traveling to this area.

In addition to college auditoriums and churches, we also began to perform in theaters when local promoters had no other places in which to present us. These theater appearances gave me a personal sense of accomplishment. Theaters were places where people with well-known names gave their performances. I began to feel that this was turning into a career.

Almost imperceptibly my fees were increasing. I reached and passed the fifty-dollar mark our good friend had had the temerity to predict for me. By the time Billy King took over the management and our tours became more extensive, the fee had mounted to a hundred dollars. It seemed quite a business then, but it must be remembered that Billy King got, out of each fee, twenty-five dollars for his work as accompanist and something additional for managing. I also had to meet traveling expenses. Fortunately, these were chiefly railroad fares. At colleges I might be put up in a visitor's room and Billy would stay in the young men's dormitory. If we appeared for a church, I would stay at the home of one of the ladies and Billy at a Y. M. C. A. or another private home. As may be clear from all this, the sums remaining after expenses were not great. But concert dates were closer together, this was more than I had ever earned, and there was the blessed fact that I was earning it by singing.

One tour led to others. My fee continued to rise, but what was more important to me, I was beginning to appear in places where one could attract the attention of music-lovers. I even got to sing in the Philadelphia Academy of Music on my own. My career was really growing.

Those were years of growth, I think, in other ways. In my travels I discovered places and people. I remember that on our earliest tours we went to remote places in Virginia where a wonderful couple, Mr. and Mrs. Lee, were pioneering in bringing education to Negro children who would otherwise have had none. Mr. Lee was head of the school, and Mrs. Lee equaled if not exceeded him in devotion, energy, and service. They must have started with little of anything except determination, and they were always close to the disaster line financially. But they persisted in their work. They were true pioneers.

They could not afford to pay the regular fee for a concert, and we were careful to give them the lowest rate, in many instances accepting only our expenses. I would not be surprised if the money came out of their own pockets, not out of the school budget. The piano they had was not in good condition. But I sang, we returned regularly, and we got more out of it than we could possibly give. In time several modest new buildings were put up. They were long overdue and were welcomed joyously.

There must be modest institutions like that all over the South, built on the determination and love of one or two persons. I wonder how many Negro children owe their basic education and perspectives to people like the Lees.

Our tours brought us invariably to Hampton Institute, one of the finest Negro schools in the country. Sometimes we appeared there twice a year. I am certain that R. Nathaniel Dett, a wonderful musician, was responsible for having us come there so often.

Nathaniel Dett was an inspiration to his students. He built the Hampton Choir so that it became famous here and abroad, where it toured. He was not content with just any music; he was careful to have his youngsters sing what was good, and he knew what was good. Some of his students, I know, went on to make reputations of their own.

He was also a composer, and I remember that at Hampton I sang one of his pieces, "Listen to the Lambs," which was for chorus and soloist. Later I appeared with his chorus in other localities. And when I was scheduled to sing a recital in Hampton, he took pains to obtain the program long in advance and go over each song with his classes so that they would be prepared to respond to the music with understanding.

He took a personal interest in my career. One night after a concert we took a drive, and he talked about music and my future. He stressed the fact that one should not compromise in matters of art, and he indicated that there might be heavy sacrifices along the way. He could not predict whether things would come out as I hoped, but he made it clear that the effort was in itself worth while.

The more I sang, the more confident I became. It is not immodest, I think, to say that I was now beginning to feel that my voice was more mature, that it was developing size and responding to Mr. Boghetti's training and the experience of concertizing. My voice was beginning to speak in a new way.

I think it was at an appearance in Washington, sponsored by Howard University, that I had a sudden awareness of enlarged capacities. The audience was mixed. In the course of a group by Richard Strauss, I reached "Morgen." When I had started to learn this song it had not seemed too difficult. I had soon realized that there was a great deal to it, and in the studio it had been drummed into me that this was a test piece. When I launched into "Morgen" in Washington it took on new meaning. The mood was set. "Morgen" seemed mine to do with what I pleased.

There are such moments in a career, when you feel that you belong to a thing and it belongs to you. "Morgen" that afternoon in Washington was like that. Everything else I did caught fire from "Morgen." As I saw the faces of that audience—a pleasantly surprised look here, a faint smile there—I felt that here was compensation for everything that had happened in the years gone by.

I now felt that I had reached a turning point in my career, and I was certain that with continued study and concentration I would be able to do whatever I undertook. If hereafter a thing failed to come off, I knew that I would have only myself to blame for having failed to apply myself.

The occasions when I sang in concert halls and theaters before audiences not confined to my group increased. Notices in publications other than Negro ones began to appear. Possibly some critics had come out of curiosity, but comments were encouraging. I became determined to make further sacrifices to push on to higher goals, not because I was proud or vainglorious but because I felt that my career thus far warranted such a decision. And so I committed myself to make the plunge and give a recital in New York's Town Hall. For this event I saved money whenever I could, and I worked hard with Mr. Boghetti to prepare a program.

The concert was arranged by a young man who lived in Harlem. I had appeared for him before at the Savoy and at Renaissance Hall. The last appearance had been a sellout, and he recommended that we try downtown. I felt I had friends in New York; I had also sung in churches, at the Baptist Convention, and for the National Association for the Advancement of Colored People—Walter White, secretary of the association, had heard me in Philadelphia and had arranged an appearance in New York.

The promoter engaged Town Hall. Mr. Boghetti gave me four new songs, including Brahms's "Von ewiger Liebe," and he assured me that I was doing fine with them. I had a great desire to sing Lieder in such a hall because Roland Hayes had done them so movingly.

On the day of the concert there was much excitement. Mr. Boghetti gave me precise instructions, when to eat (four in the afternoon) and what. He warned me to be at the hall at seven that evening. We came in early from Philadelphia, and I stayed in a room at the Y. W. C. A. in Harlem. I followed Mr. Boghetti's orders. I got to the hall at seven, and we went through some vocal exercises. I felt for all the world like a prima donna.

The tickets had been on sale for quite a while, and I

had been told that they were selling well. Billy King arrived at the hall, and I watched the clock expectantly for the starting time. I asked casually how everything was going in the auditorium and was assured that we would have a full house. Starting time came and passed, and the man who was to signal us to go out on the stage did not come. It got to be eight forty-five, and I began to feel uneasy. At nine the young man who was managing the concert advised us to begin. Billy and I walked out on the stage. My heart sank. There was only a scattering of people in the hall. I had been misled, and the enthusiasm drained out of me.

To make matters worse, the opening number was Handel's "Ombra mai fu," which we were to do with organ instead of piano. Billy King went to the organ at the side of the stage. I stood quite remote from him and felt miserably alone. I had had a lot of experience and had been foolish enough to think that I was prepared for anything, but I was only about twenty, and I had a great deal to learn.

I got to the Brahms songs. The first three were not easy, but "Von ewiger Liebe" was especially difficult. I sang the German as best I could, having learned it phonetically. I did not feel that it was bad; on the other hand, it was not like Roland Hayes's singing of Lieder. Somehow the program came to an end, though I felt it had dragged on endlessly. And the next morning the newspaper comments were not complimentary. One writer said that the voice was good, but this and that were not so good. Another said, "Marian Anderson sang her Brahms as if by rote."

I did not want people to think that I had meant to

deceive them. I was embarrassed that I had tried to sing in one of New York's concert halls without being fully ready, and I went back to Philadelphia deeply disturbed. I did not want to see any music; I did not want to hear any; I did not want to make a career of it. Do not misunderstand me. I deserved no more than I received. But I felt lost and defeated. The dream was over.

# CHAPTER 7

# A Home of Our Own

I NOW had what amounted to a complex about music. Hopes had been raised too high, and when they crashed too low I could not be objective. Perhaps I had not admitted it to myself, but Town Hall in New York had represented the mainstream of American musical life, and I had plunged into it hoping to become one of the fortunate swimmers.

I kept rehashing the concert in my mind, lingering on some points and thrusting others so thoroughly aside that I do not remember to this day which dress I wore, whether it was the one Mrs. Patterson had made over for me or a special one. I don't remember what financial arrangements were made with the young man who managed the event, but I do know that I received nothing and that he must have lost money. I thought then, and still do, that I might have done better if I had not been told that the auditorium was full. If you are sensitive, and I was perhaps too sensitive, a misrepresentation like that can throw you off balance, particularly if you feel that you have a great deal at stake.

I stopped going regularly to Mr. Boghetti's studio. I appeared once in a while, and things must have gone very indifferently. He realized how much the fiasco had shaken me, and he did not make an issue of my irregular attendance.

Mother and I talked about the whole thing, and with her patience and understanding she helped me out of my trouble. I knew that the criticism was right and that I should not have given the critics the opportunity to write as they did. I kept reiterating that I had wanted so very much to sing well enough to please everybody.

"Listen, my child," Mother said. "Whatever you do in this world, no matter how good it is, you will never be able to please everybody. All you can strive for is to do the best it is humanly possible for you to do."

As the months went by I was able again to consider singing as a career. "Think about it for a while," Mother advised, "and think of other things you might like to do."

I thought about it. It took a long time before I could confront singing again with enthusiasm, before the old conviction returned that nothing in life, not even medicine, could be so important as music.

One of my great comforts in this time of self-doubt and indecision was that Mother and my sisters and I were living in our own little house. We had taken the momentous step of buying it some time after I finished high school. It may seem that this was a chancy thing for us to do. We had stayed with Grandmother and my aunt for a number of years, moving with them from Fitzwater Street to other houses on Seventieth and Christian, on Carpenter Street, on Eighteenth Street, and on South Martin Street. Grandmother and my aunt had been kind and loving, but nothing could take the place of a home of one's own.

A small house on South Martin Street, across the way from Grandmother's, was put up for sale by an Irish family. We liked the street; it was well kept, quiet, quite desirable. Many of the people on it, Negro and white, owned their own homes. We decided to buy the little house.

When it became clear that we were serious my aunt was distressed. Even though we were going to live just across the street, she kept saying, "I can't understand it, we've lived together so long."

Mother's father had died some time before and had left her some money, and I had tried very hard to save something from my earnings. I think I had about six hundred dollars in the bank at that time, and it had taken me a long time to accumulate it. I remember that when I had gone to the bank to open my first savings account several years before I had been full of hope that my nest egg would grow with dazzling speed. When the bank informed me that the limit for a savings account was ten thousand dollars I thought that I would have to look around for a second bank in no time. My account, however, refused to shoot up and create such a problem for me. Whenever it seemed to be growing encouragingly some crisis developed, and money had to be withdrawn. I don't know how it had risen to as much as six hundred dollars when we bought the little house.

The signing of the deed and the payment of the cash that had to be put down were big events in our lives. We

were incredibly happy. In the nights before the purchase
became final I had visions that I would not live long
enough to move into the house. After the occupants left
I went into the empty house and looked around critically
and fondly. The first thing we must do, I felt, was to put
in hardwood floors.

We did not want to splurge, but Mother had taught us
that what is good is usually least expensive in the long
run. We had the hardwood floors put in, and they are still
in fine shape; Mother still lives in the little house, and I
know. We had linens, and we contracted to buy furniture
on the installment plan. And the great day dawned when
we moved in. The neighbors came to look, and they called
our home "the dream house."

We had a wonderful feeling that we could spread ourselves. The house had two bedrooms; Mother and I occupied the larger one, while my sisters had the other. We
made some changes after we had lived in the house for a
time. Ethel's young man was a contractor, and he advised
us in making our plans. We had yard space, and we used it
when we added a bathroom on the main floor. Then we
enlarged the kitchen and converted the upstairs bathroom
into a studio.

It was a luxurious feeling to have a studio all my own
at last, but the sad truth is that I could not bring myself
to practice in it a great deal. The back of our house looked
out on a street, and neighbors' houses were pretty close.
Every time I sang out I had a guilty feeling that I was disturbing our neighbors. I tried moving my studio into the
basement, but that was no better. I went back to the little

room upstairs. With occasional exceptions, the regular practicing I should have done was not done.

When the crisis over the Town Hall concert developed, my studio was a place of retreat where I could go to be alone, to think, and, I am afraid, to brood. I had never been asked or coerced to feel a sense of responsibility for the family, but, being the eldest, I knew that I should help as much as possible and was glad that I could. As my earnings increased, our situation at home had improved. We began to acquire things we had dreamed of having, and we began to be easier about having friends in to dinner. We had gone so far as to buy our first large radio-phonograph.

The changes in our family's life came gradually. Somehow a phonograph runs through my recollections of those early years. The first we ever had in our house was a small portable affair, and it came on loan. It was brought by a young man who was a friend—it would be accurate now to call him my young man, though I would have been hesitant to use that phrase then.

I was looking at a television show one afternoon recently, on which a little girl was being questioned by a master of ceremonies. "Who is the little boy next to you? Do you know him?"

"Oh yes," the little girl said.

"Is he your brother?"

"Oh no," she replied, "he's my boy friend."

She was between eight and ten, and I thought to myself, How awful to have a boy friend at that age. But when I think back to my childhood I recall being no older than this little girl when there was a little boy whom I secretly thought of as a special boy friend, though that was not the way we phrased it. And later on, when I was in my teens, I remember mooning away the time with paper and pencil, writing the names of the boys I knew—and there were many at the church—and weaving dreams around the names of those I liked most. There was, of course, a special one, but that was before I met King.

I met King—his full name is Orpheus H. Fisher, and another nickname he had was Razzle—in Wilmington, Delaware, when we were both still in school. I had gone down to appear in a benefit concert arranged by Mrs. Banton, who was active in civic affairs. After the concert Mrs. Banton took me to the home of a Mr. Fisher, where a reception was being held for some Washington friends of the Fishers. Mrs. Banton preceded me up the high front steps of the Fisher house and entered. I happened to be walking slowly. When I reached the entrance the fine-looking young man at the door stretched his arm across my path. I tried to move past him at the side, and he barred the way with his body. All through this performance he kept laughing as though it were a huge joke.

At first I was amused and then annoyed, and I was also determined to go inside. " I shall call Mrs. Banton," I said, "and I shall yell, too, if I have to."

Still laughing, he stepped aside just as Mrs. Banton returned to see what the delay was. In the house I met another young man, shorter than the one at the door but bearing a resemblance. I stayed a while at the reception, meeting hosts and guests, and then left and took a train to Philadelphia.

[ 80 ]

The doorbell rang one day weeks later, and my sister came back to say that there was a Mr. Fisher to see me.

"Mr. Fisher?" I had forgotten the Wilmington incident. "I don't know any Mr. Fisher," I said.

My sister went back to the door and told the visitor, "My sister doesn't know you."

"Oh yes, she does," he insisted. "She was in my house in Wilmington."

I went to the door, and it was the shorter of the Wilmington young men. He stayed for a while. When he left he said he would be back shortly. And he was—the same day. We saw a good deal of each other, and then one day he arrived with the taller one, his brother. After that both appeared very often at our house. One day the taller one, sitting on the same divan as I, moved his hand across the back of the seat, touched my shoulder, and, when I looked to see why, slipped me a folded piece of paper that lay under his fingertips. When I could do so without drawing attention, I opened the paper, which bore this message: "This affair between you and my brother has got to stop."

Affair, I thought—what does he mean? I'm not having any affair. But it was not long before King, the taller of the brothers, became my boy friend. He was the younger of the two. Leon was a chemist and had a modest business in Philadelphia. King traveled up to Philadelphia to attend art school. He used to come over to our house after school, and we would play records on the phonograph he had borrowed for me.

The day came when King said he wanted me to meet his family. It was a well-known, quite social family, and I was excited and nervous. I had been in his home, but this visit

to Wilmington would be different; he was very particular
about how I looked and what I wore. I still have the dress
I wore on that trip—blue cotton with little black and
white figures, made on simple lines, with small tucks serving as trimming. Over it I had on a collarless, close-fitting,
full-length white coat with three-quarter sleeves. I wore
white slippers and a large hat.

King was one of a large family—three older sisters and
three brothers in addition to Leon. When we got to Wilmington he took me to see his sisters first—each married
and in her own home—and in the evening I had dinner at
his parents' house. King did not say anything about the
seriousness of this expedition, but once we were back in
Philadelphia he made clear what he had on his mind—as
if I did not suspect.

As a matter of fact, he had suggested earlier that we
run away and get married. I was busy with the beginnings
of my concert life, and I thought that there was no great
hurry. Another day we were out strolling, and we walked
down a street of fine homes that were owned by the people
who lived in them. He stopped in front of one of the
houses.

"You know Mrs. Roberts, don't you?" he said.

"Yes."

"Let's go in and say hello to her."

"No," I said. "I don't like visiting unless people know
I'm coming."

"I know her well," he replied. "She won't mind."

"No," I said.

"Come on," he insisted and led me up the steps.

As he was about to press the button I asked, "Listen, what are you going to see her for?"

"I'm going to see," he said, "if she has a little apartment where we can live."

I got down those steps in a hurry.

We continued to see each other often. My concert work increased, and he completed art school and a few years later went off to New York to study and to work. I felt badly when he left town. I cried. He never knew this till now. My poor record as a letter-writer did not help matters much, although he phoned from time to time. I remember in one of his letters to me he said that he thought it was high time we sent our clothes to the laundry in the same bundle.

One gets swept up in a career, and one has time for little else. I went to Europe, and, when I returned, another young man whom I admired came out in a tender to meet the boat, and King heard about it. King visited me only once in the months I remained in the United States, and our conversation was brief and cool. He left, and I could not tell whether I would ever see him again. But when I was back in Europe he sent me a long letter. Upon my return to the United States he came to see me often, and presently we knew that someday we would be married. What with King's busy career as an architect and mine with its recurrent long absences from home, our wedding did not take place until 1943. It was worth waiting for.

I have been running far ahead of myself. With the borrowed phonograph, King brought some records to my house. There were "Song of the Volga Boatmen," and

Galli-Curci singing "Clavellitos" and "Una voce poco fa" from *The Barber of Seville*. This was way back in the days when high C's made no difference to me, and I would sing the coloratura runs and trills right along with Galli-Curci. That little machine sounded magnificent to me, and so did Galli-Curci. Finally the phonograph and records had to be returned, the records in an alarmingly bad state because I had played them so many times.

We did not have a phonograph again until some time later, when Sadie Johnson, a friend in Bethlehem, Pennsylvania, gave us one. And that one served until we were able to buy our own. In the meantime, however, I made a record in Camden at the Victor plant. Since we did not have a phonograph at this period, I heard the record for the first time under curious circumstances.

There was a Mr. Pasternak in Philadelphia who was interested in things musical, including the Philharmonic Orchestra, an amateur group not to be confused with the Philadelphia Orchestra, which was then being conducted by Leopold Stokowski. Mr. Pasternak was good enough to take notice of me, and through him I met a Dr. Hirsch, who played with the Philadelphia Philharmonic in his spare time. Dr. Hirsch was in the audience when I sang for the first time in Philadelphia with the Metropolitan Opera early in 1955, and he came backstage. He wanted to know whether I remembered the evenings years ago when he had had musicians visit and play in his home and when I was invited to be a guest. Indeed I remembered.

I can recall being asked to sing on several occasions. One evening when Mr. Pasternak was among the guests I was asked to sing, and I did "Heaven, Heaven." Mr. Pasternak kept suggesting that I repeat the song. I could not understand why, but I went through the song four times. Then he asked whether I thought I did it the same way each time and whether I felt I could walk into a studio and record it. I said I thought I could, and he arranged the appointment. I don't remember anything about a recording agreement; all I know is that Mr. Boghetti acted for me, and he accompanied me to Camden, where I recorded two songs, "Heaven, Heaven" and "Deep River."

I did not hear the completed record after it was issued. In fact, I was hardly aware that it was available publicly and I had forgotten it completely, I think, by the time we were busy buying furniture for our little house. I remember making our purchases in a store where the salesman was named Mr. Mann. When I chose things that were comparatively expensive he complimented me on my good taste, but no doubt he wondered how a girl of high school age would be able to pay for such things. I might add that we did not intend to spend our last penny on furniture any more than we would have on food or clothes. But we hoped to get good things, and we thought we would be able to pay for them in monthly installments. When Mr. Mann was convinced that I was earning enough money to warrant the commitments we were making, he agreed to let us have the things we wanted. That furniture is still in the little house. The wood and construction were good; we got value for our money.

We made an impression on Mr. Mann, I suppose. I remember that I once wandered off and left him talking with my sister. When I returned she was smiling, and I wanted to know why. Mr. Mann provided the explana-

[85]

tion. "I just told her," he said, "that someday you're going to have the whole family on easy street."

I made occasional visits to this store, either to pay the monthly installments on our furniture or to buy something. Mr. Mann was usually there to give us a cordial greeting. One day my sister and I were standing at the cashier's window when we heard a phonograph in the store start to play. The voice and the song were oddly familiar and oddly strange. The song I knew; it was "Deep River." The voice? There was something in it like mine, and yet I thought it was another singer. Mr. Mann came up, smiling. My heart was jumping and I was flustered, and he had noticed my surprise and discomfort.

"Do you know who's singing?" he asked.

My sister answered, "Oh, yes, it's Marian."

I did not speak, and I could not get out of the store fast enough. I felt palpitations for many minutes after I left.

When we finally had a phonograph of our own and acquired a copy of the record, I could not bring myself to listen to it except when I was all alone. I could not bear to hear my voice coming out of the machine even when only Mother and my sisters were about. I can't explain why.

In those days following the Town Hall concert our little house was like a refuge from disaster. But while I questioned myself on my vocation and drew nourishment from Mother's calmness and inner strength, I could not forget that our savings were small. I knew that I could not remain idle for long, but I could not bring myself to sing seriously.

In time the wounds began to heal. I dared to sit down

at the piano and try a song or two. Then I found myself returning to Mr. Boghetti's studio more frequently, and the business of working and repairing the flaws in one's equipment was resumed.

I determined to do something about my languages at all costs. Mr. Boghetti had a Miss Janney, who taught French in one of the high schools, come to his studio, and I concentrated harder than ever when my opportunity came to work with her. Later on I found occasion to be coached in French songs with Leon Rothier, who was a distinguished bass at the Metropolitan Opera. Mr. Boghetti was a satisfactory guide in Italian, but the German continued to worry me. For a wild moment there was a temptation to ignore the repertoire of German Lieder, but I realized that this was no solution. I loved these songs, and I knew that I would have to sing them if I was to have a serious career in music. I did not find a German teacher, but whenever I had learned a song I tried to do it for someone who had a command of the language and who could help me with meaning and pronunciation. I became increasingly aware that learning the meaning of the words was not enough. It was imperative to speak German, fluently if possible. But how was I to come to that?

The very concern with these problems helped to complete the cure. Soon I found myself singing again, accepting engagements, and touring with Billy King as my accompanist.

It was not too difficult to obtain engagements. Billy and I had kept a card file of every place we had appeared in— all the Negro schools, churches, and social organizations. We had accumulated close to two hundred cards, and he

[87]

wrote to these people, telling them we were available. Presently I was singing again. There was warm applause, and occasionally a criticism that was not too harsh. It seemed a happy time.

CHAPTER 8

# Mother

THINGS were going well again—not grandly, of course, but there were earnings, payments could be made on the installments, and a little money began to accumulate in the savings account, although there was no danger whatever that I would have to be looking for a second bank for a long, long while. Mother continued to work, as she had been doing without let-up since my father's death.

She had a job at the Wanamaker store, which did not pay a great deal but provided us with at least a small income we could depend on. We knew she worked hard, very hard, but I think we never realized how desperately hard. She never complained, either to us or to the people for whom she worked. I think she did mostly cleaning work, and I know that extra tasks were always being piled on her. They knew only too well that she would not protest; on the contrary, she would keep going, and if it was within her power she did all the chores assigned to her. We were told that other women in the work force might

[ 89 ]

complain about onerous duties, and then the supervisor would load them onto Mother.

Occasionally we went down to Wanamaker's because we had some urgent problem to discuss with Mother. We always found her working so assiduously that she would scarcely stop for a few moments to talk to us. And when she paused to listen we could see that she was not paying as close attention as she usually did at home. She had her mind on her work.

We had seen Mother going and coming from work all these years, and though we were preoccupied with our own affairs we would have been blind if we had not noticed how weary she was at times. It was borne in on me that she must be freed from her bondage, that the first thing we must do the moment we could afford it was to get her out of all this.

The day came unexpectedly, without preparation. She arrived home from work one evening, not feeling well. We had prepared dinner, but she did not eat. I was worried about her and, knowing that she would make little of her illness, I slipped out unseen and went down to the corner and rang the doorbell of Dr. Taylor, whom Mother had known when they had both lived in Virginia.

Dr. Taylor soon arrived at our house, and Mother was surprised and wanted to know how he had happened to come by. "Oh, I just thought I'd stop in," he said casually. "I see you're not well." Without asking her permission, he took her pulse, asked her questions, made an examination, and said, "I'll take a look at you tomorrow, and I think you ought to stay in for a few days."

The next morning Mother was up at her usual time.

She was sneezing and coughing and looking miserable, but she was preparing to go to work. We reminded her of what the doctor had said, but she did not see how she could stay home for a few days, with her many obligations. We were just as determined as she, and because she was really shaky on her feet she submitted.

She stayed home for quite a few days. Though she was increasingly concerned about getting back to work, even she realized that she had been very ill and needed time to recuperate. I kept thinking about the problem and considering our financial position and possibilities, and I came to a very definite decision.

I went to the telephone and called Wanamaker's. I asked to speak to the supervisor, and as I waited for her to come to the phone I felt, I must say, a glowing satisfaction. I was primed for the lady. She was a big person on her job, and maybe she had a heart, but it remained at home when she went to work. It was a good and happy moment when she came to the phone and I could say, after identifying myself, "I just wanted to tell you that Mother will not be coming back to work."

I realize that this statement could not have been shattering to her. After all, she would be able to find some other poor soul on whom to load extra work. But to us it was an event of great joy—and another turning point.

It proved to be a grand thing for all of us. It was good to come home, after being away, to find the place warm and lovely because of Mother's loving care. She cooked for us, looked after our things, kept herself busy in a hundred useful ways. But the marvelous thing was to see her comfortable and at ease, without the fearful pressure of a relentless daily grind eating away at the sources of her energy.

It is difficult to describe Mother's purity and simplicity of character, and she will find it embarrassing that I speak of her in print. But I must. A great deal of what I am and what I achieved I owe to her. Not once can I recall, from my earliest recollections, hearing Mother lift her voice to us in anger. Even after my father's death, when she was grief-stricken and sorely troubled, she was not short with us. When she corrected us she used a conversational tone. She could be firm, and we learned to respect her wishes. She did not use the rod, but she had a strap, a leather affair about twelve inches long that was plaited at the top and that had ends hanging free. If there was need to add weight to her words, Mother would scurry off and bring back the strap. She would wave it in front of us as she talked, and that was nearly always enough.

I cannot remember a single complaint from Mother. Though she toiled incessantly, she did not spend money on personal things. Her first concern was our needs. She might have wanted a dress, a coat, or a pair of shoes, but she never mentioned it. In later years, when the purchase of such things for her would have been easy and a privilege for me, she spoke not a word of her desires; I had to ask my sisters whether there was something Mother would enjoy. I no longer reprove her when she lets someone take unfair advantage of her, as I might have when I was younger. She is what she is, bless her.

She lives now in the little house we bought together more than twenty-five years ago. It is probably inadequate by many standards, but it is home to her, and she loves it.

The street is no longer what it used to be, and the neighborhood as a whole has changed. I have suggested getting her a larger house, but she is not interested. There is no necessity, she replies. My sister Alyce shares the house with her, and the adjoining house, of equal size, is occupied by Ethel and her son, Jim DePriest, now a student at the University of Pennsylvania.

It is the pleasantest thing in the world to go into that home and feel its happiness. A larger house would not in itself bring that. They are all comfortable, and they cherish and protect one another. When I phone from out of town late at night and speak to my sister, I ask whether Mother has gone to bed, and I am told, "She is right here." I remind Mother that she should be getting to bed early, and I can hear her laughing softly as she says, "Right away, right away."

I know that it warms her to have her grandson near her as he grows up, just as I think that when he gets to be a man, making his own life, he will have pleasant memories of his home and family. And perhaps Mother is experiencing familiar sensations as she watches Jim, who organized his own jazz band in high school, going off on trips with his outfit, earning money on the side.

Mother has not even asked me to help her to help others, but I have found out through Alyce about things Mother would like to do for a neighbor in need and have tried to be of use to her. None of us will ever know about all the acts of generosity she has performed for friends and neighbors without telling her family.

When the church to which Mother belongs—she remained a Methodist, though her husband and children were Baptists—wanted me to come and give a concert, the ladies spoke to her. But she did not ask me directly; she advised the ladies to communicate with my management, adding that she thought I would do it if possible. In due time I appeared at the church. A regular fee was charged, and then a check for an equal sum was returned to the church. I sang a regular program, and there was a big crowd that had a lot of enthusiasm. Mother sat in her regular seat in the church, smiling, happy, and silent. I have no doubt that she insisted on paying her way in.

I know that when I have made contributions in her name to the Widows' Club to which she belongs at her church, she has been pleased and has always made it a point to thank me.

I am running ahead of my story, but this is about Mother. As my career expanded I kept thinking of doing something special for her. Once when I was in Europe I wrote her to ask her whether there was anything she had dreamed of having from girlhood on and that she had not been able to have. I told her that at last it was within my power to give her something that could only have been imagined long ago, and that I would very much like to do so.

Mother replied that it thrilled her to have such a letter, but she did not know what I could do for her. All she wished, she wrote, was that God would lift up people to understand and be kind and that He would hold me in the highest of His hands.

I tried again, with a specific suggestion. Would she like to come to Europe? She answered that she would like to someday but did not see how she could leave the children alone. The "children," my sisters, were in their twenties. However, she spoke of my letter to some relatives and friends, and they persuaded her that the "children" could look after themselves.

Finally I got word that she would come. Knowing that travel would be complicated for her, I wrote to Billy King, who remained a friend though he was no longer my accompanist, and asked him whether he would have the leisure to be Mother's traveling companion. All arrangements would be made for him, naturally, and his only contribution would be his time. He sent an immediate reply, offering to adjust his affairs so that he could make the trip.

I met them when they arrived in England, where Mother stayed for several weeks. Then we traveled to France, and Mother remained in Paris while I went off to fill some concert dates in the Low Countries. When I returned she and I did some of the sights she had not done with Billy King.

I had hoped she would spend six months in Europe. Hardly two months were up when she said to me one day as I was dressing for a concert, "Darling, I have been thinking. I can be of no assistance to you here, and I don't want to be a hindrance. I would like to go home when it is convenient." I am sure that she had the "children" on her mind.

And so she returned home, and I wonder whether she realized how delightful it had been for me to have her there. The ladies of her church made much of her journey, and I believe they induced her to give a talk on her trip. It was probably the only time she made a speech.

Mother's influence on us was profound. She did not deliver lectures to us, but she guided us by her example. She

[ 95 ]

never tried to tell me what to do with my life; if she had any wish for my future other than my happiness, I never heard of it. Since I began to sing at a tender age and people predicted that I would be a singer, it may be that Mother thought so too. If I had wanted to study medicine I am sure that she would have done everything in her power to help me find the wherewithal. She did not seem to mind that my aunt took me to my earliest engagements; she was content to remain in the background. If I came to her for advice about my musical affairs she would say, "Darling, you know more about it than I do." But if she saw that I had to have counsel, she would find someone who could help.

Mother gave balance to the home and led us into a rich spiritual life. We knew from earliest childhood that she prayed, and she saw to it that as little girls we said our prayers. As we grew older she always asked, when she tucked us into bed, whether we had said our prayers. If we had not—and we did not know how to deceive her—she would pull back the covers and we would crawl out of bed and get down on our knees to say them.

Good habits can be fine things. If you say your prayers every night there comes a time when they grow more meaningful to you. The child who learns to repeat after his mother, "Now I lay me down to sleep," may get a little thrill out of just saying it, at the beginning. After a time he realizes that he can do nothing about keeping his own soul when he is asleep. As he says, "Now I lay me down to sleep, I pray Thee, Lord, my soul to keep," the realization comes to him that there is Someone else to whom he

[ 96 ]

can commit his soul when he cannot take care of it himself.

And later, when Mother taught us the Lord's Prayer, she put her heart into it. You tried to say it as she did, and you had to put a little of your own heart into it. I believe that Mother, realizing that she was left alone to raise three girls, knew that she had to have a support beyond herself.

Mother's religion makes her believe that she will receive what it is right for her to have if she is good and conscientious in her faith. If it does not come, it is because He has not considered it right for her. She does not question. And we grew in this atmosphere, aware that Mother indeed had a strength beyond the energies of her small body. We believed as she did because we wanted the same kind of haven in the time of storm.

It is not unusual for young people today to consider the Bible and what it stands for as things not to be taken seriously. They may be interested in themselves or in some passing fancies. They may go to Sunday school and, upon departing, leave behind them what they have heard. There are movements to prove that certain things in the Bible are untrue. What they are designed to accomplish I don't know. What I do know is this: Who is there among us who will never find himself in need of a refuge?

I may have had moments of being too preoccupied with immediate affairs to think of larger matters. But as I grew older I saw that talking to Mother helped me when I was in trouble, and then I realized, as I traveled and was away from home for long periods, that I could not always count on reaching out to her for support. The time came when I had to decide where I would find the new strength I needed. I found it where Mother had always found hers.

I believe in the basic things Mother believes in. Her God is my God. I would not condemn people who do not believe as we do. I feel, however, that each one of us must have something in which he believes with all his heart, so that he need never be absolutely alone. Mother was wise not to try to persuade us to be as she is or to do as she does; her example was such that we wished to follow in her footsteps.

My religion is something I cherish. I am not in church every Sunday, but I hope and believe that I am on good speaking terms with Him. I carry my troubles, and I don't sit back waiting for them to be cleared up. I realize that when the time is ripe they will be dissolved, but I don't mean that one should sit inert, waiting for all things to come from above. If one has a certain amount of drive, intelligence, and conscientiousness, one must use them. Having made the best effort, one is more likely to get a hearing in an extremity.

I believe that I could not have had my career without the help of the Being above. I believe, as Mother does, that He put it in the hearts of many people to be kind, interested, and helpful, and to do things that needed to be done for me and that I could not have done for myself. It would have happened anyhow, some might say. I don't believe that it would have happened anyhow.

One Sunday recently I went to church in Danbury, Connecticut, where my home is. I felt more impelled than usual to go that Sunday, I could not say why. During the service the minister said, "I have been praying since I came here to substitute for your minister that one Sunday before I left a certain person might arrive, and my prayer has been answered." He believed that his prayer was answered, and I had not known that he had prayed. I just had to go to church. All-seeing God had put things together.

I suppose you can always find manifestations if you are a believer, and if you don't believe you can find reasons to prove that the believer is wrong. But you can only travel the spiritual way you believe to be best for you, regardless of whether it is good for anyone else.

It is well that there are different roads to faith. Mother's faith has lighted the way for us in all the days of our lives, even the hardest we have gone through. Her day-to-day living and the way she accepted and greeted life and its meaning were the forces that guided us.

Mother feels especially blessed that the family holds closely together and that it does so because it wants to. We owe this blessing, and many others, to her whom I call "my little girl."

# CHAPTER 9

# Contest

CONTESTS gave my career a lift when it seemed that there would be little change in the routine of engagements that Billy King and I got through our card file. The first was in Philadelphia, and it was run by the Philharmonic Society. Each year this organization selected a soloist after a competition. I do not recall a great deal about the time I competed. I can see the room and the building in my mind's eye, and I know that the judges sat where they were not visible to the contestants, but I do not remember what I sang. At the end I received the certificate that went to the winner. As I recall it, there were not too many competitors. However, the newspapers published reports of the contest and the name of the winner, the first Negro to take first prize, and this, in turn, caused people not of my group to be curious about my capacities. When I sang in a hall instead of in a church, there were quite a few white people in the audience. Since I hoped to have a career not confined to singing to one group or on a limited circuit, the occasion represented considerable progress.

The Philadelphia contest took place, I think, in 1923. Two years later there was a much bigger affair in New York under the auspices of the Lewisohn Stadium Concerts. Mr. Boghetti offered to enter me, informing me that I would have to go to New York to compete. I agreed. He entered another pupil, Reba Patton, a soprano, and he took special pains to prepare us. He had me come to his studio several times a week to rehearse the contest pieces— an aria and two songs. The aria was the main number, and the songs were to be ready if the judges wanted to hear something else. We decided that my aria would be "O mio Fernando" from Donizetti's *La Favorita*.

It was early summer when we were working toward this contest. As usual, I kept myself busy with a lot of other activities. I had made up my mind that this summer I would learn to swim, and I went regularly to the Y. W. C. A. for instruction. Unhappily, there are skills some people just cannot acquire, and swimming has defeated me. Even today, when we have our own little swimming place in the country, I go down and stand timidly in the shallow section meant for children. I am like a stone in the water. However, I was trying that summer, and all I got for my pains was an ear infection at a most embarrassing time.

The day of the trials arrived, and I took the train to New York. Mr. Boghetti had a studio on Park Avenue in addition to the one in Philadelphia, and I went there first. He had his studio pianist, Miss Johnson, who was to play for Miss Patton and me, waiting, and we rehearsed our contest pieces. We then headed for Aeolian Hall, where the competitors were being heard.

The judges sat alone in the balcony, and the auditorium was full of contestants, teachers, and accompanists. We had not realized that there would be so many competing; we heard later that there were about three hundred. I had suspected that we would be up against some highly professional young singers, and knew that the going would not be easy. I was tense and excited, and I think Mr. Boghetti was too.

We took seats in the auditorium, assuming that the contestants would be called by name. They were called by number, and we did not have numbers. When we finally approached a table to obtain a number, we got 44—that is, Miss Patton got 44, and I received 44A. It did not calm me to know that I would be forty-fifth. As it turned out, I was perhaps sixtieth, for some numbers sheltered more than two contestants. I remember that 6 was followed by 6A, 6B, and 6C.

As we listened we became aware that the judges were not wasting time. Their schedule required them to hear something like a hundred persons a day. It was hot in New York, and the hall was not air-conditioned. One could not blame them if they were swift in their judgments, and they were competent. They had a noisy clicker upstairs, and when it sounded you knew you were to stop in midpassage and walk off the stage.

As my turn approached, Mr. Boghetti whispered that no matter what happened I must continue to the end of my aria and to be sure to sing the trill. It was lovely of him to refuse to be intimidated by the clicker, but I had been sitting there listening to the other singers, and at least six of them had launched into "O mio Fernando" and had been interrupted before they reached the middle. I made up my mind that I would not defy the rules of the contest. I would stop when the implacable clicker sounded.

I was finally called, and I began with the recitative and then launched into the aria proper, with one part of my mind waiting apprehensively for the voice of doom upstairs. It did not come. I was allowed to sing the whole aria, including the trill. There was a burst of applause from the other contestants in the auditorium because no one had gone through an entire number. An indignant voice reminded everyone that the rule against applause must be observed. Then a judge called from the balcony, "Does 44A have another song?" I sang one in English.

No one said anything to us as we left the hall. I returned to Philadelphia, and a few days later Mr. Boghetti informed me that I was one of sixteen chosen for the semi-finals and that I would have to return to New York for the next phase of the contest.

The day of the semi-finals was hot and muggy, as uncomfortable as New York can be in the summer. As Mr. Boghetti and I went to Aeolian Hall I said to him, "You know, there is something wrong with my ear."

He looked alarmed. "What's wrong?" he wanted to know.

I did not tell him that I had been trying vainly to learn to swim. "There seems to be some growth in it," I said, "and I can't pry it out." He wanted to know whether it affected my hearing, and I told him, "Not particularly, but it is very uncomfortable."

He tried to reassure me. "It won't be long today," he said. "There are only sixteen to be heard."

I sang "O mio Fernando" again, and my two songs. When we left no one gave us any inkling of how things had come out. We stopped at Mr. Boghetti's studio, hopeful that we would have some word before I took my train back to Philadelphia. As far as we knew, four contestants were to be chosen for the finals. With my ear throbbing furiously, my mind was on getting back home.

There was a telephone call, and when Mr. Boghetti hung up he rushed to me in excitement. "We have won," he shouted. "There will be no finals!" I was thrilled, but the pain in my ear was so intense that I could hardly give any sign of pleasure. I rose to go. Mr. Boghetti must have been terribly disappointed in me. He was bubbling with joy, and I was undemonstrative.

"Where are you going?" he cried.

"Home," I said.

I remember I took a seven-o'clock train. I should have been floating on clouds, but I sat there miserably intent on the furious aching in my ear. Suppose what was wrong with the ear was deep inside? Suppose it would be difficult to remedy? How could one sing if one could not hear?

I arrived home, and Mother was waiting for me. Before she could speak I set down my music and said, "I am going down to the corner to see Doctor Taylor."

"All right, darling. How did you make out?"

"Oh, all right," I said, and I was at the door.

"When do you have to go back?"

"I'll tell you when I come back."

The doctor examined my ear and told me I had quite a

bad abscess. I had been stuffing it with cotton and earplugs to keep the water out during my swimming lessons, and had succeeded in irritating and infecting it. He lanced the abscess, drained it, and put a dressing on the ear.

I was feeling better when I returned home. Mother had learned about the outcome of the contest because Mr. Boghetti, who could not contain his excitement, had telephoned to discuss it while I was at the doctor's. I was ashamed that I had been so uncommunicative, but I did not have to be. Mother's eyes shone with pride.

The newspapers in Philadelphia made a fuss about the contest the next day. When the time came to collect the prize, an appearance with the New York Philharmonic at the Lewisohn Stadium, not only my family but a good many friends and well-wishers made the trip from Philadelphia to be present.

The concert took place on the night of August 26, 1925. I came to New York early in the day because there was to be a morning rehearsal with the orchestra. Willem Van Hoogstraten was the conductor, and he was most understanding. He could see that I was not a seasoned singer, especially when it came to performing with orchestra. He probably did not have to be told that I had been chosen more for my voice than for my experience. In any case, he could not have been more attentive and thoughtful to the most famous and experienced singer.

That evening I wore a new dress purchased at Wanamaker's in Philadelphia especially for this occasion. It seemed to me quite a thing, very smart without being gaudy, and I thought, too, that its powder-blue color was complimentary to my complexion.

The time came for me to sing. It was a thrill to walk through an aisle made by the musicians and take my place right beside the conductor. As I looked out, there seemed to be a sea of faces; the stadium, I saw, was packed. There was applause before the start, and this was like a welcome and an encouragement. I will not say that I was not nervous. Perhaps deep down there was the painful memory of the Town Hall fiasco. I think, in any case, that one should never feel cocky or blasé before any appearance; it is unfortunate ever to lose that feeling of mingled excitement and anxiety. But I do not think that I was frightened; I had been singing too long and in too many places for that. Furthermore, I concentrated immediately on the conductor.

When we finished "O mio Fernando" the musicians were generous enough to tap their bows on the music stands. Even if this was only a gesture of courtesy, it was encouraging. I followed with several spirituals. As I sang I felt at ease, and I like to believe that the performance was not too bad.

If there was any expectation that this appearance would suddenly lift me to a top level of acceptance, a proper perspective was soon restored. There was an improvement, but, as always, it continued to be gradual. The newspapers in New York, Philadelphia, and cities throughout the United States and Canada took notice of the event, but there was no great splash of space. *The New York Times,* for example, devoted three paragraphs to the concert. There were these lines about the soloist:

Miss Anderson made an excellent impression. She is endowed by nature with a voice of unusual compass, color and dramatic capacity. The lower tones have a warm contralto quality, but the voice has the range and the resources of the mezzo-soprano. In passages of sustained melody the singer showed a feeling for melodic lines, while in the aria, "O mio Fernando," she gave evidence of instructive dramatic impulse. Miss Anderson also sang Negro spirituals.

That fall, when Billy King and I resumed our concerts, the effects of the contest and stadium appearance were noticeable. Almost without my realizing it, I was at a point where I had to compete with singers who were well established. It was possible to increase fees and to obtain more engagements, and the range and character of these engagements began to change. We had invitations from Canada and the West Coast. Morning musical clubs here and there asked for dates, and so did several regular concert series. Even in the South the nature of audiences changed a little. When there was a concert in a Negro school auditorium, there would be white people in the audience.

The fees went up to three hundred and fifty, and five hundred dollars in special places. There was progress. There was also a long, hard road to travel and a lot to learn on the way.

# CHAPTER 10

# Step Up

IT WAS a step up to come under the notice and management of Arthur Judson. I had high hopes that now steady advancement was assured. Arthur Judson, after all, represented the top in concert management, and when he showed an interest in my work I may have gone too far in imagining a future of unlimited rosiness.

I don't know whether Mr. Judson had taken notice of my work before the stadium contest, and as far as I know he did not hear me at the stadium. Some time later I appeared at Carnegie Hall as soloist with the Hall Johnson Choir. I sang in R. Nathaniel Dett's "Listen to the Lambs." It was a good evening; the program was fine and the audience excellent.

Mr. Judson came back to see me. He was kind enough to say that he had not been aware that I could give that sort of performance. He thought that his office would be able to do something for me, and he spoke casually of being in a position to launch me at a fee of seven hundred and fifty dollars a performance. He had offices in New

York and Philadelphia and suggested that I come to see him in either place. The Hall Johnson Choir concert took place on a Sunday night, I remember, and we made an appointment for Tuesday morning in his Philadelphia headquarters.

Mr. Boghetti accompanied me to Mr. Judson's office. It was somewhat disappointing to find that the manager was now talking in terms of five hundred dollars for an engagement. I should not have been disconcerted, because I myself had felt that the jump to seven hundred and fifty from my going fee of three hundred at that time seemed too big. However, though it was a bit of a letdown, I could readily agree to a five-hundred-dollar rate, and I believed that being associated with the Judson name would mean a great deal.

There was another mild disappointment that morning. Mr. Judson explained that on the five-hundred-dollar level I would not be under his direct, personal management. My affairs would be handled by George Leyden Colledge, although I would be known as a Judson artist.

With Mr. Boghetti's approval, I agreed to this arrangement. It took some time before the contract was signed; there were more talks, and I had to sing for a lady whose opinion Mr. Judson wanted. Mr. Colledge requested that I turn over to his office the names and addresses of the people for whom I had been appearing. The card file Billy King and I had kept was sent to Mr. Colledge; it included well over one hundred entries, and there were cards for organizations that had sent inquiries. I also promised to forward all future requests to the Judson office, and I must say that it was a pleasure to be able to reply to inquiries that the letters had been referred to them. Mr. Colledge and his associates then notified all these people of my management by Judson, adding that the fee would be five hundred dollars. Some places were delighted to accede to the new price. Hampton Institute seemed to take pride in the fact that I had come under the aegis of a major manager and was able to command the fee. Other institutions that could not afford five hundred dollars simply did not bother to have me return.

The first year under the new arrangement brought fewer engagements than I had had in the past, but with the higher fee the amount earned remained about the same. There was no question that I was on another level. When Billy King and I decided to give a concert all our own in the Academy of Music in Philadelphia, it was undoubtedly impressive to be presented by the Arthur Judson office.

There were new, unexpected expenses. The Judson office prepared a four-page leaflet containing translations and texts of songs, to be distributed to the audience. It also got out other printed matter. The bills for these things were sent to me, and I remember that the cost during the first year was some hundreds of dollars—not an overwhelming sum, but it bulked large in my finances because my total earnings were not great.

With the higher fee, Billy King had to be paid more for his services as accompanist, and this was only fair and reasonable. And I found that clothes became a bigger item: I had to have more than one evening dress. I remember that for the first Judson year I got a new dress—light blue—and I had a pair of white slippers tinted blue to match. Even in those days I tried to have clothes that were simple in design but made of good material and effective in appearance. I might add that I began to realize, particularly when I appeared in the South, how important one's appearance was. I think that my people felt a sense of pride in seeing me dressed well. I don't mean that they were unaccustomed to good clothes and a good appearance. Quite a few of them owned handsome things and knew how to dress attractively. But it made them feel good, I found out, to see one of their own pleasantly got up.

The change in my itinerary under the Judson direction was not especially marked, and it was some years before I was moved up to the supervision of Mr. Judson's main office and the fee rose to seven hundred and fifty dollars. I still appeared in churches. I still traveled as I always had.

When we went South we still got Berth 13 and we still had to put up at the homes of kind acquaintances. The great majority of the concerts were what might be called Billy King–Marian Anderson dates; they stemmed from our previous tours. Eventually there was a Judson concert, one that our card file had nothing to do with producing. Then there were a few others, but they were not many. The high hopes began to dwindle. Progress seemed to have stopped; I had substantially the same circuit of concerts but little more. I was beginning to feel that I was at a standstill.

It would have been easy to blame the Judson office, and I suppose I felt then that all that could be done was not being done. I have no doubt that the Judson office was encountering resistance in selling a young Negro contralto

to its normal concert circuits, and I had no European reputation such as Roland Hayes had acquired. But all I knew
at the time was that I was uneasy.

I went to have a talk with Mr. Judson. The idea of going
to Europe had begun to occupy my thoughts, but most of
all I wanted some reassurance from him as to my prospects.
He remarked that he had been discussing me with one of
his best friends, a woman who knew a great deal about
singing. She had informed him that I was a soprano, not a
contralto, and he suggested that I go and sing for her. If
she decided that I really was a soprano I must make the
change immediately so that the billing for the next season
could be altered. I thanked him for his friend's interest
and told him that I knew I was not a soprano. If I tried
to sing as a soprano, I added, I would be able to sustain
the role for only a short time, and then there would be no
career at all. I don't think he was impressed by my views.

I confess I was upset. My manager's uncertainty about
whether I was on the right track on so fundamental a
thing as the nature and range of the voice could have no
other effect on me. It added to the underlying feeling that
things were not going too well.

It was Mr. Judson who also advised me to study with
Frank La Forge. This advice I eventually took, and I am
sure it turned out to be profitable, for Mr. La Forge was a
charming man, a good musician, a teacher with a reputation of working with many famous singers, and a person
with excellent connections, which could be helpful to a
young singer.

It proved to be a difficult thing to do—arranging to
work with Mr. La Forge. There was Mr. Boghetti to think

about. I wanted to be as fair as possible, and I told him that Mr. Judson had recommended my going to Mr. La Forge. Mr. Boghetti was indignant. He did not see why it was necessary. There was nothing, he insisted, that I could get in any other studio that I could not get from him. When I finally decided to work with Mr. La Forge I hoped I would also be able to continue with Mr. Boghetti. But my old teacher's pride was hurt. He would not have me. It was only later, when the lessons with Mr. La Forge had stopped, that Mr. Boghetti relented and let me return to his studio.

I was warned that even an audition with Mr. La Forge would come high. An appointment was made, and I was told that if I failed to keep it I would have to pay the charge anyhow. I went to see Mr. La Forge and sang for him. He offered to teach me, but the fee he mentioned was far beyond what I had ever paid Mr. Boghetti. There was the additional consideration that I would have to travel to New York for each lesson, which would thus become even more expensive. I told Mr. La Forge that I was in no position to spend so much for a half-hour lesson. He replied that if I could come from Philadelphia early in the morning and be in his studio by nine, he would give me an hour's time for the price of half an hour.

I agreed to this arrangement, but I found I could not carry the burden of the costs. After the third or fourth lesson I had to tell Mr. La Forge that, while I appreciated the value I was getting out of the hour's work, I could not afford to pay even the half-hour fee. I did not mind getting up at the crack of dawn to be in his studio by nine. I was eager for a change that might lead to a shake-up in the apparent standstill of the career. But there were still the obligations at home, and my net earnings were not enough to support new charges.

Mr. La Forge was understanding. He said that he would see what he could do, and at the next lesson he declared, "Someone has presented the studio with a scholarship, and if you can continue to come to New York, it is yours." I am not certain who provided these funds, but I believe it was Mr. La Forge's sister, Mrs. Hall.

I worked with Mr. La Forge for more than a year. I remember sitting downstairs one afternoon, waiting to see him, when I heard a magnificent voice singing a song in German. I was unfamiliar with this song, but I thought it was by Schubert. I could hear how perfectly the singer was enunciating the German, making the words so completely a part of the music that they might have been born together. If I ever reached the point where I could sing a song like that in that way, I thought, I would be the happiest person in the world.

Then a stately, handsome woman came down the stairs. I wonder whether she was aware of the admiration in my eyes. I went upstairs and asked Mr. La Forge who she was, and he told me—Margarete Matzenauer. I was too embarrassed to ask what the song was. As we began our lesson I glanced at the piano rack, hoping to find the book of music open to this song, but the book was closed, and its cover revealed no clue. Some time afterward I encountered the piece. It was "Er, der herrlichste von allen" ("He, the noblest of all men"), the second song in Robert Schumann's beautiful cycle of a woman's love and life, *Frauenliebe und Leben.*

I mentioned "Er, der herrlichste von allen" to Mr. La Forge when I knew the song's name, and he agreed to work on the cycle with me. We concentrated on this particular song, and when Mr. La Forge felt that I had made some progress with it he took me to a recording studio and we made a disk of it. This was the first time I dared to make a recording of anything in German. Years later I was able to sing the whole cycle in public and to record it.

If I had any illusions that my German was coming along, there was a performance one evening in Mr. La Forge's studio that dispelled them. Usually these things went well. The evening that I speak of there was a full program, and there was an audience in the studio. There were other singers besides myself, and I remember that Harry Burleigh was in the gathering. I sang a German song, and something inexplicable happened: I forgot some of the words and improvised others instead. It was an uncomfortable moment. Even though I was not inclined to nervousness, the uncertainty of what I was about had thoroughly confused me. People were gracious, but the incident disturbed me. It kept haunting me and making me feel that I must find some way to become absolutely sure of my German.

Working with Mr. La Forge was pleasant. He was always kind and thoughtful, conscious of what I wanted to achieve and eager to help. He was always willing to give me a few more minutes of work, or just to talk, if the next pupil did not arrive on time.

After I stopped working with Mr. La Forge I did not see him often, although I sang several of his songs at my concerts in later years. A few years before his death he phoned me while I was spending some time at my home in Danbury. It was an agreeable surprise to hear his voice after so long a period. He was living in Darien, Connecticut, and he said, "We are not too far away, and we never see each other. I think we should do something about it." I said I would love it, and he offered to come to see me in Danbury.

I must confess that I am not one for barging in on people, for I am reluctant to take up their time. Nor am I one for correspondence; it is a fault in me. If I had written or telephoned now and then, I could have seen Mr. and Mrs. La Forge occasionally, and this would have been rewarding. I can only hope that the understanding he always had made him aware that I admired him and thought of him often.

I gladly accepted his offer to come and visit, and we set a time. When the appointed day arrived—it was winter— there was quite a bit of snow on the ground. I called and told him that the weather was bad and that I could not be selfish enough to let him drive on dangerous roads. "Marian Anderson," he replied, "we never let the weather stand in the way of doing anything we want to do." And so he and Mrs. La Forge came, and they brought me a gift—the recording of "Er, der herrlichste von allen," which I had almost forgotten.

For me it was a fine, enriching evening, but I fear that our hospitality was not quite perfect. We happened at the time to have a puppy, which we spoiled a bit because we let it stay near us all the time. I remember we were having coffee in the living room, and I heard a lot of noise in the little library. The puppy was running around, growling and having a grand time. I began to suspect that something was wrong, and I went to look. The puppy had found Mrs. La Forge's handbag, a beautiful blue velvet affair; had ripped it apart, and was playing with the contents. I tried eventually to make good the loss, although Mrs. La Forge was gracious enough to act as if dogs regularly went about tearing her handbags.

Mr. La Forge did not suggest at any time that I should convert myself into a soprano, although I remember that Mr. Judson returned to the subject after I had begun going to this studio. However, I continued to feel that I must do something more to advance my career. Europe kept coming into my mind more often, and Mr. La Forge did not discourage the idea.

I discussed it with Mr. Judson. He ended the conversation with the remark, "If you go to Europe, it will only be to satisfy your vanity."

"I will go, then, for that purpose," I said.

*CHAPTER 11*

# First Trip to Europe

THE decision to go to Europe was not taken lightly.
There was, to begin with, the all-important question
of money. We had some savings in the bank. We calculated
that, after paying for the passage, I could take about fifteen
hundred dollars with me. There would be some money
left for the family, and, with the help my sisters could
provide, it should suffice.

Mother and I discussed the matter at length. I went over
all the arguments: I was going stale; I had to get away
from my old haunts for a while; progress was at a standstill; repeating the same engagements each year, even if
programs varied a little, was becoming routine; my career
needed a fresh impetus, and perhaps a European stamp
would help. Mother, as always, was understanding and encouraging. I assured her that all I wanted was to work to
become a fine artist and that not even Europe could turn
me into a great one overnight. I don't think Mother was
worrying very much about whether I could become a great
artist. She wanted me to do well whatever I undertook to

[ 118 ]

do, but most of all, I am sure, she wanted me to be happy. I talked to friends. Billy King endorsed the idea heartily. People at the church advised me to go. My sisters gave me courage by assuring me that they could take care of things while I was gone.

Passage was bought—second class on the old *Ile de France*. There were all kinds of things to decide—what clothes to take, what luggage, what provisions to make for carrying money. As the day for departure approached, the conferences with family and friends increased. Billy King came with a letter of introduction to Roger Quilter, an Englishman who had befriended Roland Hayes. Billy told me that he had written to Mr. Quilter, who would help me to arrange things when I got to London. Lawrence Brown, Roland Hayes's accompanist, who had first suggested study in Europe to me, wrote to Raimund von Zur Mühlen. The family came to New York to see me off.

The trip was pleasant, even though I was alone most of the time. I didn't make friends aboard ship. There may have been a few pangs of loneliness, but the experience was so new and exciting that the time went rapidly. There were a good many Americans on board, but I had the delightful feeling of being at least partly in a foreign environment. At dinner one night, when steak was being served, I asked to have mine very well done. When it came, it was not as well done as I liked, and I stabbed at it without enthusiasm. The waiter wanted to know what was wrong, and I told him. He went off with the meat and brought it back done almost to a crisp, frowning disapprovingly as he set it before me. Then he observed that I did not touch the wine on the table. "You could never be the wife of a

Frenchman," he said, and I suppose that to him this was the worst that could happen to anyone.

After a few days I became courageous enough to try out my high school French. I was on deck one evening, standing at the rail, when a gentleman come up and spoke to me in French. I tried to say something light and gay about the moon and spoke of *le soleil*. He was amused, and I was embarrassed. Very soon I excused myself and went below.

We reached England, and the boat train arrived at Paddington Station in London late in the evening. I went immediately to telephone Roger Quilter. As I understood the arrangements, he would tell me where to go, and if he were not home there would be a message. The phone rang for a long time, and finally there was an answer.

"This is Marian Anderson," I said. "I have just arrived."

The voice replied, "Who?"

I repeated my name slowly. The voice at the other end had never heard it before.

"Is this Roger Quilter?"

"No, madam."

"Well, who is it?"

"The butler, madam."

"May I speak to Mr. Quilter?"

"He's in a nursing home, madam."

That was that. No message of any sort. I hung up.

What to do next? I was not traveling light. I had two coats on my arm, and an overnight bag. I had my music case on a shelf under the phone. I had my purse in my hand. I hesitated to go wandering around in this fashion, seeking advice from strangers about a hotel. Then I recalled that John Payne, who had visited our house in Philadelphia years before, had told us all that if we were ever in London he would be happy to have us stay in his home.

John Payne had been a member of a Negro theatrical company that had played in England. He had liked the life there so well that when the company left he decided that he would settle in London. I looked up his phone number and went back to the same booth and called him. His voice was like a beacon in a fog. "By all means come over," he said. "We have a spare room and can put you up."

After gathering up my things, I walked out of the booth to get a cab, and I felt relieved and oddly buoyant. It must have been eleven-thirty P. M.; when I got into the taxi I was eager to catch sight of some of the famous landmarks, but I could see little of anything in the dark, and I noticed, too, that there was no window in the back of the cab. We pulled up at 17 Regents Park Road, and John Payne was there at the door to greet me before I got out of the cab. He was warm in his welcome, and we sat around and talked for two hours. Then he arose and said, "Now I will show you to your room."

I collected my things to follow him upstairs. My music case was nowhere in sight. We looked for it, but could not find it among my things, and John Payne asked where I could have left it. In the taxi, I thought. "I know I can find it," I said, "because all I need to do is find the taxi without any window in back."

"Most of them have no windows in back," he said, and led me to my room.

I lay awake all night, trying to retrace every move I had made after arriving at Paddington Station. I sought to pinpoint the moment when I no longer had the case, and it came to me that my buoyancy on leaving the station had been reasonable because I was not carrying so much.

The loss of the case, if lost it remained, could be a disaster. It contained not only the music I had brought with me but some books, personal things that I had transferred from my bulging handbag on the boat train, and, most important of all, a letter of credit for one thousand dollars, and five hundred dollars in travelers' checks. Aside from a few dollars that I had converted into English money at Southampton, this was my whole wealth and my essential passport to a long stay in England.

I was up and dressed as soon as I heard any stirring in the house, and when I came down the lady of the house said, "Today you will devote yourself to trying to find your things."

Mr. Payne announced, "We shall go to Scotland Yard." Miserable though I felt about the loss, that magic name gave me a momentary lift.

Mr. Payne had adjusted himself to the English tempo. There was no rush about getting out and racing to Scotland Yard. We did things about the house, we made plans for my stay in England while I wondered whether there would be any stay, and then we sat down to lunch. Finally we started out. On the way we stopped at the home of a friend of Mr. Payne's. Then we resumed our errand. By this time I was in an agony of suspense.

Everybody who has read and heard about Scotland Yard has his secret image of this wonderful, mysterious place, and everyone, I suppose, is let down by the ordinariness of the reality. I was too intent on my own troubles to be let down too far, but I do remember that I was amused by the unromantic sight of an endless number of umbrella handles jutting out of an enormous bank of cubbyholes. We were admitted to an inner office, and we soon discovered that my music case had not turned up.

We went to Brown Brothers, the bank on which my letter of credit was drawn, and reported the loss. Then we went to the American Express. Of course I had not jotted down the serial numbers of the checks; there were forms to fill out, and we had to wait while a quick investigation was made to find out whether any of the checks had been cashed. As far as could be found out, not yet.

It was time to return home to dinner. We hashed over the problem again, and now I was convinced that if I could find the porter who had helped me with my baggage he would be able to lead me to my taxi driver. After dinner the lady of the house accompanied me to Paddington Station to look for the porter. I assured the station agent, after receiving permission to go onto the platforms, that it would not be difficult to locate the porter because he spoke without using his h's. I had no idea how funny this was to him.

We walked up and down, peering into the faces of porters. Finally my companion said, "Listen, dearie, they'll be running us in as bad women, so we'd better talk to a bobby."

The policeman made a sensible suggestion, to try the Lost Property Office in the station. A man behind a desk listened to my story, and before I had finished he darted behind a partition and returned with the music case. "That's my bag," I cried, and reached for it. He insisted that I describe all that was in it, and then he made me sign my name in a huge ledger where there was a description of everything in my music case. As he turned the case over to me he told us that it had been found in the telephone booth and brought in by a bobby. I tipped the man behind the desk and left another tip for the bobby.

As the man behind the desk took his tip he said, "You are lucky that this case was not sent to Scotland Yard. If you had found it there you would have been required to pay a fee of ten per cent of its contents."

Was that true? It seemed an excessive fee, but I was too happy to care about finding out. As we turned to go an elderly clerk on a high stool called out, "I beg your pardon, lady. It is my job to look into the telephone booths, and ordinarily I would have found it, but I was too busy. It's my job, you know." I gave him a ten-shilling tip.

We took a taxi—it had no back window either—to Regents Park Road. I could breathe again and settle down to a fresh beginning toward being an artist.

Roger Quilter did not remain long in the nursing home, and a few days later I got to see him. He was a tall, thin, sensitive man, an English-looking Englishman, as I put it to myself. He had a fine home, always open to musicians. It was not uncommon to go there and find his music room occupied by someone who needed a quiet place to work and study. Mr. Quilter was a cultivated man, a patron of the arts, and a fine musician in his own right. He played very well, and he had a number of charming songs to his credit.

After some days in London I took a train to a town in Sussex called Steyning, where I hoped to begin work with Raimund von Zur Mühlen. I made arrangements for lodgings at the home of Vicky Newburg, a young printer, and his wife. Vicky-bird was what all his friends called him, and he and his wife were as friendly as could be. They gave me a room on the second floor, and when I woke up in the morning the windows were frosted over and I was shivering with cold. It was winter, and there was no central heating in the house. I came down all wrapped up, and Vicky-bird was apologetic. "We'll give you a heater," he said. The heater had to be fed with shilling pieces, and it never really warmed the room sufficiently.

I got to see Master, as Raimund von Zur Mühlen was called. Having been assured that he was the best man in England for Lieder, I felt a sense of excitement and almost fear. I was shown into a large room with a piano at the far end. Master was old, and he remained seated in a big chair with a red rug over his knees. He had a cane at his side, and when he wanted your attention he pounded the floor with it. He talked to me for a few minutes and then requested that I sing something. A young Englishman who was the accompanist went to the piano, and we began. I sang "Im Abendrot," and when I was finished Master said, "Come here."

It seemed like a long walk from the piano to a chair beside him.

"Do you know what that song means?" he demanded.

"Not word for word," I said, "and I'm ashamed that I don't."

"Don't sing it if you don't know what it's about."

"I know what it's about," I explained, "but I don't know it word for word."

"That's not enough," he said with finality.

He asked me to sing something else. This time I did a song in English, with which I felt secure.

Master pounded his cane on the floor before I was finished. "Wait a minute," he called. "You're singing like a queen, and I have not crowned you yet."

He was not unkind, however, and we sat and talked for a while. When I left he lent me a book of Schubert songs and suggested that I learn the first one in it, "Nähe des Geliebten." It had several verses in German, and the book contained no English translation. Fortunately, Vicky-bird knew some German. Ordinarily he and his wife spent a lot of time cutting the pages of books just off the press, but that evening they abandoned their favorite pastime to help me with the German. Vicky-bird was stumped by some phrases, and went out and called in a friend who also knew some German. Together, we all tried to puzzle out the subtle meanings of the German poetry. It was obvious to me that even if they succeeded in doing a fair job on this song I could not possibly learn enough German overnight to be at home with the language. I thought that Master must be merely testing my capacities to work.

I did not see Master again for almost a week. He was recovering from a thrombosis, and some days he did not feel well enough to see anyone. Nor could he devote much time to me. After I had sung a part of "Nähe des Geliebten" he stopped me, though he was not too displeased with what I had accomplished. I went away from that lesson feeling that this was really right for me. The next day I went to Brighton and ordered a piano.

Master was indisposed, and lessons were postponed. I remained in Steyning for several weeks, hoping that he would soon be well enough to resume his teaching. Finally I returned to London. A few days later I hopefully telephoned Vicky-bird and got the sad news that Master had been obliged to stop all teaching.

It was a keen disappointment. After only two visits with Master, I had felt that he represented the answer to my most urgent artistic problems. Now I had to start looking for a teacher again. Roger Quilter suggested Mark Raphael, a pupil of Raimund von Zur Mühlen. I went to Raphael, who was a good teacher, and the lessons with him were beneficial. But I had traveled to England to study with Master, and I just could not help feeling disappointed.

Life in London for me centered largely around the house on Regents Park Road. I spent most of my time in it when I was not out taking lessons. I should add that I did some voice work with Amanda Ira Aldrich, daughter of Ira Aldrich, the famous actor of Othello fame. She had an excellent reputation as a voice teacher. On this I was going against Mr. Boghetti's advice. I had returned to him before I left for Europe, and he had insisted that I must not let any teacher work with me on purely vocal matters. Someone to coach me in repertoire—that he approved. But I wanted to study as much as possible.

I took my meals at the Payne home. I never ate out alone save for stopping at a Lyons Corner House for tea once or twice. I was not one for rambling around on my own. There were times when I took a bus ride alone, traveling to the end of the line and back. Otherwise I made trips around London only when I had a specific mission. For several weeks I took lessons at a place called the Hugo Institute, but they did not amount to much or go very deep.

In the evenings we sometimes went to a theater or concert. To be honest, I was careful about how I spent my money, as I wanted it to go a long way. But I do remember hearing the pianist Artur Rubinstein, and the singers Conchita Supervia, Elena Gerhardt, Lily Pons, and Elizabeth Schumann. John Payne could not have been kinder. His friends knew that Sundays meant open house, and scores of them came. Many were musicians, and these occasions were most stimulating.

I will not say that I felt perfectly at home all the time. Being busy and excited took the edge off loneliness, but there were times when I was quite homesick. Did I feel a greater sense of freedom in England than I had in the United States? A little, yes.

And having entree to Roger Quilter's home and his circle was an agreeable thing. There I met English people, composers and performers as well as society folk. Mr. Quilter did what he could to introduce me musically. Several times I sang for the gatherings in his spacious music room, with Mr. Quilter accompanying me at the piano. His visitors were warm in their reception. I sang a full program once, songs in German, Italian, and English, including several by Mr. Quilter. His friends suggested that I should appear in a concert at Wigmore Hall, and, thanks to Mr. Quilter, it was arranged. Then he and his friends were good enough to obtain an engagement for me with the Promenade Concerts under Sir Henry Wood. I have a copy of that program, and as I look at it I marvel at its length. In the first half it contained several Hungarian Dances by Brahms, the Violin Concerto by Sibelius, and Tchaikovsky's Sixth Symphony, in addition to the "Air de Lia" from Debussy's

*L'Enfant prodigue,* which I sang. In the second half there were pieces by Kodály and Handel, as well as a group of songs by me. The date, I notice, was September 16, 1930. It should be made clear that I appeared in London not as an artist of consequence but almost as a student. When I returned to the United States I had no big achievements to show for my absence of about a year. If I had done something noteworthy such as singing for the king and queen, that might have made a difference. But a recital at Wigmore Hall? That was just another appearance by an American aspirant. To people who wanted to know what had been accomplished abroad there was not a great deal to tell. Nor was there much that could be done for my career as an aftermath of England. I felt I had gained a little, but it could not be translated into practical uses such as more concerts or higher fees at home.

# CHAPTER 12

# Back to Europe

THE return home was necessary. Money was running low, and I had concert engagements which had been arranged on the understanding that I would be back. I wanted to see my family and friends.

I was disappointed that there were not more dates booked for me, and yet I had feared in my heart it would not be otherwise. Though there was more money per concert, there were far fewer engagements than in the days when Billy King and I had done our own bookings. I have a copy of a letter sent by a secretary in the management office, dated August 27, 1930, and addressed to Billy King, which lists the tour that was then ahead of me. In five months nineteen concerts are scheduled. Two of these dates are not definite because contracts have not yet been signed. Other concerts are subject to change of time, though the contracts are signed.

This could not be called a bad tour for a young artist, though I felt I had been before the public long enough not to be considered a newcomer. The sensation that I was standing still, which had led to my going to England, returned. I had not been home too long before I decided that I ought to go back to Europe.

I did not consult with many people this time. Naturally I talked with Mother, and as always she encouraged me to do what I thought best. I did not even pause at first to calculate the financial possibilities. I knew I must go, and I believed that a way would be found. Because I remained dissatisfied with my German and wanted to work on Lieder at the source, I was anxious to go to Germany this time.

I happened to be singing in Chicago at a concert under the auspices of the Alpha Kappa Alpha sorority, of which I had been made an honorary member. The appearance was not in one of the regular concert halls, but in a high school auditorium. During the performance a message came backstage that a man whose name sounded like Raphael would like to see me. I was as excited as could be. What was Mark Raphael doing in Chicago?

At the end of the concert the man arrived. His name turned out to be Ray Field. He was accompanied by Mr. George Arthur, and they were both representatives of the Julius Rosenwald Fund. They were friendly and interested in my work and aspirations. They wanted to know what plans I had for the future, and I told them that what I wanted and needed was to go to Germany. They invited me to come to the Fund offices two days later. Of course the regular questionnaire had to be filled out.

When we met again they told me that they thought the Fund would be able to offer me a fellowship. If I decided to go to Germany they assured me that a grant would be forthcoming for the trip. This was heartening. As

Mother would say, a way had been found, and I made up my mind to go.

I completed plans and then wrote to the Rosenwald Fund people that I would be thankful if I could have a half-fellowship of seven hundred and fifty dollars. The full fellowship of fifteen hundred dollars was for a year's study, but I could not afford to stay away more than six months. Since I was paying my own passage and other traveling expenses, I assumed that there would be no difficulty about obtaining a six-month fellowship.

Unfortunately I was wrong. The reply from Chicago was that the fellowship must be for a year, with the full fifteen hundred. I had been so sure my request would be approved that the refusal put me in an embarrassing position. My trunk was packed and standing in the hallway of our little house, ready to go, and my ship was to sail in less than forty-eight hours. I wired to Chicago, telling them these facts and adding that unless I could go for only six months I would be obliged to cancel the trip. Within a few hours there was a telegram in reply. The Fund would make an exception to its rule and let me go for six months: the seven hundred and fifty dollars, I was told, could be picked up at a certain bank. It was past the closing time for banks, and I had to wait until the next morning to pick up the money. There was time enough, however. The next afternoon I was on my way to New York, and in the evening I was en route to Europe on a German steamship.

I seemed to have a gift for getting myself into snarls in Europe. After my misadventures in London, I thought I was prepared for Berlin. But again I had telephone trouble. The Judson office had been good enough to supply me with the names of two men, partners in a concert management that would take care of any appearances I might choose to make in Germany. One of these men was to meet me at the station, but no one was there. I had a telephone number, and I called it at the station, but there was no answer.

Then a puzzling thing happened. To reach the street from the station you had to go downstairs. As I approached the head of a stairway being used by other people, I was confronted by a uniformed official standing in a boxed-off enclosure, who would not let me pass. I could not demand an explanation because I did not know enough German, and evidently he did not understand my English. I tried to dredge up a few German phrases from the few lessons I had taken at the Hugo Institute in London—even then I had been hoping to reach Germany. Now that I was there, all I could remember was that the word for "down" was *unten* and for "to go" was *gehen*. I finally got out the phrase *"Gehen Sie unten?"* He glared at me and snapped, *"Nein!"* Obviously that was not going to be the password. As I stood there another trainload of people poured through the station, and most of them were allowed to pass by the guardian of the stairway.

I moved away from this forbidding individual, inching toward the other side of the stairway. When another crowd of people came along I made a dash for it and, by mingling with them, got down. When I reached the street I looked around, bewildered. I clutched my music case tightly; I was not going to lose that again. No one could mistake the fact that I was a foreigner, and from the way I looked around helplessly it was obvious that I was in trouble. A woman approached me and said in English, "Can I be of assistance to you?" I told her my dilemma, and she said that she might be able to help. I am sure that she would have, but at that moment a representative of the North German Lloyd Line came up to me. He advised me where I could go to get a hotel room, and I took a cab, which drove me to an inn on the outskirts of the city. I got a large, pleasant, beautifully clean room, but I was so weary that I could not sleep. My mind was busy trying to work out plans for the next day.

In the morning, with the aid of an employe of the hotel, I called the number I had. Eventually two men arrived. They looked at me in amazement. I had no idea what Mr. Walter and Mr. Funk should look like, so I smiled and said, "Good morning."

They were blank. I repeated what I thought would be the magic word, "Judson."

They exchanged glances. "Judson?" said one. "Judson?" said the other. They had never heard the name. They were polite and remained fifteen minutes, but finally it developed that I had the wrong number, and these poor gentlemen, who were partners in a business that had no connection whatever with music, departed. Not only had I not made progress, but I had ruined their morning.

The correct number was tracked down, and at long last the right Mr. Walter arrived. I explained to him that I could not afford to stay at a hotel and that I would prefer in any case to find a room in a private home. Mr. Walter made some phone calls and located what I needed, and a day later I moved to the apartment of Herr and Frau von Edburg. They had two extra rooms, and I took the larger one, hoping that I would be able to rent a piano for it. They said that they would have no objection. Herr Matthias von Edburg, a Russian by birth, had lived in Berlin for a long time, and his wife was a German. He told me proudly that he was a Recitator.

I unpacked. Then Herr von Edburg knocked on my door. He had some papers that foreigners had to fill out. He said, *"Namen,"* and I understood that I had to fill in my name. We came to a word, *"Ledig."* I said, "What?" He replied, *"Ledig."* I filled in the blank space, writing, "Lady." What the question meant to ask was whether I was single.

Arrangements were made for me to take my meals with the von Edburgs. It was awkward at first, for Frau von Edburg spoke not a single word of English, but this was just what I needed. There were strange confusions. Once Frau Edburg said, *"Spiegel,"* to me. I understood that it meant "glass." She followed it with a clucking sound, like a chicken. I said nothing, but I wondered whether she intended to serve some chicken dish in glass. The dish, *Spiegeleier,* turned out to be eggs sunny-side-up.

I quickly acquired a pocket dictionary and resorted to it at every impasse. We all used grunts and groans and gestures, and somehow we understood one another.

Herr von Edburg did not seem to be employed extensively. In his prime he must have been an excellent performer, for he was impressive-looking and he spoke with the sonorous voice of a dramatic actor. Now and then he would break out in some sort of declamation. One day he launched into a speech that did not have the marching, ringing periods of a classic of German literature or poetry, and some of the words he used sent me hurrying to the

[ 135 ]

dictionary. I discovered that this address was aimed at his wife, and the choice of words was not exactly flattering. I slipped into my room to avoid embarrassing her, and presently the front door slammed. Frau von Edburg rushed into my room—looking for consolation, I thought. I was standing at the window that looked out on the street, and when Frau von Edburg reached my side we could see her husband striding across the street, his shoulders thrown back, every inch the Recitator. She gazed after him and said, "There goes my god."

Herr von Edburg took the trouble to coach me in German. I bought a primer, and we pored over it together. He read to me, and I read to him. He would not let me look at the side of the page that contained English translations, forcing me to plow my way through the German. It was an effective method; when I turned to the German songs I found myself more comfortable with them, and I began to detect nuances of expression in the German that quickened my grasp of the music.

My primary objective in Berlin was musical guidance in the field of German Lieder. The name most often recommended had been that of Michael Raucheisen, and I went to him for coaching. Before and during that time I had a few lessons with Sverre Jordan, who played a part in drawing the attention of a Norwegian manager to me.

One day while I was in Raucheisen's studio two strangers were admitted by my coach's mother, and they sat quietly while we finished the song we were working on. The men introduced themselves to Raucheisen, and he turned and made formal introductions to me. The two were Rule Rasmussen, a Norwegian manager, and Kosti

Vehanen, a Finnish pianist. They were traveling together, looking for new talent.

Rasmussen wanted to know whether I would be available for some concerts. I said that I might be. "If you come to Norway to sing, this man will play for you," he said, pointing to Kosti. But before they would commit them-selves they wished to be sure that I could sing an aria.

I had promised to sing that evening at a small concert arranged by Sverre Jordan at the high school where he taught, and Mr. Rasmussen and Mr. Vehanen could hear me there under something like normal performance conditions. They came to the recital, I sang an aria, and Mr. Rasmussen was now certain that he wanted me to go to Norway. The Scandinavian countries played so crucial a role in my career that I must speak of them in a separate chapter.

I wanted to give a full-length concert in Berlin and mentioned the idea to Mr. Walter. He told me that I must be presented properly, adding significantly that he understood that I had a lot of money behind me. I assured him that he was perfectly right: there was a lot of money behind me, so far behind that it would never catch up with me. (A good many Americans were coming to Berlin in those days, and some, no doubt, were wealthy.) I was convinced, however, that I would have to make some sacri-fices to sing in Berlin, for I had been persuaded that an appearance there would be important. Accordingly I did what I had never done before and have not done since—I put up the money myself. I handed five hundred dollars' worth of American Express checks to the manager, parting with them with the greatest reluctance, and he arranged a date at the Bachsaal.

Michael Raucheisen, who was my accompanist that evening at the Bachsaal, was so nervous that I had no alternative but to be reasonably calm. I remember that his mother came backstage just before we were to start, and I thought that it was nice of her to come to reassure me before my debut in Berlin. Her mission, however, was to reassure her son. As we were about to go out on the stage he muttered some incantation. I found that I was more concerned about him than about myself, and it could be that this was helpful to me, for I was not without my own concerns. I was about to sing before a German public, a group that would be alert to every subtlety of its own language and would probably know most of the Lieder by heart. It gave me a strange feeling.

I could see that the hall was filled, and I wondered how many who were there had come merely out of curiosity. We started with a group of songs by Beethoven. I had the feeling that there was no reaction after the first song. After the second there was a show of interest. By the end of the group the audience seemed to be genuinely responsive.

When we walked off the stage after this group Mr. Raucheisen was excited. "What did I tell you?" he said, though he had not said a word before. "Didn't I tell you it was going to be fine?"

We returned to the stage, and I sang a Schubert group. I had been just a shade uncomfortable with the Beethoven songs because I had not sung them in public before, but I felt much more at ease with the Schubert, which I had been doing for years. The applause was encouraging. There was enough, indeed, to cause me to return for a bow with the accompanist and then for another bow alone. In the second half I sang songs in English, and when I got to the spirituals I noticed that the public, evidently familiar with some of them, took to them kindly. After the concert people came backstage. Some asked for autographs, and a good many said pleasant things—at least, the comments I understood were pleasant.

The next day I looked through the Berlin papers but found not a single mention of the concert. I did not know what to think. Was my German still too insufficient to warrant a review in a newspaper? The von Edburgs, who had been at the concert, had nothing but praise for me. What had happened? After all, the manager had told me that it was important to receive critical notice in Berlin. Had the critics not bothered to attend? Or, even worse, had they come and decided that the performance did not deserve comment?

I could not bring myself to discuss the matter with anyone at first. But after brooding about it for the better part of a day I forced myself to speak to the von Edburgs. Had they seen anything in the papers? I asked hesitantly. Of course not, they replied. The Berlin critics are in no rush to get into print. Within a week the first notices began to appear, first in this daily newspaper and then in that weekly periodical. Most of the reviews were complimentary. One or two were not, but I had not expected unanimity.

Oddly enough, after that Berlin stay I did not sing again in Germany until 1950, when I appeared there under the auspices of our occupation authorities. I made a reconnaissance of the street I had lived in and the areas I had known well, but they were unrecognizable. Whole sections had been demolished by the bombing during the war, and the house I had lived in was gone.

Some time after the Hitler regime took power, when I was doing a great deal of singing in Scandinavia, my Stockholm manager received an inquiry from Berlin, asking whether I would be free to sing in Germany. My manager replied that I was too busy and that my schedule could not be revised to include Germany. Some weeks later there were renewed requests from Berlin. They had noticed that I was to appear in Poland, and they asked whether I could not fit in a day for Berlin. I was not eager to appear in the Germany of those days, but I wanted the satisfaction of returning under different circumstances. My manager offered Berlin a single date. The answer came back that this date would not be the best, but, since there was no alternative, it would be accepted. The fee also was acceptable. There was only one other question—was Marian Anderson an Aryan? My manager replied that Miss Anderson was not one-hundred-per-cent Aryan. That ended the correspondence.

# CHAPTER 13

# Scandinavia

SHORTLY after the Bachsaal concert there came a letter from Mr. Rasmussen, announcing that arrangements had been made for concerts in the north. There was a promise of six appearances, in pairs, with the understanding that the second of two in Norway, for example, would take place only if the first had been a success. I was to start with a pair in Oslo, follow with a pair in Stockholm, and end with a pair in Helsinki. Mr. Rasmussen decided, however, that it would do no harm, en route to Oslo, to stop and sing in Stavanger. That did not go too badly, and a concert was arranged for Bergen, where there was a similar reception. In Oslo the first concert was so well received that the second was called for immediately.

The reaction in Norway, I think, was a mixture of open-mindedness and curiosity. These audiences were not accustomed to Negroes. One of the newspaper reports described the singer as being "dressed in electric-blue satin and looking very much like a chocolate bar." Another paper made the comparison with *café au lait*. And so it went.

The comments had nothing to do with any prejudice; they expressed a kind of wonder.

This sense of surprise seemed to affect the listeners at the first concert in Oslo. I recall that there was an unexpected demonstration of applause at the end of the first group, and at the end of the first half it was almost impossible to stop for the intermission. After the first concert, the second was quickly sold out. People wrote to the manager and to me at my hotel, making special requests for things to be included in the program.

A lot of Norwegians spoke English. They kept the phones at my hotel busy, and some arrived in person to chat for a few minutes. They came to talk about their own country and mine. Some were anxious to discuss conditions for me and my people in the United States. Others wanted to speak about music; one or two persons brought flowers, and others songs which they hoped I would sing. Possibly a few came, as they might in any land, because they had nothing better to do.

I went on to Stockholm, where my appearance was to be managed by Helmer Enwall, to whom Rasmussen had delegated the chore. Director Enwall, as he is called, was younger than Rasmussen. He had vigor, enthusiasm, and vision. He felt that the name Anderson would be an asset in his country as well as in the other Scandinavian countries, particularly since I did not look in the least like a Scandinavian, and he made careful plans for my first concert in Stockholm. Because of his reputation for introducing interesting performers, the concerts he managed usually attracted a knowledgeable public.

The reaction of the first Swedish audience was, to put

it mildly, reserved. Director Enwall assured me that the concert had been a success. However, I had my doubts. Compared with Norwegian responses, this had been pallid. To prove that he meant what he said, Director Enwall swiftly arranged my second concert, and it drew a large audience. Again the reaction was not too impressive. It took me some time to discover that what Director Enwall claimed for Sweden was true: its people were slow to manifest their warmth, but it would build up into something durable.

I did not have much of a wardrobe in those days, and at the first Stockholm concert I appeared in the blue satin dress. Mrs. Enwall, who became a close friend, took me shopping so that I would have a different gown for my second appearance. We purchased a white crepe dress, which came with a long train. I had the train removed, and even though this alteration affected the chic of the dress I was not disturbed. I knew I was happier without it.

From Stockholm I went to Helsinki. The reaction there, comparable with the enthusiasm of Norway, made me feel that I would like to sing a great deal in Finland. I even tried a very simple folk song in Finnish. It was no great feat, but the audience appreciated the gesture no end. Kosti Vehanen was my accompanist. To Kosti, Finland was home; he helped to make me welcome there, and some Finns who spoke English came on their own for a visit. The second concert followed the first in Finland as a matter of course.

Kosti Vehanen played for me for the rest of that rather brief tour, and later, when I returned to Scandinavia, he became my regular accompanist. He was a well-trained musician, had studied in Germany, and spoke German fluently, and he could help me with Lieder. He also knew some French and Italian. He had been the pianist for a number of singers, including Madame Charles Cahier, a famous contralto from America, best known in Europe. A man of culture and a gentleman, Kosti Vehanen was an invaluable aid to me. It is not too much to say that he helped me a great deal in guiding me onto the path that led to my becoming an accepted international singer.

From Helsinki we went to Copenhagen, pausing in Stockholm on the way for a third concert. The news of what success I had had in Norway, Sweden, and Finland preceded me to Denmark, and the audiences were larger at the very outset. In Copenhagen nearly everyone I met seemed to speak English, and there were a good many English and American people there. One felt as if it could be an audience in America. After the first concert some Americans came backstage to say hello.

I felt very much at home in Copenhagen. Even at the hotel I was made as welcome and comfortable as if I were among my own people and closest friends. People seemed happy to be with you; they sought you out. They accepted you as an individual in your own right, judging you for your qualities as a human being and artist and for nothing else. Even the first curiosity about my outward difference was in no way disturbing or offensive, and it seemed only a moment before that dropped away.

There was an eager warmth in these people that I shall never forget. I remember that a Norwegian lady, Mrs. Signe Lund, who had been a singer, made a special trip to my hotel in Oslo the first time I was there, just to bid me welcome to her city. She brought a silver necklace, which she had received after one of her concerts, and insisted on giving it to me; I still have it. Other people sent flowers with little notes of comment on my singing. When I went out on the streets I found that strangers would follow me, then pass rapidly and return. But the way they smiled was disarming; their only aim was to be friendly.

That first trip to the Scandinavian countries was an encouragement and an incentive. It made me realize that the time and energy invested in seeking to become an artist were worth while, and that what I had dared to aspire to was not impossible. The acceptance by these audiences may have done something for me in another way. It may be that they made me feel that I need not be cautious with such things as Lieder, and it is possible that I sang with a freedom I had not had before. I know I felt that this acceptance provided the basis for daring to pour out reserves of feeling I had not called upon. I tried to remember reactions to specific songs and even to passages in songs. After a performance I would go back to my hotel room and examine the music to see where this place or that could be done more effectively. If these people believed in me as an artist, then I could venture to be a better one. I could face the challenge of bigger things.

What I got out of this tour cannot be expressed in terms of fees, but it is worth mentioning that the earnings were modest. I received the equivalent of about seventy-five dollars a concert for my first concerts. Since business was good, another twenty-five dollars was soon added. When I returned later I earned as much as three and four hundred dollars a concert, and eventually fees were ten times what they had been during the first visit. By this time I could command larger sums elsewhere, but I was bound to feel a strong loyalty to the Scandinavians.

The first visit to the north took only a few weeks, but it made a tremendous difference in my life. The full six months allotted for this European trip were soon up, and I was on my way to the United States. Some news of the success in the Scandinavian countries had reached my own country. I suppose I expected it to be of use in my tour schedule. It is possible that there would have been some such effect if the news had come from successes in Paris or London or Vienna. But American managers did not seem too impressed with what had been accomplished in Scandinavia. In any event, my tour schedule was essentially what it had been before. After completing it, I began to think of returning to Europe. I applied for the other seven hundred and fifty dollars of the Rosenwald Fund Fellowship, and I was told that it would be forthcoming.

I went back to Europe in 1933. My return was speeded by Director Enwall. One day he sent me a cable: CAN OFFER YOU TWENTY CONCERTS WHEN CAN YOU COME? I did not answer immediately. While I was deliberating there came another message from him: CAN OFFER FORTY CONCERTS. I replied that I expected to have a certain number of concerts at home that year. As a matter of fact, I knew that there would be about the usual twenty, and I did not want to give them up. Mr. Enwall answered with another cable: CAN OFFER SIXTY CONCERTS. If I had not known him to be utterly reliable and if I had not had the warm memories of the first Scandinavian tour, I might have thought that he was going wild with a kind of personal numbers game. But

I was fairly sure that if he said sixty he would have sixty dates for me. Nevertheless, I decided to fulfill my American commitments and wrote to Mr. Enwall that I could accept only twenty concerts. He agreed, and after I finished my schedule at home I returned to Scandinavia.

This time I remained in Europe for more than two years, and for a considerable part of the time I was kept busy entirely in the Scandinavian countries. I had not expected to remain so long, thinking I would come home for my usual tour, whatever its size. As work kept piling up in Europe, I wrote to the Judson office to inquire whether my American dates could not be postponed. The answer came back that they could not. The letter gave as an example an important engagement set for Philadelphia, which could not and should not be postponed. The only alternative, I was told, was to cancel. I canceled. It turned out later that the American schedule had really shrunk to about ten dates and that the one in Philadelphia was to have been under the auspices of "my" sorority.

Director Enwall was ready for me not only with the sixty concerts he had mentioned in his maximum offer, but with a lot of additional ones. Before I was through I had done more than a hundred concerts—I think the exact number was one hundred and eight—within a twelve-month period. I sang nearly everywhere in Sweden, Norway, Finland, and Denmark. I sang in the remote north of Sweden and Finland in churches of small communities. In some towns there were two and three concerts; in Stockholm there were more.

The houses were full, and the enthusiasm of the public was what it had been the first time. The only difference was in Sweden, where the reserve seemed to have melted.

Letters began to arrive from Swedish people, saying, "We wanted to be sure, and now we are sure," or, "Pardon us for being slow to recognize." But once they did recognize and were sure, they embraced me wholeheartedly. The newspapers ran caricatures, photographs, all sorts of articles about me. One piece went so far as to term the whole thing "Marian Fever."

As a guest of the Scandinavian peoples, I felt I ought to learn and sing some of the songs of their composers. Time was short on our crowded itinerary, but Kosti and I managed to work on new things now and then. He was particularly eager that I should learn some songs by Jean Sibelius, Finland's great and beloved composer. We worked on several, and I was fascinated and puzzled by one called "Norden." It was beautiful, but it was also strange and so foreign to me that I could not quite grasp it. Kosti was encouraging, and one day he said, "It would be nice to have you sing for Sibelius when we go to Finland."

"Of course," I said without much conviction.

"You wait," he said. "Maybe I can arrange it."

He could and did. We were told in advance of our visit to Villa Ainola in a forest northeast of Helsinki that we could stay with Sibelius, then about seventy, for half an hour. I would have time to sing several songs and then we would have coffee.

We were greeted warmly by Sibelius and his family. I was surprised to find that he was not so tall as his photographs had indicated, but with his strong head and broad shoulders he looked like a figure chiseled out of granite. I sang one of his songs that had a German text—"Im

Wald ein Mädchen singt"—"Norden," and several other pieces. When I was finished he arose, strode to my side, and threw his arms around me in a hearty embrace. "My roof is too low for you," he said, and then he called out in a loud voice to his wife, "Not coffee, but champagne!"

Kosti beamed, and I could hardly speak. We spent much more than the fixed half-hour. With Kosti serving as interpreter, we discussed the songs. Sibelius came to the piano to make certain points. I left feeling a glow from the meeting with so great a man, and also a rewarding knowledge that I had caught a deeper glimpse of the meaning of such a song as "Norden." It was as if a veil had been lifted, and whenever I sang the songs of Sibelius again I sensed that I was approaching them with fresh understanding.

The composer honored me by traveling down to Helsinki to attend one of my concerts. Several years later, when I returned to Finland after a long absence, he was gracious enough to send me a telegram of welcome. But I did not attempt to visit him again. One's admiration need not be expressed in personal visits; a man like Sibelius is entitled to his privacy.

Another Finnish composer I met was Kilpinen, a much younger man. I sang some of his songs in concerts, and Kosti and I visited him in his house in the country. He was a tall, wiry man, with a cigar hanging precariously from the left side of the mouth nearly all the time, whether he talked or whether he sat at the piano and played and sang. His music is quite beautiful, and quite different in style from that of Sibelius.

In Denmark I met Nina Grieg, the widow of Edvard

Grieg, Norway's greatest composer. I had sung one of Grieg's songs in Norwegian, and Nina Grieg was so pleased that she invited me to tea at her dwelling.

It was a wonderful time for me, the period of this extended Scandinavian tour. My total earnings were the highest of my career. I sent money home to my family. I bought new evening dresses and clothes for street wear. I purchased a great deal of music, and for the first time I could indulge in the luxury of having it bound in leather. I bought luggage, and gifts for friends, including Mr. and Mrs. Enwall. I did not have much time for social activities and did not go into many Scandinavian homes, but I was a frequent guest of the Enwalls. When I was in their home again several years ago, Mr. Enwall pointed to several things in his living room and said, "Do you remember that you gave us these?" I was touched that they had been accorded places of importance.

I did not have a great deal of cash on hand when the whole tour was over, but it did not matter. The enormous gratification of the acceptance of one's efforts by these people was worth a great deal.

Marian Anderson, c. 1920, Philadelphia. (Fowler Photography).
University of Pennsylvania, Annenberg Rare Book & Manuscript
Library, Marian Anderson Collection, MS. Coll. 198.

Marian Anderson singing in Budapest, Nov. 22, 1935. (Photographer: Inkey Tibor). University of Pennsylvania, Annenberg Rare Book & Manuscript Library, Marian Anderson Collection, MS. Coll. 198.

Giuseppe Boghetti, MA's teacher, Dec. 30, 1937, in Philadelphia. (Rembrandt Studios). University of Pennsylvania, Annenberg Rare Book & Manuscript Library, Marian Anderson Collection, MS. Coll. 198.

Kosti Vehanen, Aino Sibelius, and Jean Sibelius, early 1930s. University of Pennsylvania, Annenberg Rare Book & Manuscript Library, Marian Anderson Collection, MS. Coll. 198.

Anna Anderson and Marian Anderson, March 1941, with the Philadelphia
(a.k.a. the Bok) Award, in Philadelphia. University of Pennsylvania, Annenberg
Rare Book & Manuscript Library, Marian Anderson Collection, MS. Coll. 198.

Kosti Vehanen and Marian Anderson at the Lincoln Memorial, Washington, D.C., Apr. 9, 1939. University of Pennsylvania, Annenberg Rare Book & Manuscript Library, Marian Anderson Collection, MS. Coll. 198.

Marian Anderson and unidentified soldiers at Fort Logan Air
Force Base, Colorado, March 1943. University of Pennsylvania,
Annenberg Rare Book & Manuscript Library, Marian Anderson
Collection, MS. Coll. 198.

Sol Hurok, Marian Anderson, and Elsa Maxwell at MA's party on
Dec. 30, 1945, celebrating ten years of working with Hurok.
University of Pennsylvania, Annenberg Rare Book & Manuscript
Library, Marian Anderson Collection, MS. Coll. 198.

Marian Anderson greeting unidentified woman, with Albert Einstein
standing by, mid-1940s. (Photographer: O. Zane Roseberry). University
of Pennsylvania, Annenberg Rare Book & Manuscript Library, Marian
Anderson Collection, MS. Coll. 198.

Franz Rupp and Marian Anderson, spring 1951, during shooting of the "Meet the Masters" television show on NBC-TV. University of Pennsylvania, Annenberg Rare Book & Manuscript Library, Marian Anderson Collection, MS. Coll. 198.

(Left to right): Eugene Ormandy, Isaac A. Jofe, and Marian Anderson, in Paris, Oct. 1956. University of Pennsylvania, Annenberg Rare Book & Manuscript Library, Marian Anderson Collection, MS. Coll. 198.

Orpheus Fisher and Marian Anderson, Nov. 1956. University
of Pennsylvania, Annenberg Rare Book & Manuscript Library,
Marian Anderson Collection, MS. Coll. 198.

# CHAPTER 14

# Beyond Scandinavia

DIRECTOR ENWALL did not limit his vision to the Scandinavian countries. He felt that I should sing in the principal centers of Europe, and he had London and Paris particularly in mind. He wrote to the chief concert managements, asking whether they wished to arrange appearances for me.

The success in Scandinavia was not enough to impress London's biggest agency, and Mr. Enwall had to approach another manager. He was, I believe, Mr. Van Wyck. I did not sing this time at Wigmore Hall. On the other hand, I did not appear in the principal recital auditorium, Queen's Hall (which was bombed out later during the war). Later on I finally did reach Queen's Hall.

The reaction in London, though I felt that I was returning to a second home, was somewhat reserved. The reviews, which were brief in the English style, were also reserved. There was no extended comment on any point. I remember that one notice remarked that the singing showed possibilities.

I went on to Paris, appearing in the Salle Gaveau. My recollection is that this first Paris concert was not well attended. The appearance, I believe, was sold to a woman's club. When I came out with Kosti, some women were seated on the stage. I was a little surprised. There were only a few hundred people in the hall, and there were enough unoccupied seats to accommodate these ladies.

The program was very much like those I had been singing in Scandinavia. In the spot usually reserved for an aria, I had a French operatic excerpt; otherwise, there were Italian classics, songs in German and English, and a group of spirituals. It may be that the Parisians expected me to sing music of their composers, but though I had worked on my French a little with Leon Rothier in years gone by, I did not feel that I was as secure in it as I had become in German. Years later I ventured on more French material in France, and it was comforting on one occasion when the audience insisted that I repeat Debussy's song "La Chevelure."

The first Paris program was well received. Mr. Horowitz, who had been a leading figure in Berlin before the Hitler regime took over, was the manager, and he suggested a second program. This one was almost a sell-out, and Mr. Horowitz was emboldened to propose a third for the middle of June. Mr. Enwall and his wife had come to Paris for my debut in France, but they had returned home by this time, and I had to decide the question of a third concert myself. My first reaction was against it.

"Out of the question," I told Mr. Horowitz. "It's too late in the season."

Mr. Horowitz listened to this excuse and others I could

think of, and ended by persuading me. He proved his point by doing so good a job that the house was sold out the day before the concert. I was overjoyed. Other places in Europe were important, but Paris was still Paris, and its influence was not to be undervalued. And that third concert produced such flattering notices that I was certain of being "on my way." It was a "tremendous success."

I had not gone to Paris with the thought that this would be a voyage of conquest. I had gone to do my best. I had been singing long enough not to expect any miracles from any one appearance. I did not realize that this third Paris concert, which Mr. Horowitz had forced me into giving, was to produce a big change in my career. It was this concert that led Mr. Sol Hurok to me, or vice versa.

Before I had left the United States, several years before, I had tried to arrange a meeting with Mr. Hurok. I had known his reputation for daring and constructive management, had admired the boldness with which he did things, and had hoped that I could interest him in my work. But I had been unable to see him.

There I was in Paris, resting during the intermission, when Mr. Horowitz walked in with Mr. Hurok. I learned later that Mr. Hurok had happened to be spending several days in Paris, had seen the posters announcing the concert as he walked along the boulevards, and had decided to attend on the spur of the moment. This, too, was fortunate. It would not, however, be surprising to find him any place in this wide world on a given evening, examining a new attraction. So there he was in Paris at my concert, quite by chance.

Mr. Hurok said casually that he would like to see me.

[153]

Could I meet him at Mr. Horowitz's office the next day?
Could I! I don't know how I got through the rest of the
program, but, like all programs, this one also came to an
end.

With Kosti I went to Mr. Horowitz's office the next day.
I still have a vivid picture of the scene in my mind. Mr.
Horowitz sat at one side of his big desk, while Mr. Hurok
occupied the chair behind it. Kosti and I took seats in front
of it. In those days Mr. Hurok was built along generous
lines. In recent years he has slimmed himself down so that
he looks like the dapper man about town, but in June 1935
he had the impressive bulk befitting the grand impresario.
I cannot tell you how big and important he seemed to me;
Kosti and I felt inadequate in his presence. As Mr. Hurok
slowly lifted his cane, which he held at his side, and placed
it before him on the desk, his shoulders seemed to broaden.
I think I would have run away if I had dared.

Mr. Hurok's tone was calm. He wanted to know how many
concerts I had been getting each season in the United States
and how much I received for them. There were many other
questions. As I recall it, he made no mention of his reaction to my concert the previous night. At last he spoke
the words that I had been hoping to hear! "I might be able
to do something for you."

He proceeded to spell out the offer. He would guarantee
fifteen concerts at a certain fee, which was less than I had
hoped for. There was a disappointing moment, but it went
quickly. I was convinced in my heart that he could do something unusual for a performer if he took a notion to do so.

Before any firm arrangement could be made with Mr.
Hurok, however, I had to be sure that I was free. I told

him that I would have to write the Judson office to see if I could be released from my commitments. Mr. Hurok nodded and said that as soon as I knew whether I was in a position to negotiate with him I should let him know.

Kosti and I left the office. I felt like a marathon runner at the end of his race. Evidently Kosti was excited too. "Marian," he said as we reached the street, "the only thing to do now is to have a schnapps and come to life once more."

I wrote to the Judson office, explaining that I had an offer of fifteen concerts in the United States and that I would like to be released from my contract if the Judson management could not match this offer. I received a letter from Calvin Franklin, one of the officials in the Judson agency, who said that my letter had been turned over to him for attention. The Judson office could not assure me of fifteen concerts, he wrote, but if I would stay with it, he and his colleagues would do the best that could be done for me, which they knew I deserved. However, since they could not equal the offer, I was free to go if I wished.

I wished to go. I communicated with Mr. Horowitz, who informed Mr. Hurok. Eventually the details were worked out, and the contract was signed.

In the meantime, I made other appearances in various parts of Europe, thanks to arrangement made by Mr. Enwall and Mr. Horowitz. I sang in Brussels, Geneva, Vienna, and Salzburg, among other places. I have special memories of Vienna and Salzburg.

Vienna was an emotional experience to me. Schubert's songs were an inextricable part of my life and career, and this was his city, as it was the city of other composers whose music meant a great deal to me. I came to Vienna with a full

[ 155 ]

heart. To sing and be accepted here meant another mile-
stone in the direction I had always hoped to go. I made the
rounds of the places close to the lives and memories of
Beethoven, Schubert, Brahms, and the others, and I felt
that there was a special mood on me when I appeared to
sing.

The concert took place in one of the small halls of the
Wiener Konzerthaus, a building which also has a Great
Hall used for major events. The attendance was sparse. I
cared, and yet I did not care. I sang with the best I had in
me. And a strange thing happened: when I returned to the
stage after the intermission the hall was full. I did not
know then how this transformation had taken place. I
learned later that another concert was in progress in the
Great Hall and that during the intermission, which occurred at the same time for both events, people in my audience spoke so excitedly of what they were hearing that
people attending the concert in the Great Hall came to
hear the second half of my concert.

The sight of this suddenly enlarged gathering did something to me. Whatever it was, I could see that there had
been a change in the audience too, particularly after Bach's
"Komm', süsser Tod." There were people who were dab-
bing at their eyes.

I like to feel that the work I do is sufficiently prepared so that it is pleasing from a vocal standpoint.
But beyond that, I know that a pleasing rendition is
not all I must give. There are things in the heart that
must enrich the songs I sing. If this does not happen—and
it does not always happen—the performance is not fulfilled.
With "Komm', süsser Tod" that day in Vienna, I had

[156]

probably found the key to the heart. And the audience knew. You cannot fool an audience.

In Salzburg I had the great good fortune to sing for an audience that included Arturo Toscanini. My singing in Salzburg at festival time is a story that had its beginning many years before in Philadelphia. As I have mentioned, one of the people who befriended me there was Dr. Hirsch, whose son taught at the Curtis Institute. Madame Charles Cahier was on the Curtis faculty for a short time, and Dr. Hirsch arranged that I should sing for her. I remember that one of the things I sang was Cyril Scott's "Lullaby," and my final note was not secure. This was then a rare occurrence for me, and it must have happened because I was under emotional stress. Madame Cahier had been understanding, and she had advised me to go to Europe to study. I encountered her again when I was spending many consecutive months in Europe, and I spent some time studying with her, particularly the songs of Mahler, which she understood very well because she had studied them with the composer himself.

Madame Cahier introduced me to an American woman, Mrs. Moulton, when I was in Austria, and Mrs. Moulton thought it would be nice if I sang a program one afternoon in the ballroom of one of Salzburg's hotels. I agreed, and a date was fixed. Madame Cahier and Mrs. Moulton were hopeful that the Maestro would attend, and I was hoping that he would not. I held him in such high esteem that I felt I could not possibly do anything of interest to him.

The day finally came, and I was ready to begin the program when I was told that Maestro Toscanini had indeed arrived. I was as nervous as a beginner. I thought that I would try to find him, and then I decided that I would not. I was in a state by the time I got out on the stage.

At intermission time Madame Cahier appeared backstage with Maestro Toscanini. The sight of him caused my heart to leap and throb so violently that I did not hear a word he said. All I could do was mumble a thank you, sir, thank you very much, and then he left. Madame Cahier, however, was not so nervous. She heard and told me of Maestro's words: "Yours is a voice such as one hears once in a hundred years."

It was enough, more than enough, that he addressed such words to me. If it had been up to me, I would not have allowed his comment to be made public. I certainly would not have allowed it without asking his permission. But it was already news before I had any power to intervene. I had the other half of the concert to sing, and there were people clamoring to find out and report what Maestro Toscanini had said. He was the dominant personality in Salzburg and the musical world at large, and it was news that he had seen fit to come to a concert by a singer who was not yet well known.

There is no doubt that such praise from Maestro Toscanini was a tremendous help, but I have often wondered what he thought of its being used publicly, and I have been embarrassed at the possibility that he might have felt I was taking unfair advantage of his good will of the moment. Had I met him again, would I have had the courage to ask him? I don't know. I went to some of his concerts. The last time I was close to him was when I attended a program he played with the N. B. C. Symphony at Ridgefield, Connecticut, some years ago. I actually started backstage to see him, but there was such a crowd that I decided I could spare him this intrusion. This, however, I know: there were people in that gathering who were closer to him through friendship and association, but none more admiring or indebted than I.

I continued my appearances in Europe that fall, and then began to prepare for my return to the United States to sing under Mr. Hurok's management. I have been asked on occasion why I was so glad to return to America. Some people have wondered why I did not decide to make my permanent home in Europe, which had accepted me, as others of my group had done on occasion. No such thought ever entered my mind. It has been suggested that if it was Mother and my family that concerned me, I could have brought them over to live in Europe with me. Again I can honestly say that I never considered such a plan. Moving the family would have meant uprooting it, and I had no right to place my career ahead of my family's interests. Their world could not revolve entirely around my affairs. But the family was not all. There were other people to be considered—all the friends and neighbors who had believed in me. They had not helped me and had faith in me just to see me run away to Europe. I had gone to Europe to achieve something, to reach for a place as a serious artist, but I never doubted that I must return. I was—and am—an American.

It might have been playing it safe to remain where things were going well, but I was more eager than ever to return. I wanted to come home, and I knew that I had to test myself as a serious artist in my own country.

# CHAPTER 15

# Home Again

A DIFFICULT, even painful decision had to be made
before the return home. Kosti Vehanen had been
my accompanist in Europe, appearing with me in Scandinavia and other European countries. Billy King had been
my accompanist in the United States. Who should be my
accompanist when I came back? Because I had been working most recently with Kosti, I felt more at home with
him in the new programs. With his help I had made considerable progress in the weaker phases of my repertory.
On the other hand, Billy also had been a good and faithful
friend when I needed one.

The issue went deeper, and I was aware that, whatever
the decision, it would be open to misunderstanding and
would be criticized by some. If I did not use Billy King
some of my own people might be offended. And particularly in the South, where I knew I would be singing,
people might take offense that a white man was serving
as my accompanist.

I knew in my heart that the right decision would be

the one taken on musical grounds. I put the matter to Kosti, feeling that he should be prepared if he came. He was eager for the assignment. Indeed, he was troubled that he might not have it.

"Marian," he said, "if I can come and play only the first pieces on the program, I will charm them so that they will want me to stay."

And so it was. Kosti Vehanen came, and he stayed. I think he did charm people, and he remained with me for the next five years during my American as well as European tours.

We knew several months before the return that the date fixed for the first homecoming concert was December 30 at New York's Town Hall, and we began preparing the program in September while we were still in Europe. There were concerts to be given during this time, but we spent every free moment studying our repertory and laying out all manner of possible programs. We worked with concentration and diligence. Kosti gave a lot of thought to every detail of program arrangement, trying to balance each group for maximum effect. He selected certain songs which he called the *Schlagers,* those that would make the biggest impression, the knockouts. He made suggestions for songs that would begin each group and for the pieces that should come in the middle. He wanted nothing left to chance. I agreed with him, of course, and before we sailed we had the program for the New York concert prepared.

We continued to work on board the ship. We applied to the purser for the use of a room with a piano and discovered that another passenger who was a singer had made a similar request. Fixed times were allotted to each of us.

On the third day of the voyage I was relaxing out on deck when I noticed that it was almost time for my rehearsal. I hastened to the stairway, intent on getting down to my room to pick up my music. The sea was rough that day, and as I started down, my hands touching the rail very lightly, the ship lurched. I lost my balance, stumbled, reached for the rail, and tumbled down the stairs. My ankle seemed to buckle under me, and I actually saw stars. I had always believed that such stars were things seen only in the comic strips, but I saw them. The first thought that entered my mind was, I wonder if I can do that concert? And the next was, Why not?

No one was in sight, for which I was thankful. I got up and put my weight on my left foot. A twinge of pain shot through the ankle. I limped along a passageway, and then Kosti was there, wanting to know what had happened. I said I felt all right, but he could see that I didn't. He sent for the doctor, and the ship's physician arrived in my stateroom with a nurse. They examined the ankle and told me to be careful with it. We did not have our rehearsal that day or the next, when quite a bit of swelling appeared on the ankle. I remained in my room, keeping my weight off the foot as the doctor suggested. But I had promised to appear in the ship's concert. When I pointed out that I was *hors de combat,* arrangements were made to bring me down to the salon in wheel chair and elevator, using back passages. I did not want to be seen publicly in a wheel chair, and I did not want anyone to know of my trouble. I wore a long dress, which covered the bandaged ankle. The piano in the salon was not far from the door to which I had been wheeled, and I stood up and hobbled over to do my singing. Then I returned to my room, where I remained until debarkation time.

On the day of arrival I took off the bandages, and the ankle did not feel too bad when I stood up and walked about. I had a pair of elegant brown sport shoes, which I had purchased in Stockholm, and I was as fond of them as of any shoes I had ever had, including the Buster Brown pair of my girlhood. In any case, I had to wear them that day, and I had a costume that went well with them. I had not been home for a long time; I knew that there would be many special people to meet me at the pier, and I did not wish to alarm anyone. Oh, yes, there was vanity in it, too.

I walked off the pier, went through customs, and had all the excitement of seeing my family again. Dr. Burleigh was there, and so were friends from Philadelphia. I was too excited to give much thought to my ankle. Then we traveled down to Philadelphia. The reunion in our house there was a thing of joy; neighbors came in, and we had a fine evening.

The next morning—it was a day or two before Christmas—I awoke and looked at my foot. There was no swelling around the ankle, but my toes had turned blue and green, and there was a numbness in the foot. I became frightened; my sister called a cab, and we went to the hospital, where the foot and ankle were X-rayed. There was a break in the ankle, and I was outfitted with a cast that covered the leg up to the calf and left the toes sticking out.

"Is that my foot?" I asked the doctor as I looked at the X-ray pictures.

"There's no reason why it shouldn't be," he said.

[ 163 ]

Then he told me that the cast would have to stay on for six weeks. I returned home, feeling a gnawing sense of desperation. I was equipped with a pair of crutches, and learning how to get around with them was difficult and did not add to my tranquillity. I realized that this New York concert after the long European sojourn was most important, and I knew that Mr. Hurok had made careful plans to launch me under his management. I did not want to sing unless I was in perfect shape physically, and yet I did not see how I could not sing. As I hobbled about I realized that there was no great pain. I could manage if I wanted to. The cumbersome crutches were a nuisance, but there seemed to be nothing to do but make the best of the situation.

I drove in to New York two days before the concert. We hired a heated automobile for the trip, which took almost five hours because the weather was stormy. A registered nurse accompanied me. The doctor had recommended that the toes and upper leg should be massaged regularly to keep the circulation moving, and the nurse was to attend to this task.

I went to the Y. W. C. A. in Harlem and tried to rest. The next morning there was an interview with the press in Mr. Hurok's office, and I came down for that. I was careful to get myself seated comfortably behind a desk before the visitors entered, for I did not see why it was relevant to have them know of my accident.

On the day of the concert I wanted very much to be staying somewhere near the hall. There was a young woman I knew who occupied a suite at the Algonquin Hotel. She had phoned me in Philadelphia and had asked when I would be coming to New York. I had been vague at that moment, and she had said that she would be leaving her suite for some days and I would be welcome to use it. I did not know that she had broached the idea to someone in authority but had not received approval, and when I arrived at the hotel I got a cool reception. I should say that Frank Case, the owner of the Algonquin, later changed all that, and for some years I had a suite of my own there whenever I was in New York.

I remained at the Algonquin the night of the concert and the following night. The nurse stayed with me and helped me to move about as I dressed. I wore a black and gold brocade evening dress, which reached the floor so that no one in the audience would know there was anything amiss.

We were at Town Hall early, and a good deal of time was spent discussing the problem of how to get on and off the stage without causing undue excitement. It was decided that the curtains should be kept drawn as I was wheeled onstage. When I stood up and took my place in the bend of the piano, putting my weight on my feet without the aid of crutches, there was little difficulty. The pain was not intense, but there was some. I would not agree that an announcement should be made to the public, explaining my difficulty. To tell the audience I was singing despite a broken ankle would smack of searching for pity, and I was not there for pity that night. I was there to present myself as an artist and to be judged by that standard only.

As the curtains were pulled apart I looked out apprehensively, fearful of what the public might be thinking of these dramatics. I could not tell. At the end of the concert many people came backstage—not only my family but also such musical friends as Mr. Boghetti and other persons from my city, as well as other men and women. Those who didn't know the reason for my apparent immobility had found out from others who did know, and I realized that many in the audience had not taken offense at the ostentation of the drawing and parting of the curtains. But when I began to sing I had no such comforting knowledge. I was both fearful and hopeful.

We began with Handel's "Begrüssung." A friend of Kosti's had given it to me in Europe, and I knew that it was rarely sung in concert. It begins with a long, sustained tone that builds to a crescendo. To do it properly you must be a rather calm person. To start a program with it you must be sure of yourself. The first tone of your first number can make a decisive first impression. I had no reason to fear it, for I had done it often in Europe, and if I had not had a nagging feeling that the plaster cast might impede my freedom I would have sung that tone without any restraint at all. Having decided to give the concert, I did not think I should change the carefully arranged program just because of this tone. I had gone over the music before going out on the stage to immerse myself in the mood, and I was as ready as I could be.

The opening tone and the rest of "Begrüssung" might have been freer. But when I was finished with the song I had the feeling that I had done it worse on other occasions.

I felt, too, after that song, that the audience was with me. I cannot stress too strongly how significant a role the audience plays in any concert. Although I sing with my eyes closed, I have a picture of the audience out front. The lights on the stage carry well into the front rows, and you can make out the expressions on the faces of your listeners before you start and after each number. After many years of singing in public you develop a knack of finding the people who are with you, and you are able, you think, to pick out those who stand apart from you, determined to be shown. Often you choose an individual or a group, strangers all, to whom you sing. Of course you sing to and for all, but there may be one person who is unlike the other ninety-nine. This person, you sense, wants to be brought back into the fold and you can help bring him back. And so as you sing you have to be so deeply convinced of what you are doing that the person for whom you are singing will be convinced.

It was like that at Town Hall that night. I do not recall what the particular person I was trying to reach looked like. I do not know what the full program was, number by number; I could look it up, but it is not necessary. In the telling now, it is only the mood that needs to be remembered. When I reached the intermission—by which time I had sung my Schubert songs and had not been too uncomfortable with them—I had mingled feelings. Part of what I had done had gone as I had hoped; part had not. On average, I would have said that it was more right than wrong. There was a responsiveness in the audience that lifted the spirit, and I did not worry so much about the drawing and pulling apart of the curtains at the end of the first half and the beginning of the second.

I will make no bones about the fact that the program was devised so that there would be opportunity to show whatever I was capable of doing, including low notes and high. In Schubert's "Der Tod und das Mädchen" there is a low D that I felt to be effective when done well. In the spiritual "The Crucifixion" there are several low F's. But the program was not put together to make an impression with individual notes. It was selected to include music I liked, music about which I had a conviction. "The Crucifixion," for example, was more than a song. It contained a spiritual message. Maybe there was something extra in "The Crucifixion" that night; maybe there was something extra in all the spirituals at the end of the program. I do not know. When I reached them I felt as if I had come home, fully and unreservedly—not only because they were the songs I had sung from childhood but also because the program was almost finished, and I had survived.

After the visitors left the artist's room backstage I felt a sense of weariness and repose. People had been generous in their comments. There were words of praise from some who had not needed to utter them. But I did not delude myself. I knew that this was not the end of the quest to be an artist. It was, I felt, a beginning—a new beginning.

There was exhilaration in the flattering reviews the next day, but there was also the weight of greater responsibility. When I returned to Philadelphia and several days had passed, taking the keen edge off the excitement, I got out my music. I studied the songs I had sung at Town Hall, examining my singing in retrospect to check where I had not done as I would have liked and where a point had been exaggerated or undervalued. Here was a song that should have begun more softly and ended more powerfully. There was another that had not been all of a piece. I thought back to the spirituals, and I felt that in some places I had touched too lightly on the essential feeling, missing its depth. Had I given passages in them the character of art songs, which is not their nature at all? I feared that I might have. I resolved to be more careful.

It was borne in on me that I had now stepped up to another level. I had been singing a long time, moving from one step to the next almost imperceptibly. My career had seemed to follow an almost natural course. But if there has been one appearance that seemed like a leap forward, this Town Hall event was it. I resolved to make myself equal to the challenge of this new sphere. I tried to arrange stronger programs, if stronger programs were possible. I realized that it was inevitable now that I would be compared with established concert artists and that I had an obligation to seek for constant improvement.

Mr. Hurok had planned my first season under his management with great care. He hoped to have about fifteen dates for me that year. He also arranged an extra concert at Carnegie Hall to take advantage of the excitement generated by the Town Hall appearance. Though the plaster cast still encumbered me, I filled my engagements. Curtains were drawn and parted in halls that had them. In auditoriums where there were no curtains I managed to hobble on, and this was worse than the business of the curtains. The public knew of the shipboard accident and was kind enough to make allowances, but I could not get it out of my mind that it looked a bit as though I were "putting on."

As events developed, the fifteen concerts Mr. Hurok had hoped for did not pan out, but this did not worry him. I have since learned from another source, not from Mr. Hurok, that when he returned to America and reported that he had signed me a person who knew the concert business had told him, "You won't be able to give her away."

Mr. Hurok was not disturbed. He had faith in his own judgments, and he did not hesitate to take big risks in support of them. The normal thing in the music world is for the performer to defray the costs of a New York concert, but Mr. Hurok did not follow routine. He met all the expenses himself. He never bothered to tell me how he made out on the event, but I learned later that the gross receipts at the box office were about nine hundred dollars, a good deal less than the amount he spent.

He and his staff went to great pains in arranging the next New York concert at Carnegie Hall. Again there was no discussion of who would pay what bills; he met them all. There may have been a profit from this one; I never knew. What counted was that Mr. Hurok was satisfied that things were progressing well.

I cannot thank him too much for the consideration and taste with which he handled everything. There was dignity in all things, in the publicity that was sent out and in the auspices he approved for appearances. He did not care if he took a loss on the first season. He knew, by the way, that I was planning to go back to Europe several months after my return because I had commitments there. He was not worried that this might mean passing up dates we could have. He was building for the future. He did not accept any offer that came along simply because it meant a quick fee. He was concerned whether a concert would be right for me. If he arranged for an appearance in a concert course, he made sure it was one of the best. If I was billed outside of a regular concert series, he saw to it that much was made of the fact that this was to be a special attraction.

Best of all, Mr. Hurok brought a deep personal interest to my career. There was the kind of friendship that you do not look for in managers. Mr. Hurok, of course, is not just a manager. He is an impresario who takes chances whenever he believes in the artist or the ensemble. He has undoubtedly had some failures, but if one examined all the people and attractions he has managed one would find that his record for presenting good and successful things is amazing.

He made a determined effort to get certain doors opened to me. I remember that I had always wanted to appear at the Philadelphia Forum. Mr. Hurok turned the trick. It was gratifying that after my appearance the Forum asked for my return the next season, of its own accord.

In later years Mr. Hurok may have held up a date for me with some series because he hoped to get an opportunity for a young artist. If he did, I do not mind; indeed, I am flattered. It would be only justice that my success should be used to help others as I had been helped.

I suppose I will never know all that Mr. Hurok and his staff did for me. I am indebted to people like the late Mae Frohman, in Mr. Hurok's office, who was in charge of the booking of my tours and who handled all the details with tact and imagination. The office has shielded me from some facts in the course of the years, and I know that Miss Frohman looked into each offer to make sure that my best interests, both personal and artistic, would be served. Once she made a trip South with me. I suspect that the office was uneasy about how things would work out, and Miss Frohman went along to smooth any difficulties. She never told me what she was concerned about or what she had to do to protect me. On another occasion she accompanied me on a tour of South America, and even though she was fulfilling her job of looking after my affairs, she managed to be a delightful traveling companion all the way. Others, such as Anne Opperman in the Hurok organization—all, in fact—have given me friendship and loyalty, and I thank them all. Perhaps they took their cue from Mr. Hurok, but I think they did extra things out of their great fund of good will.

It may not be rare for one performer to remain under one management for more than two decades, but I am sure that there have not been many relationships of this sort that have been as amicable and gratifying. Consider the question of contracts. Mr. Hurok and I had detailed contracts at first. After a while a new contract would arrive at my home, and I would lay it aside, meaning to read and sign it at my leisure. Somehow I would forget. I cannot remember when I last signed a contract. Mr. Hurok usually signs the one which he sends me, but if he didn't, I would not be disturbed.

In June 1955 I happened to be in Paris. I had just come from Israel via Spain and stopped in Paris to appear as soloist with the Israel Philharmonic, which was visiting France. Mr. Hurok happened to be in Paris too, and he phoned me that he would like to take me to dinner. We went to one of his favorite restaurants, and anyone who knows him knows that he is a marvelous host and has a gourmet's knowledge of the best eating places in most parts of the world. He recalled that it was just twenty years since our first meeting in Paris. We reminisced about our artistic partnership, and he toasted it with champagne.

I owe more than I can say to this fabulous man. There must be other performers who were better equipped for a great career and who were simply not lucky enough to have Mr. Hurok at the helm.

# Russia

WHILE I was singing in the United States early in
1936, Mr. Enwall in Stockholm and Mr. Horowitz
in Paris were busy making engagements for me, and three
months after my return home I was on my way back to
Europe for a well-booked tour. I had already traveled a
great deal in Europe, singing all over the Continent. I had
even made a trip to Poland, the Baltic countries, and
Russia.

Mr. Enwall arranged the first trip to Russia, and he and
his wife accompanied Kosti and me. We gave only about
six concerts on that occasion, three each in Leningrad and
Moscow. We entered Russia by way of Finland. It was
January, and when we got out of the train at the border
town I thought I'd never experienced such cold before.
The snow was piled high on all sides. The few steps from
the train to the customs shed were enough to congeal one.
The eyes burned, and the threads of hair in the nostrils
actually froze.

We rode to Leningrad, and there it was just as icy. A car

met us and drove us to a hotel, and I was ushered into a suite with an enormous bathroom. It was not long before a young woman arrived. She spoke English well, and she had come to obtain a copy of the program I planned to offer.

I gave it to her with some curiosity as to her reaction. She also wanted the texts of the songs in order to make Russian translations. When I pointed out that some were in German and Italian she was not fazed; she knew several languages. I had been warned before setting out for Russia that I would not be permitted to sing spirituals or any other songs with religious connotations. Nevertheless, I wanted to do the kind of program I did everywhere. The young woman looked at my program but said nothing. "Ave Maria" was on the list, as were four spirituals.

The hall was packed for the concert. When I looked out through the wings I could see that there was a microphone on the stage, and I protested that I did not need amplification. I was assured that it would be turned off while I sang. Before we began, the young woman who had come to the hotel walked out on the stage and addressed the audience. She read the names of the songs in the first group, pronouncing the Italian titles and providing Russian equivalents. Kosti and I performed the group, and came offstage. The young woman went out to announce the second group—this was the Lieder, ending with "Ave Maria." When she got to this song, she identified it as "Aria by Schubert."

When the time came for the spirituals she did not say much about them to the audience beyond giving the names. I would guess that she mentioned their Negro origin, but I doubt that she stressed their sacred meaning.

I went out and sang them, and then the concert was presumably over. It was quite a distance from the piano to the stage exit, and as Kosti and I walked off, not looking back, we heard a swelling noise. It grew in volume and intensity, and when we reached the artist's room it had mounted to horrifying proportions. It sounded as if the building were being torn up by its roots.

"What on earth is going on?" I asked.

"I don't know," said Kosti, looking as bewildered as I surely did.

The young woman came into the room and asked us to go out on the stage again. We did, and what we saw astonished us. Half the audience—the half that had sat in the rear of the house—had rushed down the aisles and had formed a thick phalanx around the stage. Those nearest the stage were pounding on the board floor with their fists. Deep voices were roaring in Russian accents, "Deep River" and "Heaven, Heaven." We did several encores with the throng almost underfoot. It was disconcerting for a few moments, but how could one resist such enthusiasm?

On the second visit to Russia, starting in May, we remained several weeks, singing in Leningrad, Moscow, Kiev, Kharkov, Odessa, and Tiflis. In Moscow the great theater director Konstantin Stanislavski sent a gorgeous spray of white lilacs. I met him at a tea. I gathered that many important people in Russia's artistic life were present, but I cannot possibly recall the difficult Russian names. There was an entertainment, including a dramatic reading. Then Stanislavski came up and drew me aside, with an interpreter.

Had I ever thought of singing in opera?

I nodded.

How would I like to study *Carmen* with him?

I was touched and thrilled by the offer. I told him I would like to think about it. And I did think about it. I had thought vaguely about the possibility of opera, even of *Carmen*. But I had not considered seriously that I would be able to manage the acting, and I had no doubt whatever that I could not do the dancing a good Carmen must do. I was young, and time stretched invitingly before me. What was the hurry? I would return when there was more time. At the moment I had a tour to complete and many engagements in other European countries. I was not even free in the summer. Furthermore, there was no fixed operatic commitment. If I had stayed several months in Russia to study the role, I suppose an occasion to perform it would have been found. In Brussels there had been an invitation to do opera, but it had not gone beyond the discussion stage.

I told Stanislavski that I would be interested, but time passed too quickly. I did not return to Russia. Stanislavski died. I lost an invaluable opportunity, and I have so regretted it. It would have been wise to grasp that opportunity even at the expense of postponing the tour.

Another impressive figure I met in Russia on this visit was Mikhail Ippolitov-Ivanov, composer of the familiar *Sketches from the Caucasus*. We were invited to his home for dinner. He was a bulky, bearded man, and from his place at the head of a huge, round table he presided over his company with a sultan's benevolence. Steaming plates of food were brought in by a stout woman who was rounder than the host. He had a fork with the longest handle I have ever seen, and he used it to spear the bread on the plate in the center of the table and then to hand it across to a guest. He wielded the fork as though it were a sword and he a skilled swordsman. It was a lively dinner, and afterward there were music and conversation.

I also met a man named Ustishov, known as the "jazz king" of Russia. Kosti and I went to his apartment. We discovered that Ustishov's band included an Englishman and an American. But the young man I remember best is the Russian, also a member of the band, who had a mouthful of silver teeth. I do not know whether this was a fashion for Russian jazz performers or whether silver was used for fillings because gold was not available. But when this young man smiled it was like looking into a metal mouth.

I have been asked whether I met the principal leaders of the country or was heard by them. Not so far as I know. At one Moscow concert, however, there was a great to-do backstage before Kosti and I began the performance. We were told that a very important person would be in attendance. When we began our program we could see that the huge center box had its crimson curtains drawn. We assumed that the box was unoccupied, but we were assured between groups that the drawn curtains were a sign that it was occupied. Somebody whispered that Stalin was in the box, but no one was sure.

One constantly encountered strange things in Russia. In Tiflis I was to appear with orchestra, but the ensemble was away on tour and did not return until the day after our scheduled rehearsal. At the last minute our concert was postponed a night. People had congregated in the outdoor theater, but they went home with no indication of protest, and the next night they came back, filling every available seat.

To while away the time we were taken to hear local singers and instrumentalists, and these were fascinating. Kosti said he had not encountered such instruments before; he assumed that they went back to primitive times. The singing was especially interesting. There was a young woman who sang with endless curlicues and trills in the vocal line, and though the voice was not cultivated, her skill and control were spellbinding.

At the hotel I found a food I liked and requested it again the next day. When it was brought to our table it bore no resemblance to what I had eaten the day before. How could such a drastic change occur overnight? I found out that a new chef had been installed suddenly.

Then there was a fantastic trip to Kislovodsk, a Black Sea resort, for a short vacation. By the time we reached our destination I wished we had never started; in fact, I wished by then that I had never journeyed so far from home.

First of all there was the problem of getting there from Tiflis. We drove out on the Georgian highway to a point where we were to pick up a plane. We stopped beside an open field; there was no indication of an airport. We waited for a long time and finally a small plane landed on the remote edge of the field. Two ancient, horse-driven carts appeared; the baggage was loaded into one, and we clambered into the other. We plodded out to the plane and helped the pilot load the baggage. There was one other passenger, and he sat beside the pilot. Kosti and

I were on a narrow seat in back. We flew over mountains, and the pilot, perhaps to amuse us, did stunts. It was the roughest plane ride I ever took. I became ill early in the trip, and by the time we landed I was so miserable I could hardly walk or talk.

We were taken to a hotel, a busy place full of people. The third passenger went along with Kosti and me. Though we had no idea who this man was, the desk clerk assumed he was part of our party. Kosti, who knew a few words in Russian, asked about our reservations, and the clerk responded with a knowing smile.

"You see, Marian," said Kosti, who was trying to keep my spirits up, "everything is all right."

We were led to the elevator, but it was out of order and we had to climb three flights of stairs. We noticed that the third passenger was following us, and we assumed that each of us would be led to his own room in due course. We followed a young Russian down one long corridor and another, and then he threw open a door to a large corner room. With a bow and sweeping gesture, he indicated that we were to enter. We glanced in. There were sleeping accommodations for three. Kosti and I looked at each other, and the young man waited politely for us to enter.

"What will you do?" Kosti murmured.

"The first thing I'm going to do is find out about having a bath," I said.

Kosti nodded commiseratingly. He led our fellow passenger downstairs. I found a bathroom down the hall and had my bath. Kosti was gone a long while, but when he had finished his conferences he had things straightened out. We got separate quarters, Kosti and I, in a scientists' housing development some miles away, and these were quite pleasant.

The Russians did not think twice of throwing travelers into close proximity even though they were strangers to one another. Taking a train out of one town, I was told by an interpreter that I would have to share my compartment with another person.

"Oh," I said genially, "I understand that you can't always expect to be alone, considering what traveling conditions are."

The interpreter looked relieved. "I thought you'd mind," she said, "because the other person may not be a woman."

Kosti hastened away to make inquiries and returned, smiling.

"Marian," he said, "you have a nice officer in your compartment."

I stood with my mouth open. Kosti grinned. "You were going to have a nice officer," he added, "but I talked him out of it. Now you have me."

One got used to curious Russian customs, the buying of food at stations during train stops and the drinking of tea from a glass, à la Russe—it was poured from a samovar in the coach. One even got accustomed to being paid in bulky packages of paper rubles. The ruble notes came in small denominations, and a mass of them was packed tight and wrapped in old newspaper. Each bundle looked like a large brick. We were not paid after each concert; a lot of bundles were delivered after several appearances. I did not know what to do with them. I tried lining a suitcase with the packages, and the thing became too heavy. I made no effort to unwrap each brick and count the rubles; I wasn't sure that I could, and I feared it would take forever.

We knew that we could not carry any rubles out of Russia or exchange them for a foreign currency in Russia, and we sought to spend them there. I bought some jewelry and two evening wraps. People sensed that I had a lot of rubles and came to my hotel, offering to sell valuable personal possessions. Such transactions were frowned upon by the government, and I did not relish furtive dealings. When I left Russia I had something like five thousand rubles, which I had to declare. They were deposited in a Russian bank at the border, and I received a slip of paper confirming that I had the money on deposit. It is still on deposit, but I doubt that I can find the paper to confirm it.

I went to see opera, ballet, and theater performances in Russia, and the most vivid memory is of a presentation of a Rimski-Korsakov opera for an audience of children at the Bolshoi Theater in Moscow. The staging was something extraordinary, and I was delighted to see a house full of boys and girls. But my delight changed to concern. Shortly after the lights went out a faint silhouette of a tiny figure slipped down the aisle and into a seat not far from me. Then a tall figure followed it and presently returned, leading the little figure firmly back up the aisle. It turned out that the child had tried to crash the performance and had been caught. The child looked so wistful and unhappy as she passed back up the aisle that the performance was spoiled for me. Although I was assured that the little girl could get to see a performance if she applied at the proper place, I wanted her to stay.

Russian audiences, particularly in the winter, were extraordinary. Men and women entered a hall, looking like monstrous, stuffed creatures. They went to the cloakroom and peeled off heavy overcoats that had interlinings of fur. Then they took off their boots, which had newspapers stuffed into them, and put on their good shoes, which they carried in paper packages or in their pockets. When they were ready to take their seats they looked like different people.

I have been asked whether the Russians, because they have produced a wealth of fine low voices, were especially responsive to me because of the nature of my voice. There was no inkling of that. Indeed, I heard some exceptional voices—sopranos and tenors—in the Russian opera houses.

I would say that the Russians were particularly fond of music and were delighted to welcome anyone from abroad. Were they especially attentive to me for propaganda reasons? In any case, it would make no difference to me. I sang in Russia for the same reason I have always sung anywhere else—to make music. After all, it proved that one of my people could be raised up freely in the United States to do the work the Lord had given him the gift to do.

# CHAPTER 17

# Easter Sunday

THE division between time spent in Europe and in the United States changed gradually. In my second season under Mr. Hurok's management there was already more to do at home, and less time was devoted to Europe. Soon there were so many concerts to do in the cities of the United States that a trip abroad for concerts had to be squeezed in. There is no doubt that my work was drawing the attention of larger circles of people in wider areas of our country. Fees went up, and I hope that I was making a return in greater service.

Mr. Hurok's aim was to have me accepted as an artist worthy to stand with the finest serious ones, and he sought appearances for me in all the places where the best performers were expected and taken for granted. The nation's capital was such a place. I had sung in Washington years before—in schools and churches. It was time to appear on the city's foremost concert platform—Constitution Hall.

As it turned out, the decision to arrange an appearance

in Constitution Hall proved to be momentous. I left bookings entirely to the management. When this one was being made I did not give it much thought. Negotiations for the renting of the hall were begun while I was touring, and I recall that the first intimation I had that there were difficulties came by accident. Even then I did not find out exactly what was going on; all I knew was that something was amiss. It was only a few weeks before the scheduled date for Washington that I discovered the full truth—that the Daughters of the American Revolution, owners of the hall, had decreed that it could not be used by one of my race. I was saddened, but as it is my belief that right will win I assumed that a way would be found. I had no inkling that the thing would become a *cause célèbre*.

I was in San Francisco, I recall, when I passed a newsstand, and my eye caught a headline: MRS. ROOSEVELT TAKES STAND. Under this was another line, in bold print just a bit smaller: RESIGNS FROM D. A. R., etc. I was on my way to the concert hall for my performance and could not stop to buy a paper. I did not get one until after the concert, and I honestly could not conceive that things had gone so far.

As we worked our way back East, continuing with our regular schedule, newspaper people made efforts to obtain some comment from me, but I had nothing to say. I really did not know precisely what the Hurok office was doing about the situation and, since I had no useful opinions to offer, did not discuss it. I trusted the management. I knew it must be working on every possible angle, and somehow I felt I would sing in Washington.

Kosti became ill in St. Louis and could not continue on

[ 185 ]

tour. Here was a crisis of immediate concern to me. I was worried about Kosti's well-being and we had to find a substitute in a hurry. Kosti had had symptoms of this illness some time before and had gone to see a physician in Washington, who had recommended special treatment. It was decided now that Kosti should be taken to Washington and hospitalized there.

Franz Rupp, a young man I had never met before, was rushed out to St. Louis by the management to be the accompanist. I had a piano in my hotel room, and as soon as Franz, who is now my accompanist, arrived, we went over the program. I was impressed by the ease with which he handled the situation. He could transpose a song at sight, and he could play many of my numbers entirely from memory. I found out later that he had had a huge backlog of experience playing for instrumentalists and singers. He assured me that I had seen and heard him in Philadelphia when I had attended a concert by Sigrid Onegin years before, as he had been her accompanist.

Mr. Rupp and I gave the St. Louis concert, and then we filled two other engagements as we headed East. Our objective was Washington. We knew by this time that the date in Constitution Hall would not be filled, but we planned to stop in Washington to visit Kosti. I did not realize that my arrival in Washington would in itself be a cause for a commotion, but I was prepared in advance when Gerald Goode, the public-relations man on Mr. Hurok's staff, came down to Annapolis to board our train and ride into the capital with us.

Mr. Goode is another person who made a contribution to my career the value of which I can scarcely estimate. He was with Mr. Hurok when I joined the roster, and I am sure that he labored devotedly and effectively from the moment of my return from Europe for that first Hurok season in America. His publicity efforts were always constructive, and they took account of my aversion to things flamboyant. Everything he did was tasteful and helpful. And in the Washington affair he was a tower of strength.

Mr. Goode filled me in on developments as we rode into Washington, and he tried to prepare me for what he knew would happen—a barrage of questions from the newspaper people. They were waiting for us in the Washington station. Questions flew at me, and some of them I could not answer because they involved things I did not know about. I tried to get away; I wanted to go straight to the hospital to see Kosti. There was a car waiting for me, and the reporters followed us in another car. I had some difficulty getting into the hospital without several reporters following me. They waited until I had finished my visit, and they questioned me again—about Kosti's progress and his opinion of the Washington situation. Finally we got away and traveled on to New York.

The excitement over the denial of Constitution Hall to me did not die down. It seemed to increase and to follow me wherever I went. I felt about the affair as about an election campaign; whatever the outcome, there is bound to be unpleasantness and embarrassment. I could not escape it, of course. My friends wanted to discuss it, and even strangers went out of their way to express their strong feelings of sympathy and support.

What were my own feelings? I was saddened and ashamed. I was sorry for the people who had precipitated the affair. I felt that their behavior stemmed from a lack of understanding. They were not persecuting me personally or as a representative of my people so much as they were doing something that was neither sensible nor good. Could I have erased the bitterness, I would have done so gladly. I do not mean that I would have been prepared to say that I was not entitled to appear in Constitution Hall as might any other performer. But the unpleasantness disturbed me, and if it had been up to me alone I would have sought a way to wipe it out. I cannot say that such a way out suggested itself to me at the time, or that I thought of one after the event. But I have been in this world long enough to know that there are all kinds of people, all suited by their own natures for different tasks. It would be fooling myself to think that I was meant to be a fearless fighter; I was not, just as I was not meant to be a soprano instead of a contralto.

Then the time came when it was decided that I would sing in Washington on Easter Sunday. The invitation to appear in the open, singing from the Lincoln Memorial before as many people as would care to come, without charge, was made formally by Harold L. Ickes, Secretary of the Interior. It was duly reported, and the weight of the Washington affair bore in on me.

Easter Sunday in 1939 was April 9, and I had other concert dates to fill before it came. Wherever we went I was met by reporters and photographers. The inevitable question was, "What about Washington?" My answer was that I knew too little to tell an intelligent story about it. There were occasions, of course, when I knew more than I said. I did not want to talk, and I particularly did not want to say anything about the D. A. R. As I have made clear, I did not feel that I was designed for hand-to-hand combat, and I did not wish to make statements that I would later regret. The management was taking action. That was enough.

It was comforting to have concrete expressions of support for an essential principle. It was touching to hear from a local manager in a Texas city that a block of two hundred tickets had been purchased by the community's D. A. R. people. It was also heartening; it confirmed my conviction that a whole group should not be condemned because an individual or section of the group does a thing that is not right.

I was informed of the plan for the outdoor concert before the news was published. Indeed, I was asked whether I approved. I said yes, but the yes did not come easily or quickly. I don't like a lot of show, and one could not tell in advance what direction the affair would take. I studied my conscience. In principle the idea was sound, but it could not be comfortable to me as an individual. As I thought further, I could see that my significance as an individual was small in this affair. I had become, whether I liked it or not, a symbol, representing my people. I had to appear.

I discussed the problem with Mother, of course. Her comment was characteristic: "It is an important decision to make. You are in this work. You intend to stay in it. You know what your aspirations are. I think you should make your own decision."

Mother knew what the decision would be. In my heart I also knew. I could not run away from this situation. If I had anything to offer, I would have to do so now. It would be misleading, however, to say that once the decision was made I was without doubts.

We reached Washington early that Easter morning and went to the home of Gifford Pinchot, who had been Governor of Pennsylvania. The Pinchots had been kind enough to offer their hospitality, and it was needed because the hotels would not take us. Then we drove over to the Lincoln Memorial. Kosti was well enough to play, and we tried out the piano and examined the public-address system, which had six microphones, meant not only for the people who were present but also for a radio audience.

When we returned that afternoon I had sensations unlike any I had experienced before. The only comparable emotion I could recall was the feeling I had had when Maestro Toscanini had appeared in the artist's room in Salzburg. My heart leaped wildly, and I could not talk. I even wondered whether I would be able to sing.

The murmur of the vast assemblage quickened my pulse beat. There were policemen waiting at the car, and they led us through a passageway that other officers kept open in the throng. We entered the monument and were taken to a small room. We were introduced to Mr. Ickes, whom we had not met before. He outlined the program. Then came the signal to go out before the public.

If I did not consult contemporary reports I could not recall who was there. My head and heart were in such turmoil that I looked and hardly saw, I listened and hardly heard. I was led to the platform by Representative Caroline O'Day of New York, who had been born in Georgia, and Oscar Chapman, Assistant Secretary of the Interior, who was a Virginian. On the platform behind me sat Secretary Ickes, Secretary of the Treasury Morgenthau, Supreme Court Justice Black, Senators Wagner, Mead, Barkley, Clark, Guffey, and Capper, and many Representatives, including Representative Arthur W. Mitchell of Illinois, a Negro. Mother was there, as were people from Howard University and from churches in Washington and other cities. So was Walter White, then secretary of the National Association for the Advancement of Colored People. It was Mr. White who at one point stepped to the microphone and appealed to the crowd, probably averting serious accidents when my own people tried to reach me.

I report these things now because I have looked them up. All I knew then as I stepped forward was the overwhelming impact of that vast multitude. There seemed to be people as far as the eye could see. The crowd stretched in a great semicircle from the Lincoln Memorial around the reflecting pool on to the shaft of the Washington Monument. I had a feeling that a great wave of good will poured out from these people, almost engulfing me. And when I stood up to sing our National Anthem I felt for a moment as though I were choking. For a desperate second I thought that the words, well as I know them, would not come.

I sang, I don't know how. There must have been the help of professionalism I had accumulated over the years. Without it I could not have gone through the program. I sang—and again I know because I consulted a newspaper clipping—"America," the aria "O mio Fernando," Schubert's "Ave Maria," and three spirituals—"Gospel Train," "Trampin'," and "My Soul Is Anchored in the Lord."

I regret that a fixed rule was broken, another thing about which I found out later. Photographs were taken from within the Memorial, where the great statue of Lincoln stands, although there was a tradition that no pictures could be taken from within the sanctum.

It seems also that at the end, when the tumult of the crowd's shouting would not die down, I spoke a few words. I read the clipping now and cannot believe that I could have uttered another sound after I had finished singing. "I am overwhelmed," I said. "I just can't talk. I can't tell you what you have done for me today. I thank you from the bottom of my heart again and again."

It was the simple truth. But did I really say it?

There were many in the gathering who were stirred by their own emotions. Perhaps I did not grasp all that was happening, but at the end great numbers of people bore down on me. They were friendly; all they wished to do was to offer their congratulations and good wishes. The police felt that such a concentration of people was a danger, and they escorted me back into the Memorial. Finally we returned to the Pinchot home.

I cannot forget that demonstration of public emotion or my own strong feelings. In the years that have passed I have had constant reminders of that Easter Sunday. It is not at all uncommon to have people come backstage after a concert even now and remark, "You know, I was at that Easter concert." In my travels abroad I have met countless people who heard and remembered about that Easter Sunday.

In time the policy at Constitution Hall changed. I appeared there first in a concert for the benefit of China Relief. The second appearance in the hall, I believe, was also under charitable auspices. Then, at last, I appeared in the hall as does any other musical performer, presented by a concert manager, and I have been appearing in it regularly. The hall is open to other performers of my group. There is no longer an issue, and that is good.

It may be said that my concerts at Constitution Hall are usually sold out. I hope that people come because they expect to hear a fine program in a first-class performance. If they came for any other reason I would be disappointed. The essential point about wanting to appear in the hall was that I wanted to do so because I felt I had that right as an artist.

I wish I could have thanked personally all the people who stood beside me then. There were musicians who canceled their own scheduled appearances at Constitution Hall out of conviction and principle. Some of these people I did not know personally. I appreciate the stand they took.

May I say that when I finally walked into Constitution Hall and sang from its stage I had no feeling different from what I have in other halls. There was no sense of triumph. I felt that it was a beautiful concert hall, and I was happy to sing in it.

The story of that Easter Sunday had several sequels. A mural was painted in the Department of Interior Building in Washington, commemorating the event, and I was invited down for the unveiling. I met Mr. Ickes again, and as we talked and as I studied the immense mural the impact of it all was unmistakable. More recently I was in Kansas City for a concert, and a young man phoned me and asked whether he could come to see me. He had competed as a painter in the mural contest, and had won second prize. The purpose of his visit was to offer me the painting for the mural that he submitted in the contest. It was a huge picture and, like the prize-winning work, contained a message. I could not find space for so large a painting in my home, and I sent it to the Countee Cullen Foundation in Atlanta. Countee Cullen was a gifted American Negro poet who died prematurely.

I do not recall meeting Mrs. Franklin D. Roosevelt on that Easter Sunday. Some weeks later in 1939 I had the high privilege of making her acquaintance. It was on the occasion of the visit to this country of King George VI and his Queen, and I was one of those honored with an invitation to perform for the royal guests.

While waiting to sing I was in Mrs. Roosevelt's room in the White House. There was a traveling bag on a chair, and the tab on it indicated that she would soon be off again. I can still see it plainly.

Knowing that I would be introduced to the President, I tried to prepare a little speech suitable for such an occasion. When I met him, he spoke first. "You look just like your photographs, don't you?" he said, and my pretty speech flew right out of my head. All I could say was, "Good evening, Mr. President."

After the concert for the visitors was over, we were told that we would be presented to the King and Queen. I had returned to Mrs. Roosevelt's room to prepare myself. It occurred to me that it might be the right thing to curtsy. I had seen people curtsy in the movies, and it looked like the simplest thing in the world. I practiced a few curtsies in Mrs. Roosevelt's room. An aide came to call me, and I happened to be the first woman in line to meet Their Majesties. I remember that I was looking into the queen's eyes as I started my curtsy, and when I had completed it and was upright again I had turned a quarter- or half-circle and no longer faced the queen. I don't know how I managed it so inelegantly, but I never tried one again, not even for the king.

As I approached the center of the receiving line, there stood Mrs. Roosevelt, and at her right His Majesty the King. Mrs. Roosevelt put out her hand and said, "How do you do?"

I met Mrs. Roosevelt a number of times in the ensuing years, in New York, at Hyde Park, in Tokyo, and in Tel-Aviv. When I was in Japan several years ago I heard that Mrs. Roosevelt was about to arrive. I knew from my own experience with the Japanese that an extensive program would be arranged for her and that there would be an abundance of flowers waiting for her everywhere. I thought that an orchid might be the thing to get for her, so I went down to the lobby of the Imperial Hotel, intent on obtaining the orchid. But Mrs. Roosevelt arrived ahead of schedule, entered the hotel, and walked up several steps to where I had been caught standing before I could complete my errand. She stared at me. "Well, how long have you been here?" she asked.

I told her, adding that I was making a tour in Japan.

"When are you singing in Tokyo?" she asked.

"Tonight," I replied.

She turned to the people who were escorting her. "May I hear Marian Anderson tonight?"

I hesitate to think how her hosts had to rearrange their

plans for her that evening, but she was at the concert. I know how crowded her schedule must have been, and I am sure that she did not have many minutes to herself. I shall never forget that she took the time to come and listen again.

When I was in Israel, more recently, Mrs. Roosevelt was there too. She was staying at the same hotel in Tel-Aviv, and she had left word at the desk that when I arrived she would like to be informed. We managed to have a brief visit, and soon she was on her way again.

She is one of the most admirable human beings I have ever met. She likes to have first-hand information about the things she talks about and deals with. Her bags seem to be ready for travel at any moment. Wherever she goes there is praise for her and what she stands for. I suspect that she has done a great deal for people that has never been divulged publicly. I know what she did for me.

Once when I was occupying the artist's room of a hall the stage manager told me with great enthusiasm that Mrs. Roosevelt would occupy the same room two days later. And so on the large mirror I left a greeting, written with soap.

# CHAPTER 18

# Songs I Sing

M AKING a program is like having to choose what to
wear from an inexhaustible and infinitely varied
wardrobe. Very few people can command such wardrobes,
but a singer has that kind of repertory to draw upon.

One has to have the audience in mind, and one must
never forget that an audience is many people, some who
are deeply musical by nature and cultivation and others
who have little musical background and wish only to be
entertained. I seek to put together music that will appeal
to both sorts of listeners. At the same time it must be
music that I believe in. It must be good music; it must be
music with which I feel at home; otherwise I cannot reach
others with it. There are thousands upon thousands of
songs. The situation is like that of the woman and the
wardrobe. If she has a blue dress and a black dress she does
not have much trouble choosing; if she has fifty dresses
she has a problem.

I begin with Schubert, the composer I love best. I go
through the seven volumes of his songs. There are hun-

dreds of them, and each seems to be more beautiful than the last. I do this in the summer when I am on vacation, and at the end of several weeks I have so many Schubert songs selected that I could fill an entire program with them.

Early in my career, when I was not too sure of my German, I did not dare attempt an all-Schubert program. Now I don't undertake one because so many songs by other composers pull at me for attention. After setting aside a batch of Schubert possibilities, I look at the Brahms songs and make a tentative selection; then at Schumann, Hugo Wolf, Richard Strauss. All I can use from these composers is eight to twelve songs, depending on how many different programs I prepare for any season—at the most there are three or four in the United States.

I go on to the French songs, beginning with Debussy. Then I look at some Spanish selections, and next I turn to the Italian songs. Here again I am in trouble. There are too many things, and they are so beautiful.

The greatest problem is in English songs. I like to do a group by American and English composers in addition to a group of spirituals, but the choice is difficult. There is not such an abundance of fine things in this classification, or else I have been looking in the wrong places. As for modern things, I have to confess that I cannot cope with them.

My accompanists and I have spent many, many hours on the group in English. We have taken down book after book of songs and examined countless new ones, some sent unsolicited. I have tried to have at least one new song by an unknown American composer on my programs each year, but this practice has to be suspended at times. Going through stacks of new songs in manuscript leaves one groggy after a while. Some songs can be understood, others cannot. Sad letters come with them. "This is my first song," a typical note will say. "I have not had any formal education in music, but I think this is a song absolutely made for you."

When I was working with Kosti Vehanen on the preparation of a program, he would write down on a separate slip of paper the name of each song we had selected as a possibility. We would study the slips, numbering them in the order that they appealed to us, and then he would organize them into groups, with the last song in each group making a strong climax. Each group was constructed in the same way. Presently we had a program—on paper.

Then comes the task of learning the program. Some of the songs I have chosen I may have sung in other seasons. I know them, or knew them well once. It does not matter. We try to prepare each song afresh.

Each singer has his own way of learning a song. I like to hear the melody first, to get something from the music before I have begun serious work on the words. Then I read the poem apart from the music; I want to know what it is about. I want to know something about the way in which the song was written. I try to saturate myself in everything that relates to it. When I put words and music together I try to reach deeply into the mood. If I concentrate, and if there is nothing in the song to create unexpected difficulties, the task is not hard.

It is not always easy, however, to concentrate; your mind has to be free of distractions. Household and family obligations have their rights, and do occupy my thoughts a great deal, and other calls on my time may intrude. No matter how study has gone during the day, I take the songs to bed with me. Just before one is ready to sleep there comes the time of complete relaxation, and one lives the mood of the music. Suddenly one is wide awake, completely lost in the spirit of the song, and in a few hours, while all is still around one, a great deal is accomplished.

Music is an elusive thing. I may work on a song every day for a week while nothing much happens. Then suddenly there is a flash of understanding. What has appeared useless labor for days becomes fruitful at an unpredictable moment. But I do not tackle the most difficult songs first; I try to master those that appeal most directly and give me the least trouble, leaving the preponderance of time to those that resist me.

It is impossible to say exactly how long it takes to prepare a full program. Certainly I devote weeks, even months, to the job. When the program has been organized so that it has a fixed order, we begin working on it by groups. Franz Rupp comes up to my home in Connecticut, and he and his wife occupy the guest house. Franz and I work for several hours in the morning, and after an interval for lunch we work for two or three hours in the afternoon. There is a longer break for dinner, and then we put in another hour or so around nine in the evening.

After all the groups have been learned we assemble them into the completed program. As we go through the entire list it occurs to us that some things are not going well or are not suited to each other. Occasionally a song is dropped, and something different is chosen. I may have set aside a certain song for a later season, but I may look at it again and realize that it merges better with the other things we have assembled.

After this final change we go through the entire program again and again. There is no limit to the number of times one would like to do this. Our objective is to make the whole program a part of ourselves, to probe as deeply as our poor powers will permit into the secret mood of each song.

The feeling and message of some songs have escaped me for a long time. I remember that when I was working in Mr. Boghetti's studio he gave me Schubert's "Ave Maria" to learn. It seemed to me the longest and most drawn-out thing I had ever encountered. I did not know any German, and I struggled with the three verses, but I could not come to grips with the song. I tried it in public on several occasions, and I had the impression that it missed out with the audience in some inexplicable way. I laid it aside.

About five years later, when I was in Europe and preparing a new program with Kosti, we found we needed another song for the German group. "Ave Maria" was mentioned, and we took it out and tried two verses. This time it sounded promising. I had the sense that at last the time had come for "Ave Maria." I took it back to my hotel, studied the words, and immersed myself in the music, and within a few weeks I tried it in a concert. It worked. For more than a year and a half I had "Ave Maria" on every program. If I returned for a second or third concert to a city and omitted the song from the printed list there were requests in great numbers that it be included. Invariably it was done as an encore. Even today it is almost always requested and is always a highlight of my programs. With so much repetition of a song one is bound to grow into it.

With "Ave Maria" it was a question of having little understanding of the song at the outset. Schubert's "Gretchen am Spinnrade" is a song to which I was immediately attracted, but I could do nothing with it at first. I put it away sadly. There came the happy day when I was in need of this sort of song and picked it up again. It is amazing that what you have been unable to reach can suddenly lie clear and approachable. It is as if the subconscious mind has been wrestling with the problem all along. In an instant you feel like a clairvoyant. The song is yours; you feel free with it, and may even dare to bring a personal communication to it.

I had a similar experience with Schubert's "Der Erlkönig" and "Ungeduld," and Richard Strauss's "Morgen." I tried over "Ungeduld" several times, thought it was beautiful, but not for me. Then one day I felt that I must have it on my program. "Morgen" was deceptively simple —just two pages. I tried it, and it was tremendously difficult. I worked on it with Mr. Boghetti and with Billy King, who had a clear idea of the way Roland Hayes had sung it. It went well in the studio, but not in public at first. Then suddenly at a concert it seemed to be mine.

On the other hand, Schubert's "Der Tod und Das Mädchen" came naturally and easily. Perhaps I should have been suspicious of that, but once I began to work

with it I did not have to put it back on the shelf. I was
drawn to the song because it packs so much drama into
a brief span. I felt that it had to be acted rather than
sung; by that I mean that the voices of death and the
child must summon up the drama and that the singer must
use her own voice so as to suggest those two. Death is
making an overture to the child and does not wish to
frighten her, and the final phrase before the low D is the
last appeal, the more insinuating and terrible because it
is so soothing. I found it exciting to attempt capturing
this mood, and I was fortunate not to have any difficulty
with the low D. I never underestimated the importance
of that note and I knew that the singer who did it right
had to be very steady inside.

With this song, as with others, one must be careful
that, with so much practicing and planning, spontaneity
is not lost. One must leave something to be achieved at
the performance, whatever that magical thing is; otherwise one does not reach the public as one should.

And if one is lucky enough to convey what one had
hoped to, the good fortune must not be pressed. I am
reminded of a time when I sang "The Crucifixion" in
Oslo. This spiritual is one of the most deeply emotional
of all the songs I know. In its simple words and moving music it captures the terror and tragedy of that
awful moment. I felt it all that night. I was so deeply
stirred myself that I was on the verge of tears, and I believe that some in the audience did weep. There was so
much applause that I could not go on to the next number,
so I sang it a second time. I was not happy with the

repetition. One critic the next day wrote that it should not have been repeated, and he was right. When you have been given something special in a moment of grace, it is sacrilegious to be greedy.

Another time I myself was moved to tears was as I sang the spiritual "Trampin'" at a concert in the United States. So many things are bound up in that spiritual.

> I'm trampin', I'm trampin',
> I'm trying to make Heaven my home.
> I've never been to Heaven but I've been told
> That the streets up there are paved with gold.

I saw an army of people who were bowed down and whose only solace was the march along the road to Heaven— to the things they never had. Why the emotion came upon me so intensely that night I don't know, but there it was. And when you feel it so strongly you can give a convincing rendition.

The odd thing was that when I had tried this spiritual at an earlier concert it did not go well. I had liked the song, and, feeling that it should be pitched low to convey the impression of people tramping, I had had it transposed downward so that I would have to sing a low F. The low F had not imposed any difficulties, but somehow the performance had not clicked. I had wanted badly to do it right. The auditorium that night in the Dunbar High School was small, and there were many people there I knew. As I rode home on the train I kept thinking about this song. Should I continue with the transposed version, or should I drop the spiritual entirely? I decided to try it again, and it went. I searched myself to find out why one performance failed and the other succeeded. If you know a thing thoroughly why does it not emerge the same way each time? The answer is a mystery to me, if not to other performers. One night the proper mood is on you, the next it isn't. And that happens even with the songs one loves the most.

Everyone has his favorites. I suppose mine are "Ave Maria," "Begrüssung," "Komm, süsser Tod," Bach's "Es ist vollbracht," "The Crucifixion" and, perhaps most precious of all, the spiritual "He Has the Whole World in His Hands." This spiritual was brought to my attention by Marion Kerby, collector of folk songs of the Negroes and the mountain people. An English musician, Hamilton Forrest, provided a piano part that fits the words like a glove. In many places, even where the audience did not understand English, the song has had to be repeated.

This spiritual reminds us not to lose sight of the fact that we have our times of extremity and that there is a Being who can help us at such a time. It takes in everybody. It speaks first of the wind and the rain. No one can stop the rain, no matter how rich or poor, brilliant or stupid he may be. "He's got the wind and the rain in His hands, He's got the whole world in His hands." It goes on, "He's got the lying man, He's got the gambling man, He's got the crap-shooting man in His hands." That takes in most of the transgressors. Then it comes to "little bits-a-baby." Who will protect them when mother and father can't? Then "He's got you and me, brother, in His hands. He's got you and me, sister, in His hands. He's

got everybody here in His hands. He's got the whole
world in His hands."

It is all there in that spiritual. I chose it not alone
because I thought the audience would like it, but because
it had a cry, an appeal, a meaning to me. It is more, much
more, than a number on a concert program.

*CHAPTER 19*

# Notes on the Voice

IT MAY have been an old Brazilian custom. On one of my tours of South America there was a knock on the door of the artist's room in the Rio de Janeiro hall during the intermission, and a voice called out, "Dr. So-and-so to see you." I replied that I did not know any such doctor. The door opened, and two Brazilian gentlemen walked in. They were dignified and courtly; they talked in Portuguese, which I did not understand at all; and there was no clue as to what they were there for. Finally they got out a few words in English. At last I understood that they wanted to look down my throat.

I was a bit startled. Perhaps it was the Brazilian way to check on singers' throats during intermission, and I did not wish to seem a churlish guest in a strange country. I opened my mouth. Dr. So-and-so stared down my throat, and then he talked in rapid Portuguese to his companion. Dr. So-and-so stepped aside and made room for his friend, who waited for me to open my mouth again. I obliged. Then he turned to Dr. So-and-so and made some comments. They stood chattering animatedly. Then they turned and shook hands with me in the friendliest fashion, bowed ceremoniously, and walked out.

What had they come to find out? Were they medical doctors? If so, they had come unprepared for a serious examination, for they looked down my throat with the naked eye. I shall never know what they thought of what they saw, because I did not understand a word they said. One can only suppose that something they heard that evening made them wish to investigate. So far as I could make out, they were just curious.

I have never stopped to consider my voice as a thing apart. Having sung from childhood, I took it for granted. Even the range I had as a youngster did not seem extraordinary to me. I remember once that a young woman came to Philadelphia as a pianist, and after the concert she visited our home. There were a number of people in the living room, and this young pianist played some numbers. Without reflecting, I hummed along with her music, softly and quite low. She turned to a young man sitting near me and said to him, "I didn't know you sang."

"I'm not singing," he said.

"Well, who is?" she wanted to know.

I confessed that it was my humming that she heard.

As my career grew I could not, of course, behave as though my voice would take care of itself. Any voice needs attention, training, and cultivation. A singer needs a knowledgeable person to listen to him objectively. I have always felt that a vocal coach was extremely useful. You do not hear yourself as another does. If you are not watchful little kinks may appear in the voice on which you do not put sufficient importance at first. But if you do not take corrective measures they can become bad habits.

In recent years Steffi Rupp, my accompanist's wife, has helped me as a vocal teacher. She is wise, thoughtful about the voice, and clever at preparing special vocal exercises that fit my requirements of the moment.

A vocal coach can be a positive inspiration to a singer. Years ago I worked for a time with Edythe Walker, an American soprano who had a particularly successful career in Europe. After Mr. Boghetti died I went to her for checking. If I ever teach singing I would like to teach it as Miss Walker did. She did not adhere to a strict schedule; if she felt you needed more time she did not think twice about spending an hour and a half with you instead of the allotted half-hour. I do not blame other teachers for keeping to a schedule, of course. They have their livings to make, and they are fortunate to be so successful that all their time is in demand. It is, I suppose, a luxury to do as Miss Walker did—take only a few singers and work with them as the situation requires. It was Miss Walker who made me feel that I could take the top notes of "Ave Maria" pianissimo without any trouble. She gave me a feeling of security.

It may be that my lifelong aversion to practicing when anybody else is around has had its effect. Some time ago when I visited Israel I had a suite in Orchestra House. My living room was isolated, and it contained a piano. I could practice at any time of day or night without disturbing a soul. I practiced alone every day, and the benefits of that work were very rewarding.

I am sure that my voice would have benefited from

top to bottom if I had been determined to practice every day while I was on tour. But I could rarely bring myself to work out in a hotel room; there was always the fear of disturbing my neighbors. I was equally reluctant to practice in the private homes that were hospitable enough to put me up. I would wait until we could go to the concert hall, or I would try to get the use of a room isolated from the guests in the hotel. There have been many occasions when I did not practice as I should have, contenting myself with reading the words of a song as I hummed the music to myself.

I wish I could be as indifferent to outsiders as Franz Rupp, my accompanist. If there is a piano backstage in a concert hall he uses it. He sits down and warms up. It does not worry him too much if some strains from the piano can be heard out in the auditorium by some in the assembling audience.

For a performer there is nothing like being wanted. As far as the ego is concerned there is no such thing as being wanted too much. But there comes a time when one's physical resources are stretched to the limit and when a voice needs time for rest and recuperation. The business of touring and appearing in public is both enormously exciting and enormously wearing. Incessant traveling can take its toll of energy, and if you are lucky enough to give an exciting performance the stimulation is so great that sleep is impossible until the early hours of the morning. Then, as you arise early to catch a train, there is the worry about how you will feel at the next concert. You can only hope for the best, but you must never neglect that solid foundation that is essential for a professional performance, no matter how you feel.

One has to learn to take criticism, particularly the published sort, as it comes. When certain writers observed in the early thirties that there was unevenness in my voice, I asked myself whether they were right. I listened carefully and decided that they were, and I worked hard to correct the fault. Constructive criticism can alert a singer to bad habits in the making, and I am grateful for such comments. On the whole, however, it must be said that a serious person does not wait for the words of the critic; he checks himself. Deep in his heart he knows what his standards should be, and he strives to be faithful to them. He knows before anyone else whether he is straying in vital matters.

For the rest, criticisms are part of the game. There have been times when I felt wonderful and thought the job well done, only to find the next morning that a critic thought otherwise. There have been other times when the position was reversed, when I did not think too well of my performance, only to discover that a critic had considered it outstanding.

I have been one of those fortunate singers who do not have to baby themselves. I do not behave much differently on days of performances from the way I do on other days. If there is shopping to do, I do it. If possible I try to eat fairly early before a concert. I like to have dinner at five o'clock, but if it is not feasible I eat at six or later.

I remember that Mr. Boghetti used to lecture me on proper procedure. "Eat at four-thirty on concert days," he would say, "and have a good steak." That was fine advice if you could afford steaks. Furthermore, I stayed often in private homes, and it was hardly the thing to tell a hostess, "I'll come and stay with you if you will serve steak at precisely four-thirty." I have no doubt that some of these kind, generous people would have gone out of their way to be obliging, but I could not bring myself to lay down conditions.

We always ate well as youngsters, as I have indicated, even though steaks were rare items on our menu. I got into the habit of eating when it was convenient and I was hungry. I heard a young singer on television recently describing the way she prepared herself on the day of a performance, and evidently it was a day-long affair. That is perfectly all right for her, but I think I would end up by being out of sorts if I made too big a fuss over myself or my voice.

I do not fret over having people smoke in the same room with me. I have had accompanists who had a cigar or cigarette going beside them at the piano while we practiced, and I did not mind. It is true that I would not care to have anyone smoking in the artist's room just before or during a concert, but smoke is something you have to learn to live with. There are halls that become filled with smoke when doors are left open during inter-missions. They are not comfortable, but you go out and sing anyway.

On concert days I like to rehearse in the afternoon, usually in the hall. Just before a concert I like to warm up with a few exercises, if I can have privacy. I go through some scales, and if I am to start with a piece that poses difficulties I like to warm up well, using the piece in question. But I have ventured out with only a bit of humming and concentration on the music in my head, which is not always sufficient by any means.

Unpredictable things happen even when you have taken all the necessary precautions. For a radio date on a national network we rehearsed my numbers thoroughly shortly before the performance. My voice was in quite good condition, I thought, and the rendition likewise. Came the performance two hours later, and in the first number, which had gone well in rehearsal, a tone broke at the start. Why? My only explanation could be that I had spent the time in an unventilated room filled with stale, smoky, dried air, and did not have a sufficiently good warm-up. A friend asked, "What happened on that first note?" There was nothing to say. I could not answer, "You should have heard how well it went in rehearsal."

I have seldom taken special drinks or preparations for the voice, but I have used a mentholated spray when I have felt a touch of hoarseness or a cold coming on. I have also tried a good gargle. There have been times when I carried a Thermos bottle with hot tea and had a cup with honey and lemon between groups. But these were measures taken when I felt that my voice was under particular strain. As a rule I have not worried myself with drinks, sprays, or gargles. If there is something wrong it is best to go to a doctor and get at the source of the trouble.

Wear and tear on the voice are inescapable. There comes a time when one has to cut down. It is heartening to have more requests for performances than one can fill, but one can do only so much work. In the years when I did a hundred concerts or more a season it seemed a wonderful accomplishment. When I look back on that kind of schedule I realize how silly it was. How could I be at my best every night? How could I forget that I was being judged just as severely on nights when I was not up to par as on other nights? One can be naïve at a time when one is old enough to know better. It is flattering to hear that there are scads of concerts booked and lots of tickets sold, and you do not wish to be a temperamental prima donna who throws up engagements at small provocation.

My health through these years has been something for which I thank the Lord. I do not remember missing any engagements at all until 1935. I had been through a season of a hundred concerts without a sniffle or sore throat, but I finally came down with a cold in Vienna. I tried desperately to fill my dates, while getting expert medical advice, but I was evidently thoroughly run down, and my throat did not respond to medication. There were some cancelations. Mr. Enwall in Sweden relayed the bad news to Mr. De Koos in Holland, saying, "The wonder has come to pass—Marian Anderson has a cold and must postpone her concerts."

The excitement of the performance must be an aid in helping a singer overcome wild fluctuations of temperatures in auditoriums. You get to work and forget.

In the first ten years or more with Mr. Hurok I did not miss an engagement because of illness. There was one that I missed some years ago in Sacramento, California, and illness was given as the reason. It is time to tell the truth.

I was in San Francisco, staying at the Fairmont Hotel. One evening I had a friend to dinner, and we went to the Tonga Room. Here the patrons were entertained in lively fashion. The room had a pool, and music was provided by a Hawaiian band on a raft which was drawn slowly from one side of the pool to the other. From time to time, when the musicians were resting, a storm would be staged with effects of wind, rain, thunder, and lightning.

We were seated at a table beside the pool. The food was good, the entertainment amusing, the visit with my friend pleasant. We were there a long time; indeed, we sat through three or four storms. Finally we left, and I said good-by to my friend and went to my room and to bed.

The next morning there was a call from the concert agency's field representative in that area, asking where we had been the night before and why we had not kept our date in Sacramento. Presently the newspaper people in Sacramento and San Francisco began to call for explanations.

Mr. Jofe, my traveling manager for years, who had received all these calls, phoned me at eight in the morning. Usually he does not call before ten. I knew something was wrong, and indeed it was.

"Something terrible has happened," he said.

All the terrible things that could happen flashed through my mind. I hated to find out what this was, but finally got up enough courage to ask.

"We had a concert in Sacramento last night," he said.

"What?"

"We had one—I mean we should have had one."

"What happened?" I asked.

"They were in the hall, and they waited." He groaned.

Sacramento had called the hotel. I suppose they had rung my room and paged me while I was sitting through those storms.

The explanation was simple enough. The signed contract, which Mr. Jofe carried, stipulated a certain date, which was changed by an agreement between the New York office and Sacramento. Notice of this change, which meant that the concert was to take place a day earlier, did not reach us in time. We were counting on the original date.

Sacramento was gracious enough to set another date. All was forgiven, and I trust it will remain so now that the whole truth is out.

*CHAPTER 20*

# On the Road

ONE of the first things to be considered in preparing for a tour is one's wardrobe. If special gowns are to be designed and made they must be ordered even before the work on the program begins. As soon as I get the itinerary for the next season—this happens early in the spring for a tour to start in the fall—I think about my clothes. They are really my working uniform, and one owes it to the public to make everything about the occasion as agreeable as possible within the limits of one's endowments. No one needs to tell me that I am not a glamour girl, and I do not try to dress like one.

I keep a notebook, not too completely, about the dresses I have worn in specific places each year. More often than not I have to rely on my memory. I try to make sure that I will not wear the same gown in any town on successive years.

I begin by checking how many times I shall be singing in New York and order a new dress for each occasion. There have been times when I have sung three or four times a season in New York. This does not mean that I think less of other cities. New York simply serves as a useful point of departure, and a dress that has been worn in New York is just as new to an audience in another city that has not seen it before.

Several years ago, when I had dresses made to order the designer prepared his sketches in June and July, and by August we were ready to choose materials for color and fabric. My measurements were in his studio, and the final designs were turned over to the dressmaker. When the time came for a fitting the gown might look a little fuller than it had in the drawing with the slim model, and I would remember that I was once slimmer, too. After the final fittings the dress would be delivered, ready to be packed, and I would not try it on again until concert time.

More recently the procedure has been quite different. After the tour in the United States and Canada we are off to some other country and return about the end of June. After a short rest I call the designer, who puts things in motion. He and the companies that execute the sketches may be working at top speed on one or more Broadway productions involving several dozen costumes. By the time the drawings are approved and other steps taken, my next tour is not far off, and things become rushed. Last year I had a fitting at eleven in the morning on the day of a flight to Rome, and the costumes were sent to the airport just in time for the six-o'clock take-off. This was the closest shave.

As the other dresses for the trip, I take along those that were new the year before and were worn on tour in only a very few places. I make sure that they are all in excellent shape. The first impression on an audience is the visual one, and one should wear what is right for one's type. I like a dress to be easy and comfortable to wear, and I like to feel that nothing about it will hinder me in any way when I sing. I like simple, tasteful clothes; I do not go in for things that dazzle, for I am not a dazzler, and I pay much more attention to my concert costumes than to my everyday clothes. I have threatened at times to spruce up my daily wear, but somehow have not succeeded.

It is not necessary to splurge on evening gowns. A few may cost more than they should, and I may have a lot of them—I keep telling people that they are a necessity of my craft. I remember that when we were building our house in the country my husband observed, "I don't think we can build a house around your evening clothes."

I have not kept count of how many dresses I have— more than fifty, I would guess. Many are stored in the cellar, in oversized suitcases, a wicker basket, and a special chest. If I ever get the time I shall go through the lot and give some away.

The prices of gowns increase each year. In the beginning I bought ready-to-wear dresses. I remember one I bought in a Philadelphia store for a hundred and twenty-five dollars. This was when I was earning money from regular concertizing, but it seemed like a large sum to pay, and I had to make the purchase on the installment plan. The dress was a black satin with a trimming of imported black lace and an embroidery of red roses and green leaves down the side. The first photographs used to promote the tours were taken in this dress.

This was my first expensive gown, and I bought it at a shop that advertised exclusive things. I realized that it would be wise to have dresses that would not be seen on someone else. The Philadelphia shop, no matter what it advertised, could not make just one dress of any design. The solution was a designer. Madame Cahier introduced me to Ladislas Czettel in Vienna. He had told her that he wished to design some dresses for me, and I went to his studio.

He had three sketches ready, and I ordered the first. This dress was white satin. Its only decoration was a long panel on the left side, which could be thrown over the shoulder, where it hung to the floor and formed a suggestion of a train. The panel could also be draped around the arms and shoulders, and it could be worn as a collar. I wore that dress at every opportunity. Only a year ago someone asked me what had happened to it. Naturally I still have it. I can't get into it any longer, and I doubt that I ever shall, but I would not give it away. It represents too much to me.

That dress cost seventy-five dollars. When Mr. Czettel came to the United States later his prices went up, as they should have, for in Europe the poor man never charged enough to make his business sufficiently profitable. In time his dresses came to three hundred and fifty dollars. The gown I wore in the New York concert in 1935 was designed by him.

After Mr. Czettel there were Paul Engle to serve as designer and Minna Owens to carry out the design. In recent years Raoul DuBois has been the designer, and Karinska, who is wonderful, has been the dressmaker.

Years ago, when Mr. Czettel was the designer, Karinska executed some gowns, and so did the Eaves Costume Company.

The most I have ever paid for a gown is eight hundred and twenty-five dollars. Though the people who worked on it deserved all they received, I have never quite got over the fact that such a sum for a dress is a tremendous extravagance.

The reward, I may say, is that people seem to be interested. When I reach a town, an interviewer may ask, "What color gown are you wearing tonight, and who designed it?" I tell him. If this should be a new place on my itinerary I go to the auditorium to look things over, rehearse, and check acoustics. I may notice that the background of the hall will clash with the color of the gown I planned to wear, and I get out another that will be more suitable. And people who have read the paper find that I am not wearing what I said I would wear. This is not a tragedy, but women, who are interested in these things, don't like to be misled.

Once the dresses are selected for the tour, other clothes and equipment are made ready. A tour covers north, south, east, and west. One is in fiercely cold and pleasantly warm climates by turns and needs fur coats as well as light evening wraps. Traveling clothes and street wear for the same wide range of weather conditions have to be carried. In times gone by I have been accompanied on a tour by more than twenty-five pieces of luggage. I have tried to systematize things and cut down on baggage, but the count still goes too high. When you travel by plane the excess-baggage charges mount up; once this fee was three hundred and fifty-eight dollars. I keep trying to eliminate things, and I find that one dress for traveling can do the work of five. A jumper with several blouses makes for changes of costume. I used to carry a floor-length karakul cape with a sable collar, and an ermine wrap with a black velvet lining that could be reversed and made to do for two wraps, as well as several other coats. I now take along fewer of these outer garments.

But the things I have taken with me on tour! I had an electric hot plate and a Pyrex dish or two, useful for brewing tea and boiling eggs. It is not always easy to get food when one wants it en route. Since I do not usually go down to the dining room, I try to make a light supper of soup and crackers for myself, particularly if room service is not geared to help you early enough. Once I even went out and bought an electric oven, but I thought better of using it and did not try it out until I got home.

Believe it or not, I carried a sewing machine with me on tour at one time. I made simple slacks and summer dresses to wear when I was at home puttering around in the garden. When we were building our new home I offered to make curtains while I was on tour. It was quite a business. The curtains were chintz and had linings and interlinings, and I took along the materials as well as the sewing machine. It was awkward to get the right base to set the machine on, and the cutting of the curtains had to be done on the floor.

My husband scoffed at the idea of my undertaking such a job on tour. He bet five dollars that I would not finish the curtains, and I won. It got so that the minute I arrived in a hotel I opened the bag with the curtain materials. On a free day in a strange town I spent my time pinning hems and interlining, sewing, making pleats. Fortunately I like working with my hands.

For a time I dragged along a tape recorder. It was useful, too. I would have the accompanist record his part of a song, and at night, before retiring, I could go over some songs without taking the time of the pianist. But some hotels had direct current, and the machine needed alternating current, so after a while this equipment was left at home.

An item I always have with me is a sleeping bag. I acquired it years ago in Sweden when I toured in the far north, where the nights can be bitterly cold. It rolls up into a light package, and I take it along even when I go to southern localities. If I do not need it there for warmth I can always put odds and ends into it that I cannot find space for elsewhere. I find the bag useful on trains. There are never enough blankets for me; I happen to get cold feet easily. I used to try hot-water bottles, but the sleeping bag is more convenient.

Before I learned to systematize my packing I used to toss things into suitcases as I took them out of drawers and closets. Once on the road, I would find that I did not have things I needed and that I had all sorts of objects I did not need. Now I make a determined effort to get everything out in the open where I can take stock before packing. I try also to show some will-power by returning a few things to the closet.

It is one thing to pack and take off. When you arrive at a destination the question comes up—how much to unpack? A lot depends on the length of the stay and the number of appearances you are to make. If you sing with orchestra there may be two concerts, and you have to get out two gowns. If the pause is as much as four or five days the unpacking and repacking constitute a major operation, for nearly everything is opened.

You generally arrive at a town in the morning. While you wait for your breakfast to be brought to your room you take out the gown you will wear that night. It is easiest to have the hotel valet do the pressing. Sometimes you must wait until you see the auditorium before you choose a dress. Then it is too late to send the dress to the valet. In that case I press the dress myself.

I always carry an iron with me—another of the impedimenta of touring. I use one that will take alternating or direct current. Few hotels provide ironing boards in their rooms, and I have even gone so far as to carry a small board in a suitcase. But it was a bulky object, and I learned to dispense with it. I now have a big Turkish towel in my luggage. I place newspapers over a suitcase, spread the Turkish towel on top, and over the towel a piece of sheeting or a linen towel that I have for this purpose. Then I do the dress. The skirts of most dresses are long and wide, and the surface to work on is small. It takes some time to do the job, but, when it is finished, the dress is not too badly ironed.

There are occasions when I can use a bureau in a hotel room as an ironing surface. If there is a glass cover I am always careful to remove it. I do not own a hotel, and I would not want to, judging by the way people abuse property that is not theirs. If the bureau is not high enough

I place a suitcase on it. I try to be meticulous about not making burns in hotel furniture.

All this may sound like a cumbersome way to get a dress ready, and it is. But after many years I have learned not to mind. And it is comforting that, come what may, your clothes will be ready for you on time and they will look acceptable.

There is a hazard in traveling with so much luggage: you must be sure that you do not mislay or lose something vital. That is a task in itself. Many of our trips start in the morning, and you stand on a station platform, half awake, going through the motions of counting possessions. You count twelve pieces, and you cudgel your memory. Did you have twelve or was it really thirteen? Once we went off without my sleeping bag. I might have been able to wait patiently for it until it caught up with me some days later, if it were not for my bad habit of sticking odds and ends into it. That day my bedroom slippers, a bottle of bath soap, and a number of other things were nestling in the bag.

In Italy some time ago I was busy saying farewell to some friends at the station and let someone else look after the baggage. When we got to our destination in another country we were met by friends, and again we chattered away as our things were taken off the train and sent on to the hotel. Eventually I got to my room and looked around.

There's something wrong in this room, I thought. What can it be? Then it came to me: I have too much space to walk around in. Something's missing in my baggage.

I made a check, and the hatbox was gone. The hatbox, alas, contained a lot of other items besides hats. To begin with, it was a combination hatbox-shoebox, and it was not strange that there were shoes in it as well as hats. I had, of course, managed to fill every cranny. There were stockings, handkerchiefs, veils, and what-not in the hatbox.

Getting that bag returned was like negotiating a treaty between nations. There were telephone calls in which a word could scarcely be heard. There were telegrams, special emissaries to the airport, *pourparlers* with customs officials. After some days the hatbox was safely in the company of my other luggage, and I promised myself that I would always check everything carefully myself.

In Israel I blundered in a fresh way. I remembered to take the right luggage but forgot to make sure that everything I needed was packed into it. I was to make an appearance in Haifa with the Israel Philharmonic, and a number of cars made the trip from Tel-Aviv. In our car were the conductor, Paul Kletzki, Jofe, and several men from the orchestra.

Halfway to Haifa the awful realization dawned on me. "Gentlemen," I said, "my dress is in Tel-Aviv."

We were to stay just one night in Haifa, and I had packed carefully, leaving the evening gown that I would wear at the concert hanging neatly behind a door. I had thought that I might be able to carry it on my lap in the car and thus avoid the bother of having it pressed in Haifa. When I left my quarters the door was open and my mind was on other things. The men of the Israel Philharmonic behaved as if dresses left behind were routine.

Luckily the distance was short, and a call to Tel-Aviv produced a messenger with the dress.

I keep making resolutions to travel light, but I also keep thinking of things I need on long journeys. I was about to leave for a trip to South America once when I remembered my Bell and Howell movie camera. I rushed back and got it, plus four packs of film. Usually I don't take the movie camera; I try to content myself with a still camera. My husband stood and watched me as I got my possessions together. The luggage was in the car, and now I was dealing with the things I would carry myself. I had a small Pan-American bag in which I carried all manner of things, including a portable radio. I hung the movie camera over one shoulder and a large handbag stuffed full of things over the other. I picked up three coats and threw them over one arm, and bent down to take hold of the Pan-American bag.

"How far do you think you can go with all that around your neck?" said my husband.

He relieved me of the movie camera, and I felt five years younger.

# CHAPTER 21

# Good Companions

I HAVE not kept count of all the performances I have
given over the years, so I know only that they are well
over the thousand mark. As for the mileage covered by
train, car, ship, and plane, it must be in the hundreds of
thousands. For a good many of those performances I have
had two faithful and delightful traveling companions—
Franz Rupp, my accompanist, and Isaac Alexander Jofe,
who has been not only a friend but also the touring
factotum almost as long as I have been under Mr. Hurok's
management. There was one long trip Franz did not make
because all the engagements were with orchestra. When
he joined us he looked at Jofe and me with a happy grin
and said, "Now the family is together again."

When Kosti Vehanen returned to Finland in 1940 it
became necessary to find another accompanist. Franz Rupp
was chosen out of three strong candidates. Though he
had played several concerts with me in 1939 during Kosti's
illness, we had not worked together through the period of
preparation of a program. Now we worked on new pro-

grams, and some suggestions were his. The first tours served to acquaint us with each other. For years we did our preparatory work on the farm; now we do more of it in New York.

In the beginning Franz played, for my taste, much more as a pianist than as accompanist. He is a thorough and excellent musician, but I found myself hampered. In German songs, for instance, the tempos suddenly became different from those I had been taught and grown accustomed to. Franz had good and sufficient reasons to back up his choice of tempos. This, moreover, was his native music; he was steeped in it. And so I restudied some of the German songs I had done before.

For years Schubert's songs had been my favorites, and each year these were the first from which we made selections for my programs. These songs are rewarding for pianist and singer alike, and Franz was of tremendous help to me. I welcomed his criticism of my renditions of Schubert's songs and sought the proper way to achieve a better understanding and performance.

Franz has the rare capacity to adjust his musical approach to the needs of the occasion. He is an excellent accompanist, and he is a fine concert pianist. These are decidedly different musical occupations, requiring distinctive orientations; he can manage each with flexibility. He has played piano recitals in Japan, South America, and Scandinavia with effectiveness. Such performances provide him with the larger outlet for his talents that he needs; they enable him to stay fresh as a musician.

In years gone by I have known him to spend free evenings playing chamber music with amateurs. In Chicago there was a physician who played the violin and who gathered other string players at his home for evenings of Haydn, Mozart, and Beethoven. When we were in that city Franz would join these musicians, playing trios, quartets, and quintets with them. I have no doubt that they deferred to his musical taste and experience, and I am sure that he rejoiced at the opportunity to make music.

Franz is generous to musicians. He keeps his ears open for young performers and composers of promise. If he feels that they are striving conscientiously, he goes out of his way to encourage them and to recommend them to influential people. He has used his spare time to play accompaniments for young artists.

His years in America have mellowed him, but nothing has changed the orderliness of his mind and habits. Somehow he finds time not only for touring with me but also for practice, study, and coaching of pianists as well as singers.

As a traveling companion Franz is jolly and really good company. He double-checks our itineraries, and he has been known to emerge from his examination of timetables and maps with suggestions to save time on our journeys. He is meticulous about reading up on the places we pass through, and is insistent on taking time out for sightseeing excursions. It was Franz who worked out a scheme that enabled us to make a side trip to the Grand Canyon in the course of one of our tours. I kept telling myself that this was a sight to see, but I kept postponing it. Franz cut through the inertia and the difficulties of a tight schedule. When we are in Europe, of course, Franz is in his element as a knowing guide.

Franz Rupp has also elected himself the agent in charge of finding places for rehearsal while we are traveling. He checks on the pianos for the performances. There have been times when he has had to make last-minute changes and arrangements to get the right instrument. He has even learned how to tune a piano so that we will not have to depend on others in an emergency.

From the moment that Jofe assumed some of the responsibilities of my travels I knew I had someone I could rely on, for he had traveled a great deal before. I think he had always worked with musicians. He adores them, and they adore him.

As soon as the roster of dates for a season is fixed, Jofe arrives to work out the itinerary with me. If you have a concert in one town on a Monday and the next in another on a Thursday, he wishes to know where you prefer to spend the free day or two. You might have friends in one town and not in the other, or one town might have superior hotel accommodations. Jofe is prepared to make the most comfortable arrangements. He is a student of railroads, knowing even the branch lines, and he works out a plan of travel that involves the least wear and tear. He usually looks after the luggage, and when he does no item goes astray. He sees to it that taxis are ready on time and that bills are paid, and he is watchful that there are no exorbitant charges.

There was the occasion when Franz, Jofe, and I took a taxi from the railroad station to a hotel, and the charge was thirty-five cents per passenger. When we were ready to leave the hotel and the town Jofe ordered two taxis— one for us and one for the baggage. A seven-passenger car arrived, and the driver insisted he could handle us and our baggage, while Jofe complained that he had asked for two vehicles. The driver succeeded in getting us and all our baggage into the car, and we rode the short distance to the station. Franz and I got out and walked down the platform, while Jofe remained to supervise the removal of the luggage. We noticed that Jofe was arguing with the driver. I moved farther away; I did not want to hear what was going on. Finally Jofe joined us, and he was annoyed.

"That fellow charged me two-fifty for the same trip that cost a dollar-five yesterday," he muttered. "So I objected."

"How did it come out?" I asked.

"I had to pay him," said Jofe. "He says to me, 'What are you yelling about? I paid two twenty-five for a ticket to her concert, and I'm not yelling.' "

Jofe knows most of the local managers on our route. He makes it his business to call on them, to entertain them, and to be their friends. I am sure that he has built up all sorts of good will for us, and although he does not report everything that happens I know that he has spared me many embarrassments.

Jofe looks after all preparations backstage before a concert. He sees to it that the piano is moved to the right place, making sure that the light does not shine into the accompanist's eyes. He checks the dressing room, the stage entrance, and even the lighting—he knows that a light straw spot is best for me, regardless of what I am wearing. He confers with the electrician, and if there is no straw spotlight he complains but compromises with the next best. Then he goes out front and supervises the adjustment of the spotlight. And when it is time to go to the hall he is ready to escort us and has a car waiting. He looks me over to see that all is well. I have no doubt that he casts a judicious eye at Franz, making sure that he has the necessary music, though Franz could probably play through the whole program without a printed note before him.

Jofe loves music and musicians. He likes to raise his tenor voice in song, for he studied to be a singer. I remember that I had a recording machine in the living room of a suite in a Montreal hotel. Jofe came in while I was in the bedroom and noticed that the machine was ready for recording. He could not resist. In a booming voice he began to record "Dein is mein ganzes Herz." I tiptoed to the door and peeked through a crack. There he was, a tall, stout man, gesticulating like mad in front of the machine. I have that disk in my collection, and on it I have written the title "The Big Tenor."

Jofe knows the melodies of all the songs I sing, and in most cases the words, whether in Italian, German, French, Spanish, or English. When he stands in the wings during a concert he sometimes sings along with me, though in a subdued tone that will not disturb me. Occasionally he takes a seat in the auditorium in one of the front rows, and even if I cannot make out his features I know where he is from the way his head bobs up and down and his clenched fist pounds out the rhythm on his knee. He is too engrossed to be self-conscious.

Jofe listens to me in rehearsal most attentively. If he does not hear the words clearly from the back of the house he informs me. If he thinks that I am not doing justice to a note or a phrase he comes forward and tells me, and he does not hesitate to sing it for me as he thinks it should go. He may rush backstage as a concert nears its end to suggest an encore that he thinks would go well in this particular community.

If he is not around when Franz and I make up a program, I call him and tell him what we are planning. He makes no secret of his opinion. Occasionally he is present at a program-making session, and he takes part in the discussion.

"No good," Jofe will say about a number. "The song does not make much of a point, and it isn't anything you should do." Then he turns to Franz. "And you should know better than to let her sing it," he says.

"What's wrong with it?" Franz replies.

"Everything."

"We need some good music," Franz protests.

"Who says it's good music?" Jofe demands.

In the end there may be some changes in the program. Jofe wants things that are melodic, sure-fire. Franz may be attracted to a composition that shows musical originality. Both really want things for me which are convincing.

Jofe has never been too tired to look after things that needed doing at the last minute. If we are in a small town where the hotel's dining facilities close down before a concert is over, he scouts around to find out where food can be obtained. He knows that I like a light supper after singing because I have not had much in the way of dinner. He will try to have the hotel leave something in my room if there is no other way, or he will hurry off to a restaurant in an out-of-the-way corner of town and return with a parcel of hot sandwiches and hot drinks.

I used to listen to young singers but found it led me into difficulties. In recent years Jofe and Franz have given auditions to young men and women on the road when they could spare the time. Jofe has made himself endlessly helpful to some of these people, telling them the hard facts of what living in New York costs and means, where they should study, what they should do about planning a career. I have known him to encourage them to visit him in New York, and he has gone so far as to keep an eye on them. When they are in a hurry to succeed he is likely to caution them, "Take things easier and go a little deeper, and you will have something to build on."

Watching him, I once suggested that he ought to set up an office devoted to counseling young people who wanted to go into music. "It would be a good business," I said.

He received the idea coolly. "Who wants advice?" he said.

Nevertheless, Jofe is always ready with it. When I was looking for a place in the country he knew a real-estate man I should go to. When I was fixing up my music library in more orderly fashion than I had ever kept it, Jofe came up to the country to supervise the preparation of an index.

He is always gay. He loves to dance, and at a party he is one of the attractions. When the three of us make part of a journey by car instead of train or plane, Jofe hires the automobile and does the driving. He sits there contentedly, and presently begins singing Russian songs in a voice that gets louder as the miles slip by. He loves children, and wherever we go he pauses to make friends with little strangers. I once sought Franz's advice about what to give Jofe for Christmas, and he said, "A live baby."

If it were up to hospitable friends there would be receptions after every concert. I try to keep them to a minimum. It becomes an exhausting thing to stand in a receiving line shaking hands with hundreds of people. I like people, and it would be a pleasure to meet many of them, but one tries to give everything one has at every concert, and when it is over one is spent. If I do make a rare exception and accept an invitation I always tell the hostess that I would like it very much if Jofe and Franz could come with me, and they are invited too. You can depend on Jofe to have fun at these affairs.

Occasionally when I have a free afternoon I go shopping, and Jofe comes along if he has nothing better to do. I do not bother with big things as a rule, though I once bought a set of rattan furniture in Hawaii and had it shipped to Connecticut. If I buy anything at all it is small —dishes, silver, knickknacks. I picked up glasses in Sweden, porcelain in Denmark, enamelware in Norway, and dishes in Finland.

When we are all on the road together Jofe and Franz and I may get together for a leisurely dinner on a free evening. I like to retire to my room around nine or ten in the evening to make telephone calls to my mother in Philadelphia and my husband in Connecticut. The telephone is my greatest extravagance; I call any night from any point in the United States. I remember making a call to Philadelphia from San Francisco, and after I had finished the operator rang me to say that the charge for that call was fifty-seven dollars and thirty cents. This was a real visit, and I talked with every member of the family. It is on long train trips that my good companions and I hold our most extended powwows. If Jofe has been displeased with the way I have sung at a concert he tells me all about it on the train. There is too much to do after a concert, and there is time to burn in the course of a long haul. The three of us do not agree necessarily on the criticism, and we get into a spirited discussion, although I must say that the two men relish arguments more than I do. Their conversations, of course, are not confined to music. They talk politics, economics, literature, anything at all. They are both lively and sharp-witted—Franz Rupp, who describes himself as a "Yankee mit accent," and Jofe, with his hearty interest in all aspects of life.

When arguments die down the two men read. Once on the way to Oklahoma City we had a little excitement that provided us with train talk for many days. Our train rammed into another, and passengers were tossed about and injured. The engine and several coaches had jumped the track. Our car remained on the rails, and we were only slightly shaken up, so we tried to help those who were hurt, and I remember that this was one occasion where my hot-water bottle proved of some use. I managed to find it in the baggage in my compartment, and Jofe delivered it where it was needed.

To kill time on some trips we took to playing cards. It would be no understatement to say that I am no card shark. To be honest, I have no card sense at all, and I am hopeless when it comes to games. But I agreed to try when Jofe and Franz urged me. After a while I noticed that before every game there was something of a tussle between the two men. I could not understand why. I would not say that tempers flared, but there is no doubt that the ironic comments were meant to be cutting. I finally figured out that they were sparring over position; each wanted desperately to sit where I would be discarding. How wise they were!

# CHAPTER 22

# The Highest and the Lowest

THANKS to the skill and thoughtfulness of my manager and his staff, I have been spared and shielded. They have not told me every hazard they have encountered and overcome in arranging things for me. They have not told me of difficulties in making reservations. They have not let me in on all the problems they have met with local managers or committees. And I am grateful.

I know, of course, that there have been difficulties and problems. I look at the itinerary, see that I am scheduled to stay at a certain hotel in a certain city, and sense that an exception has been made. It is better not to know for sure. It is more comfortable not to think about it if I can avoid it. I have a performance to give, and if my feelings are divided I cannot do my best. If my mind dwells even partly on the disconcerting thought that I am staying where I am not really welcome, I cannot go out and sing as though my heart were full of love and happiness.

And yet the work must be done. If I suspect that an

exception is being made for me I go into the hotel not with triumph but out of necessity. I try to leave behind a conviction in those with whom I have had contact that their attitudes were not based on knowledge. It may be that if they discover that they are wrong about an individual they will begin to realize that their judgment of a group is equally fallacious.

I have gone into places where, without being told by my traveling companions or manager, I discovered at once that an exception was being made for me. For I could feel the cold breeze that blew from the persons who were waiting on me. After my stay some of these very people who were distant at the outset were more cordial and remarked, "We were glad to have you. Please come again."

In this life many people on both sides of the fence, I have found, are eager to jump to conclusions. They do not bother to get facts. They do not take the trouble to make the simplest kind of personal associations that will help them to form intelligent points of view. All too often there is a shying away, almost a fear of getting to know one another. I do not mean that we can all be expected to become friends overnight, or that it is even desirable. I do mean that in some cases that there is an aloofness, an apartness, even a mutual suspicion based on nothing but unstated fears and misunderstanding.

A local manager once said, "Miss Anderson, my daughter has become aware of certain problems. She would like to do something to bring about better relations. She is in high school, and she does not know any Negro children. What would you suggest that she do?"

My suggestion, for what it was worth, was that the girl

should speak to a faculty adviser or to a representative of a student council, who would get in touch with a person in a similar position at a school with Negro girls of her age. The two girls would then be provided with one another's addresses, and, if they chose, they could try writing. In letters there might be less embarrassment, and they could speak freely. Eventually, if they felt like it, they could arrange to meet personally.

I learned later that this suggestion was followed. The girls corresponded, and after a time they became acquainted. This does not mean that a scheme like this would work so well for others. But the only hope for all of us is that we will attempt in good faith to rid ourselves of unknown fears in matters where it is possible to discover that the fears are often groundless and unreasonable. Fear is a disease that eats away at logic and makes man inhuman. A great many of us go out into the world, where we encounter people of whom we know very little. It may be that we care less. But there comes a moment when indifference cannot be maintained and when one has some personal position to take. At such a time it is fine to have some knowledge of why we act as we do. If you teach a child what is right and the child elects to do what is wrong, you know that you have at least done your duty. And if you have taught the child what is right, often he acts right when it is necessary for him to do so, for he finds it difficult to do otherwise.

To return to hotels, I have heard that in some cases where exceptions were made for me exceptions were later made for one or two others of my group who applied for reservations. That is a little progress. On the other hand, there are cities in which only one or two hotels out of many are open to us. And I might add that we are not always restricted to second-class hotels. In some cases the owners or managers of the first-class hotels are the more hospitable.

Once a reservation is made, it is firm. I can recall one painful situation, and I hope I never encounter anything like it again. We arrived at a hotel in a small town, and the man at the desk pushed the registration pad out to the men who were with me. Jofe immediately moved it toward me.

The man at the desk was indignant. "You know we can't take you in here," he said to me.

"What do you mean?" said Jofe.

"She knows better," the man behind the desk said. "She knows I can't take her."

"We have a reservation," said Jofe.

The man at the desk was speechless. He checked and found that Jofe was right. It seems that this man had purchased the hotel between the time our reservation had been made and our appearance in his lobby.

I was given a room. When I got to it and saw what it looked like, I wondered why he should have been so concerned.

The next morning, having given our performance the previous evening, we came down to check out. Something had changed. The man and the woman who had been behind the desk with him the previous day were both pleasant and talkative that morning. But I had not much to say. I had not come to this town or hotel to make conversation.

In another town at another hotel there was an executive who was, if not antagonistic, at least unpleasant. There was an air about him that could not be misinterpreted. But reservations were accepted each year, and since my concert management had troubles enough I did not object to having the reservations renewed at this hotel. I do not make a practice of entertaining when I am on tour. Occasionally, however, there are friends I like to see, and I invite them over. At times people arrive uninvited, and while I like to know who is coming and when, it is not an unforgivable sin to call without warning. This particular day a Negro friend arrived without previous notice. When he called on the house phone I invited him up. I need make no apologies for him, but I would like to make it clear that his character would measure up to anyone's.

The next year, when we were due back in this city and a request for a reservation at this hotel was made, we were informed that there would be no space because all rooms were being turned over to people attending a convention. When the request was repeated, another reason was given. Neither reason could really stand up. In any case, it was not necessary to stay at this hotel; there was another to go to.

There are some people around whose minds never change, and they are not in the least bit interested in having them changed. But one does not live in this world alone. Whatever we have may depend upon what many other people have done to make it possible—food, clothing, and even the way we live and work. A cleaning woman makes a contribution to the well-being of the most successful executive by keeping his offices free of dirt and clutter. Even a great draftsman needs the help and accuracy of the man below who makes preliminary drawings. The most dazzling fashions in the Paris salons depend in great measure on the work of the *midinettes*. Even the highest needs some contribution from those he may regard as the lowest.

I have found that there are all sorts of people in the world, and the great majority are kind and thoughtful. In hotels you meet courteous and gracious people working as managers, desk clerks, waiters, bellboys, telephone operators, and maids. In some hotels I pick up the phone shortly after arriving and, without identifying myself, ask for room service. The operator says, "Miss Anderson, you're back. We're glad to have you." Some attend the concerts and send their programs up with the waiters to be autographed. Bellboys, who have been known to look the other way when a lot of baggage had to be handled, often make a beeline for our things. It is not because we overtip—not exactly, but we do pay well for good service.

As I have said, I take my meals in my room. That is my preference. If I wanted to take them elsewhere I would. I assume that there are hotel managements that are happier to have me dine in my room. It is not because they have any objections but because they feel other guests might complain—or so the explanation would go. If I were inclined to be combative, I suppose I might insist on making issues of these things. But that is not my nature, and I always bear in mind that my mission is to leave behind me the kind of impression that will make it easier for those who follow.

[244]

On one occasion I arrived in a Southern city where the local manager, a woman whom I had never seen before, met me at the station and addressed me by my first name. There was also a young woman there who had offered to be my hostess. She approached me and said, "I am Mrs. So-and-so, Miss Anderson." The difference in attitude made no impression on the manager.

The next day I went over to the auditorium to rehearse. Jofe and Franz seemed to be furious. We had our rehearsal, but their mood did not become brighter.

"I don't know what it is," I told them, "but if you want to keep it to yourselves, all right."

I returned to my hostess's home and got ready for the concert. When I arrived at the hall I did not see the local manager. The hall was full; there were some fifteen hundred persons, and they were wonderful. When we finished the German group there was tremendous applause. Franz Rupp and I returned for a bow. The applause grew louder. We went off and returned, and this time, as is my custom, I took my accompanist's hand. For a split second the house was quiet, and then there was a deafening outburst of applause. After the intermission I sang an aria, and the response was so enthusiastic that Franz and I went out again hand in hand. The audience reaction was the same after the English group and after the spirituals. I sang encores after each, ending with "Ave Maria." At the finish Franz and I took a final bow together.

The manager did not show herself backstage. We went straight to the railroad station and took an overnight train. At last the men decided to tell me what had angered them.

Before I had arrived for the rehearsal the lady manager had appeared and had demanded, "Where is she?"

"Do you mean Miss Anderson?" Mr. Rupp had asked.

She paid him no mind. "I understand," she said, "that she goes out on the stage holding her accompanist's hand, and we won't stand for that here."

"Miss Anderson would not think of coming here and telling you how to run your business," Jofe replied. "She has been on the stage long enough to know how to take care of her own business."

I never sang in that town again, and it may not make any difference. But there were fifteen hundred people in that hall for whom one person was making a decision, and they had shown that they could make their own. It struck me that this one woman was assuming a heavy responsibility in thinking that she could decide for them.

In another Southern city we gave a concert that elicited an unusually hearty response. It grew so enthusiastic as the evening went on that I was obliged to sing encore after encore. Even the singing of "Ave Maria" would not induce these people to cease their demands for more. I went out and sang an old American song, "Carry Me Back to Ol' Virginny." When I reached the last stanza I invited the audience to join me, and it did with wonderful eagerness and unanimity. A local person backstage was indignant at the temerity of one of my group asking white people in the audience to join me in song. Again it turned out that this person was speaking for himself. Indeed, the local newspaper published an editorial the next day congratulating performer and audience.

One encounters differing attitudes on trains. I was in

a drawing room once, and the conductor came and collected the ticket, closing the door after him when he left. A young waiter who had heard we were on the train came back of his own accord with a glass of freshly made orange juice. He left the door open when he walked out. At that moment the conductor came by and reached in and shut the door. Jofe got up and opened it. The conductor seemed to find occasion to walk by frequently. He came along presently, and he closed the door again. The young waiter returned to collect the empty glass. As he emerged from the drawing room he ran into the conductor, and we could hear the latter. "That door's got to be kept closed," he barked.

One does not quite grasp why this was so important to him. However, such things have been fairly rare. I have found more often the opposite reaction among people working on trains. Mostly there have been conductors who have said, "If there is anything we can do for you, let us know."

I recall one odd incident. A conductor came along, took the tickets, and closed the door. I didn't mind; it was pleasant in the compartment. In the meantime I had rung for the waiter, and when there was a knock on the door I was surprised to see the conductor.

"Just found out who you were," he said. "Glad to have you on board."

Then apparently he went down the train, telling other passengers about my being among them. I myself heard him telling someone, "Do you know who's back there?" And so this seemed to be an invitation to autograph-seekers.

It is comfortable or uncomfortable to be an exception, depending on the grounds for it. I keep thinking of other people, so many that one cannot imagine them all, who are good and fine and whose unimpeachable characters entitle them to every consideration. I do not regard riding in a Pullman as a mark of superiority. It indicates simply that you can afford to travel in this way, just as, if you wish to go to a theater, you may be able to afford to purchase the best seats. And even if you want to indulge in some luxury for the good of your soul, why should not one have the privilege as well as the other?

All in all, travel has been pleasant. In one Southern town I stayed in an elegant apartment hotel, and everything was just as agreeable as one could wish. On the other hand, I do not mind putting up at private homes and am grateful for the warmth and hospitality of my people. When I do there are many who come to pay their respects, and this is a lovely tribute to have. But hostesses have a way of making their hospitality so fabulous that one must be on guard against such things as eating too much delicious food and becoming much too stout.

Over the years the audiences for my concerts have been changing. Whereas they were almost entirely my own people at the start, later they were predominantly white. I appeared on concert courses, which means that patrons buy tickets for a season's series in advance, without knowing who the performers will be. In some Southern towns the Negro community no doubt was not circularized, and when it discovered that I was to appear it was too late to get series subscriptions, and single performance tickets were available only for out-of-towners. Furthermore, my people had to sit in restricted areas, and once the tickets in these sections were disposed of no further provision was made for extra patrons.

I was never very happy about singing in halls where segregation was practiced. Some years ago I decided that I had had enough, and I made it a rule that I would not sing where there was segregation. I am aware that this decision made it difficult for the sponsors of local concerts in some cities where I had appeared. They did not feel that they could venture to present concerts on any basis other than the old one—with an invisible line marking off the Negro section from the white, from orchestra to topmost balcony. One could not expect them to take a poll of their patrons. This was their business, and there are plenty of other artists. For myself it meant the loss of several engagements a year. I am sorry to give up warm and enthusiastic audiences. I do not feel, however, that these audiences are irretrievably lost because I am standing on principle. I may be able to go back someday and sing to nonsegregated audiences. If not I, someone else surely will.

In the meantime there have been at least four communities—one in Virginia, one in Kentucky, and two in Florida—where I could appear before nonsegregated audiences. In Florida the concerts took place in the auditoriums of Negro colleges, but in both these gatherings there was a high percentage of white persons. Some of the latter called to ask whether there were reserved seats, which is the expression used to connote segregation. They were told that they could sit anywhere they wished, and they ordered tickets anyhow. In Virginia and recently in Kentucky there was no segregation in the town auditoriums.

Even in the old days, of course, no segregation was practiced backstage. All sorts of people came to ask for autographs backstage without incident. I remember one woman whose attitude was somewhat disconcerting. She stood apart from the others in the artist's room and waited until everyone had gone. Then she came up.

"Since I'm back here," she said, "I'll take an autograph."

I bent over her program, and as I wrote she said, "I still don't understand why you didn't sing 'Chattanooga Choo Choo.'"

My own people always streamed backstage almost triumphantly. They were so delighted at the recognition I was getting that they felt the auditorium was theirs for an evening. Even as I was finishing my last number they started backstage. They were not accustomed to coming backstage, and some who came from the balconies wandered around, trying to find their way. Parents, I discovered, made great sacrifices to have their children hear me. They brought them backstage, and some did not bother to ask for autographs. "This is the lady we were telling you about," one would say. "This is Marian Anderson," another would tell his children. "Shake hands with her, and you can always say that you shook hands with Marian Anderson." I have heard of one woman who scrimped, saved, and borrowed so that she could take her children to my concert. What could be more touching and humbling?

There are also correctives to pride. I was in Houston, Texas, for a concert, staying at a private home. My hostess had a friend down the street, a woman who had taken pains to expose her five-year-old grandson to the finer things of life. She was planning, indeed, to take him to my concert, and she had seen to it that he was led to look at good things on television at home.

"I'm going to take you to hear Marian Anderson," she told the boy. "Did you ever hear that name?"

The child looked at her thoughtfully.

"Don't you remember?" she continued. "She was on TV."

A light began to show in the boy's eyes.

"Marian Anderson," the grandmother persisted. "Of course, you remember."

The boy smiled. "Oh, yes," he said, "she's the blonde who did the rumba."

There is the story of a Negro woman in a Western town who heard that I was to appear in the regular concert series. I was listed with the other performers who would appear, but no definite dates were announced. This woman came to the committee office and asked for my date. She was told that it would be announced later. Since she did not look as if she could afford expensive tickets, she was advised to make her reservation early and she was told that she could do so with a small deposit on a ticket.

Several weeks later she returned. "I want to know when Marian Anderson is coming," she said.

A committee member told her that an announcement would be made in due course and urged her to reserve her ticket. Again she left.

A few weeks later she returned. This time she was told that there were few tickets left and virtually no time for installment buying. The date would be announced in several days, and there could be no guarantee that there would be a ticket available for her.

"Why don't you leave some money now, even twenty-five cents?" she was asked. "You won't be able to get into the concert if you don't."

"I'm not interested in coming to the concert," the woman replied. "All I want is to know when she gets here, because I have six kids I want her to educate."

# CHAPTER 23

# East and West

IF YOU are fortunate your services are in demand, and you get to see something of the world. You learn to be flexible, for the habits of other peoples are different from those in your own country.

In Spain, for example, I found a different conception of time. My concert began at nine-thirty in the evening, and because the man in charge of the lights in the hall insisted on handling them his way, the program dragged on past midnight. After each group this person would turn up the hall lights full. The audience got up after the second group and walked out, taking a twenty-minute intermission we had not planned on. When it returned, I sang an aria. After the aria it was time for my usual intermission, and I might have skipped it, but the printed program provided for it. The audience, not in the least disturbed, arose and took another long break after hearing one number.

This experience was a minor one compared with what happened to Yehudi Menuhin in Mexico City. He was giving concerts there when we arrived, and his wife invited me to attend. His performance was scheduled to start at nine in the evening. When we reached the hall we found the place jammed with people clearly not the Menuhin audience. On the stage children were doing little dances and songs. In the auditorium were their families. It was a program of a mother's organization, I believe, and the affair did not end until eleven at night. Believe it or not, the Menuhin audience, which had gone off to stroll or have a bite, appeared at that hour and quickly filled the hall as soon as the other crowd disappeared, and it sat there until after one in the morning, excitedly listening to the violinist. I should mention that Menuhin's success kept him there overtime, and this was his third or fourth *despedida*.

When in Mexico, I had my movie camera with me and took it along on my one and only visit to the bullfights. Just as the first fight was to start I adjusted the camera, prepared to record everything. I poised the camera, but when the bull charged my heart jumped with fear. I tried to hold the camera firmly, but my hand shook. I kept it going, even though there were moments when I had to avert my eyes and did not bother to take proper aim. The strange thing is that the roll of film came out rather well. When I got home and looked at my handiwork, I was horrified by the gruesome record I had made, and I have never looked at those films again.

The most sympathetic memory I have of Mexico, however, is of the way people greeted me. When I walked down the street or when I strolled through the market, they would smile as they recognized me and call out gently, "Ave Maria, ave Maria."

Two places that I visited in recent years made especially deep impressions on me. At the outermost extremes of Asia, they offered remarkable contrasts, and yet in their eagerness to hear our music—in fact, any good music—they were very much alike. I speak of Japan and Israel.

Our start for Japan was as breathless as it could be, thanks to my decision to do some last-minute shopping in San Francisco. Our plane was to leave for Hawaii at noon, and I discovered the previous night that I lacked some vital things. I was up early the next morning and in the store the moment the doors were opened. I kept picking up this object and that, and when I got to my hotel Jofe and Franz were frantic. We got to the airport at the last possible minute.

We paused in Hawaii for several concerts. Then we landed briefly on Wake Island, where we met Chester Bowles and his wife, returning from India. I had visited him when he was Governor of Connecticut, and we had a brief chat before resuming our trip.

In Tokyo there was a crowd to greet us at the airport. I thought that some celebrated dignitary was being expected, but it turned out to be for us. Representatives of the Japanese Broadcasting Company, which was sponsoring my concerts, were there, as well as people from the American Embassy, and many others. Two delightful little Japanese girls in doll-like costumes came forward to present bouquets. Since the Japanese are assiduous photographers, we had to wait while dozens of cameras were pointed at us.

We finally got into Tokyo and we stayed at what I called the Frank Lloyd Wright hotel. On the way over I had imagined how different and exotic Japan would be, but when I looked around I did not have that feeling at all.

The Japanese are indefatigable planners. My schedule was as rigid as a railroad timetable. Days were laid out in units of three—one for sightseeing, and this was planned down to the minute; one for a concert; and one, praise be, for rest.

I remember that Mr. Furukaki, president of the Japanese Broadcasting Company, took us to dinner the first evening in a large, beautiful establishment that did not look like a restaurant. As our car drove up there were servants waiting to sprinkle water before us. Then at the steps there were cloth slippers to wear in place of our shoes. We walked into a room that was simple and unadorned. In the rear was an alcove with a fine etching hanging on the wall. Underneath it there was a fairly tall vase which contained a single flower. That was all, and it was a sermon on what can be accomplished with simplicity and taste.

We sat on the floor. After a while several girls brought in tables and pillows. Then came the food, and presently more girls whose business seemed to be to attend to the guests—principally, I would say, the men. These girls were poised demurely on their knees, and their grace was very beautiful. This was not a geisha house, by the way. As far as I could make out, it was a rather special place for the entertainment of special guests, with dancing and singing girls performing their ancient art.

The programs we offered in Japan were almost exactly like those in America. They had asked long in advance for all the things we do, specifying Schubert and Brahms and

Handel and, among the spirituals, "Deep River." The way the Japanese listened was extraordinary. The concentration was intense and the quietness almost uncanny. No one seemed to stir, and at first I was conscious of the deep silence and immobility. They were not upsetting in any way, but they made me feel that a similar intensity was expected of me.

When we left Tokyo to appear in other cities we found ourselves traveling as a party of eight. A young woman was provided as an interpreter, and there were four men to serve us in other capacities. One young man was sent along to be banker and cashier; he carried the money and paid bills at hotels, restaurants, and shops.

On one of our sightseeing trips we were taken to Kyoto, the holy city, where we visited the head of the Buddhist Church, Count Olani, and his wife, a beautiful woman who is the sister of the Empress. We were allowed to see the inside of the temple. I will not try to describe its beauty; I could not do it justice.

We were invited to visit the royal palace, where I sang for the Empress. When we arrived at the palace we were taken to a reception room. We heard a car pulling into the drive, and Franz hurried over to the window, eager to see the Empress arriving, but he was told that one did not look out of windows when royal personages were appearing.

Before we performed for the Empress a special entertainment was put on. The court orchestra, of ancient instruments unfamiliar to us, played for us, producing strange and eerie sounds. The musicians wore fantastic costumes, and then in the garden on a platform some male dancers appeared, wearing even more fantastic costumes, and they did some unusual dances.

When it was our turn we were led into another room, which had rising tiers of seats. There was a stairway in the center of this arrangement, leading to the topmost seats. At the apex sat the Empress, and on either side of her was one of her children. Below her at her left sat the women of the court, and below her at her right the men.

I sang four or five German songs, ending with "Ave Maria," an aria, then a group of spirituals. When the performance was finished, the Empress made her exit, and we were led back into the reception room. We were soon summoned into an adjoining chamber, where the Empress received us personally, asking about our tour and our reactions to Japan. We were then presented with gifts from the Empress. I received a hand-carved figure of a No performer. The No theater is an ancient Japanese institution, and its players have a fascinating tradition. This figure of camphor wood, about a foot high, was exquisite in detail, with the traditional mask over the performer's face and the fan in his hand, all painted with delicacy. The figure, standing on a lacquer tray that had carvings of chrysanthemums, was handed to me ceremoniously. On another tray there was a beautifully decorated lacquer box, which was presented to Franz.

When we returned to the waiting room, after making our adieus to the Empress, our gifts were ready for us, packed in lovely boxes. It was all done with the style of an ancient ceremonial. Somehow that was a major impression left by Japan. Though it has become Western in many ways, the essence of an old tradition remains.

In Israel I found the spirit of a new tradition in the making. Things did not begin auspiciously. I had left America feeling ill, and the doctor had suggested that I had a small virus. I had assumed that I would shake it off quickly, but it turned out to be a full-grown virus. In Tel-Aviv I found that I was not getting better. I went to have medication, and the diagnosis was that I had congestion of the trachea. Inhalations twice a day and rest were prescribed.

All this was embarrassing. It meant the postponement of the start of our performances. I had agreed to appear with the Israel Philharmonic, which plays in a small hall that seats no more than a thousand and which has ten different subscription series to accommodate its public. In the end I caught up with the subscriptions and made additional appearances on tour. There were also four recitals when Franz Rupp joined us.

The audiences in Israel were something special. They were made up of people who had found a refuge and a home there, and their hunger for music was exceptional. But no audience was more remarkable than those we had when we performed at two kibbutzim, those pioneering agricultural communities created by dedicated men and women who have had the faith and energy to cause a desert to bloom.

Jofe, who has brothers, a sister, and nephews and nieces living in Israel, had prepared me for the kibbutzim in advance, but the reality transcended his ardent description. At one of these places we happened to arrive just before the start of the Passover. We were invited to be guests at the traditional seder, ceremony of prayer and feasting. It was held in a large hall, and everyone in the community, some thousand people, joined in a common celebration. The seder and the gathering were impressive and moving.

The other kibbutz was at Ein Gev, a remarkable place on the Sea of Galilee. We reached it by a little boat, and the boy who handled it seemed too young to be entrusted with such a job, but he managed it skillfully. The kibbutz is at the bottom of a hill, and beyond it rises the mountain, which is part of Syria. The lights were on at concert time, and the Syrians had been notified that there would be an entertainment, lest they become nervous that something ominous was afoot. The performance took place in a shell with a crowd seated before us. The roof for that shell, the floor for the stage, and the piano had been donated by musicians who had appeared there and who had been stirred by the indomitable spirit of these people.

I was impressed by the emphasis this kibbutz put on music. I was even more impressed by the thought and attention the kibbutzim devoted to the children. It was evident in a short visit that there was no end to the sacrifices the grown-ups were prepared to make so that the children might grow up in happiness. It was noticeable, too, that these children were not being spoiled. As soon as they were old enough they were given tasks to do in accordance with their capacities.

While I was in Israel a number of singers came to see us and discuss their problems. I realized that there was a great deal of potential talent there, and I contributed part of my fee to the setting up of a small scholarship each year for a gifted person.

We were privileged to meet the President of Israel, Itzhak Ben-Zvi, and his wife, who invited us to tea, and the prime minister, Moshe Sharett, and the widow of the first President, Mrs. Chaim Weizmann.

I took occasion to make a pilgrimage to Jerusalem. I did the Stations of the Cross. I was in a group of English-speaking people, and at its head, oddly enough, was a priest from Philadelphia, Father Patrick. We went to Gethsemane, the Mount of Olives, and the Dead Sea, and visited the River Jordan, which had tremendous implications for me. I remembered the words of the spiritual— "The River Jordan is so wide, I don't know how to get to the other side." It turned out, in fact, to be quite narrow and muddy and was a bit of a disappointment. I went to see the walls of Jericho—another name that had all kinds of meaning for me. I thought of the spiritual's lines, "Joshua fit the battle of Jericho, and the walls came tumbling down." But the walls were not high any more. Archaeologists were doing some excavation in the area, and, seeing the results of their work, I realized that the walls must have been high after all.

And it came to me that the Negro made images out of the Bible that were as vaulting as his aspirations. He had a desire to escape from the confining restrictions and burdens of the life he led. The making and singing of a song constituted an act of liberation, even if it was one that lasted only briefly in the imagination. He expressed his emotions and dreams in terms that were closest to him—

terms from the Bible. He could see Heaven and Jerusalem and Calvary and the stone that was rolled away from the tomb. Being oppressed and persecuted, he dreamed of a city called Heaven, which would be a new home of peace and love.

I could see in Israel the geographic places that represented the reality, and they stirred me deeply. I kept thinking that my people had captured the essence of that reality and had gone beyond it to express in the spirituals the deepest necessities of their human predicament.

# CHAPTER 24

# Those Who Listen

A PERFORMER makes contact with an audience in various ways. There is nothing more certain than the feeling you have when your listeners are getting something out of your renditions. It may be that they are not getting too much, and you sense that too, if you are conscientious. What is it? You cannot put your finger on it, but you know it is there.

Call it, if you like, radiation. You may go to a concert feeling below par. As you step out on the stage your audience's eagerness to hear and accept you before you have uttered a sound is a lift. You sense yourself being pulled up abruptly. And as you sing you find more and more strength coming to you from the audience. By the end of the evening the concert that you feared would not be much has turned out to be one of your best.

I have never been able to analyze the qualities that the audience contributes to a performance. The most important, I think, are sympathy, open-mindedness, expectancy, faith, and a certain support to your effort. I know that my career could not have been what it is without all these things, which have come from many people. The knowledge of the feelings other people have expended on me has kept me going when times were hard. That knowledge has been a responsibility, a challenge, and an inspiration. It has been the path to development and growth. The faith and confidence of others in me have been like shining, guiding stars.

You yourself do not know how you reach other people. You may sing in less than your best form, and some people will come back and say, "Your concert was the best I've heard you give." This does not mean that they are ignorant about music. It suggests that people bring an eagerness to hearing that illuminates a performance for them far more than the performer has any right to expect.

Audiences differ. In such cities as New York you have a cosmopolitan audience. As you travel westward you notice that audiences become more outgoing. They seem to be more eager to be entertained, and they are less sophisticated. An audience in the East has had a great deal more experience with musical performers of all sorts, and it may be harder to please. But in all these matters there has been a tendency in recent years toward an equalization of experience, thanks to the spread of good music.

I shall always remember an audience in Minneapolis. We had appeared in a small Michigan town and were not scheduled to appear in Minneapolis but thought it would be most comfortable to spend two days of rest there. I remember that when I got into my hotel room I picked up one of those booklets that describe goings-on in town and noticed that Vladimir Horowitz was playing that night. Jofe phoned Mr. Lombard, who runs the concert series at the University of Minnesota, and for whom we had appeared a number of times, and asked whether any tickets for the pianist were available.

"The place is sold out," he said, "but you are welcome to sit in my box."

"We are three," Jofe reminded him.

"I understand."

"Could we find a place somewhere at the university to do some work on some new things?" I asked.

"Come over to the auditorium," he said, "and we'll arrange it."

When we got there he said, "I have something to ask you. Horowitz may not be able to play tonight. Would you be willing to appear?"

"Absolutely not."

"Please don't say no yet. Let me know what you think when you finish your rehearsal. I have a feeling Horowitz will not play tonight. Mrs. Horowitz has promised to phone me at six. I wouldn't like to turn an audience away, and it's too late to reach anybody else."

"I don't think a singer should replace a pianist," I said.

"Please consider it," Mr. Lombard pleaded.

I returned to the hotel and phoned the Hurok office in New York to tell them what was up and to ask for their suggestions. "We leave it up to you," they said.

Soon Mr. Lombard phoned with the bad news—Horowitz could not play. I consulted with Franz. He was for it (so was Jofe) and could probably have given a fine piano recital on his own. I decided that I would sing, though I went to the hall troubled. What would an audience think of getting a singer in place of Horowitz, of all artists?

Mr. Lombard, a master psychologist, handled the situation tactfully. He spoke to the audience, making an impromptu address the like of which I had not heard. He explained the suddenness of Horowitz's illness and then built up the substitute, without identification, until the audience had no alternative but to regard itself as fortunate indeed. He did not mention my name until the very end. As I walked out there was thunderous applause.

Mr. Lombard had offered to make refunds to any patrons who were not content to have a singer instead of Horowitz. But he had spellbound the audience; I understand that only a half-dozen people asked for their money back. His speech had excited me, too. He had keyed us all up so that everything I did had fire and was welcomed warmly. I had to announce each group. At the end many people came backstage for autographs, and I found myself signing my name across the program of Vladimir Horowitz. The next day Mrs. Horowitz telephoned to thank me for this act of comradeship. Mr. Lombard deserved a vote of thanks for his eloquence.

One of the rewards of being a public performer is the recognition by so many strangers. In some cases they become friends. One evening at Carnegie Hall a man with a sensitive face and beautiful white hair came backstage. He was Albert Einstein. He was soft-spoken and understanding, leaving me with a feeling of humility.

Several years later I received an invitation from him through Franz Rupp, who had known Dr. Einstein and had played sonatas with him, to use his home in Princeton, New Jersey, where I was scheduled to appear. I accepted, and when I arrived he came downstairs to welcome me into his home. His daughter, Margot, had prepared a room for me in which I could rest and change into my evening clothes. She also brought up a tray of food.

Dr. Einstein, who did not go out much, attended the concert. Afterward there was a reception, which a group of my people had arranged. Dr. Einstein was invited as a matter of form, but no one expected him to go, and no one, of course, would have been offended if he had begged off. But he went there too. And when I returned to his home he was waiting up for me, and he sat and talked for a time.

In January 1955 I was scheduled to sing in Princeton, and again there was an invitation to feel free to use the Einstein home. Dr. Einstein was not downstairs when we arrived, and I could understand that—indeed, I was glad that he was not putting himself out for us. Margot Einstein led me upstairs. I had not been in my room more than five minutes when there was a gentle knock on the door. I opened it, and there stood Dr. Einstein. He had come to say, "How do you do" and "Glad to have you back." This time he did not go to the concert. Afterward, when I left his home, he came out of his room to say good-by. This, though I did not know it, was really good-by.

There is another man I remember whose warmth was always like a reward for all the years of effort. He was Fiorello H. La Guardia. I met him while he was Mayor of New York, through the good offices of Hubert T. Delany, who looked after my legal affairs at the time. I remember that Mayor La Guardia asked me to appear on the programs he was arranging, and one could not say no to him. As I sat on the platform he would whisper information about the cause for which we were appearing, talk about music, be flattering about my singing. He was so vibrant that the brief meeting with him made you feel that you were living with greater awareness.

Mayor La Guardia was not the only one to call on me to help in this cause or that. It is good to know that people feel they can call upon you and that you can be helpful. One acceptance is an invitation to others, all worthy causes, but after a time it becomes impossible to respond affirmatively to all. Your work remains to be done and does not leave you a great deal of spare time. When it is possible, you appear. But you soon realize that a request turned down may cause offense or misunderstanding. I have found that the best thing to do is to channel all requests through the Hurok office, which has a clear idea of all my engagements and knows from long experience just how much, if anything, I can take on in addition.

The public makes contact with one in the hall, backstage, and through the mail. There are letters from people who wish to praise or to criticize. There are messages from people who ask for contributions ranging from money for homes, businesses, church repairs, sewing machines, and phone bills to help in paying for a stay at a private summer resort. I wish I could respond favorably to all, but, no matter how much I might earn, it would not be enough. I once got a letter from an organization, an excellent one, which said, "Our drive needs twelve thousand dollars more to go over the top. Will you please be kind enough to send us a check for that amount?" It would be a wonderful thing to be in a position to make such gestures, and I would not need to be asked.

There are letters from people who think they have discovered new and better ways of producing the voice. There are letters from young singers seeking advice, and from older ones who feel that they are well qualified but never had the right opportunity. One such missive ended with these words, "You had your break, now give me mine."

A good many notes from people who attend my concerts discuss the songs on the program, telling me which they liked and which they did not. They want to know the details of putting together a program. They make requests for songs on future programs. They discuss your clothes, and they ask for information as to where a gown was made. They want to know where you learned to walk on and off the stage. To this last one my answer is, "Nowhere. It's the way I walk. I had no training."

You get letters that are tremendously moving. A woman who had just lost someone very dear to her wrote, "You need not answer, but I just want you to know that I was feeling very badly, and I heard some of your recordings and they helped me." When people pour out the fullness of their hearts you know that something precious has been accomplished.

But the public is a diverse body. There are elements in it that do not let you remain self-satisfied. Once Jofe came backstage to report an incident he had witnessed during a concert. A young couple had stalked out of the hall in the middle of the program; the girl was indignant, and the boy was following her in great concern. As they reached the outer door she flung her printed program to the ground in evident disgust. Apparently she felt that this sort of music and performance was not her meat.

The generous interest of the public is wonderful to have, but I must admit that the flow of letters is a bit of an embarrassment to me. I would like to answer them all, but I am one of the world's worst correspondents. My husband has attempted to answer some for me, and my sisters now take care of some. I do not have a secretary to travel with me; occasionally I bring in a girl for a few days and dictate a lot of replies.

The problem, however, is never solved. I always withhold the letters from friends, since I feel that they should be answered personally. There comes a day when I determine to do letters. I get out a yellow pad and write a first draft. Then I may be called away for a moment, and the next thing I know, I am involved in more pressing duties. I console myself with the thought that the letters are written; all that remains is to make fair copies and send them off. Somehow, that task is delayed endlessly. I fear that I have lost valuable friends in this way, though most people seem to understand and forgive.

People are wonderful. There is no stopping their impulses for generosity. I cannot get over the recurrent phenomenon of people who pay their way into my concerts and then go to the trouble of sending personal gifts, which mean a great deal to them and so much to me. A woman in Canada came to the hall—against her doctor's orders, I learned later—and brought a doll she had fashioned with her own hands. It had a charming little dress made of lace, and a sweet bonnet, and everything about it indicated that much thought and affection had gone into its making. I have received hand-embroidered handkerchiefs from strangers, a beautiful feather fan from a woman who said that my records had meant much to her son in the last days of his life, a Chinese wall hanging, sketches made during a performance, carved figures of myself, lovely plates, bits of jewelry, a plaque from a radio listener in New Haven, an African figurine, and a most unusual score of Brahms's "Alto Rhapsody," in which a young woman had copied and colored all the notes from the first to the last in keeping with her emotional reaction to the music—a fantastic work. One woman sent me a lovely old pin with a note: "This has little monetary value, but it was my mother's favorite piece of jewelry, and I would like you to have it for your mother."

Among the audiences that I remember with special vividness are those I sang for during World War II—in hospitals and in military establishments. In some sections of hospitals I sang where there was no piano. In Topeka, Kansas, I sang for wounded men who, I was warned, could not remain seated and listening for more than fifteen minutes. But they would not permit me to leave after fifteen minutes, and their medical guardians thought it would be good for them if I continued. That performance lasted forty-five minutes, and I was more touched than the audience.

I remember that I sang in a hospital where a boy from Texas who had lost both legs said to me, "I am going to get my legs soon and go home to Dallas. Do you ever sing there?"

I said I did.

"Well, I'll come to hear your concert and look you up."
And he did, bless him.

I sang in Korea—on a hospital ship off Inchon, in a
hospital on shore, in a facility for troops of the Republic
of Korea. In one place there was a pedal organ instead of
a piano, which Franz Rupp played cheerfully and remarked at the end that he had walked ten miles in that performance.

In the United States I sang for the WAC at Oglethorpe
and at Sheppard Field in Texas at an air-force ceremony.
That appearance at Sheppard Field I shall not forget. We
were in San Antonio for a concert, and we were told we
would be flown to the air-force installation. Franz, in his
infinite wisdom, decided to go by car. Because it meant
being able to start later, Jofe and I were to go by plane.

Mrs. Black, the wife of a colonel who had made all the
arrangements, came along to serve as an escort. The plane
was so small that it looked as if it could not possibly hold
all of us. We got in—Mrs. Black, Jofe, the pilot, and I—
the engines began to hum, and we took off. The young
pilot seemed to be delighted to have Mrs. Black at his side;
he talked and talked. Part of the time he had his hands on
the controls, and part of the time he didn't. I was nervous.
How long would it be before we reached our destination?
We put down at Waco to refuel and I whispered to Jofe,
"I hope he stops talking when we get up again."

We had been aloft for a few minutes when Jofe and I
saw sheets of white, whirling like a fan, near one of the
engines.

"Do you see what I see?" I said to Jofe.

He tapped the pilot on the shoulder, and the young man took a look and exclaimed, "My God, it's the gasoline."

The plane took a turn as if it were spinning on a dime. We got back to the Waco airport safely and discovered that a gasket was missing. Eventually we reached Sheppard Field, not a moment too soon. Franz Rupp, who had started out early, was there, somewhat rested after a bumpy drive.

There were thousands of men on the field, and they made a wonderful audience. I found this to be the case everywhere. One did not have to sing down to these men; One could sing the things one sang regularly, and they seemed to be delighted. I remember that in Korea two lads approached me for autographs. They seemed to be in a hurry, and I made some mention of that. One of them grinned. "We went AWOL for this concert, and we have to hurry back to the front before we're missed."

Another audience that lingers in my memory was one of workers in a California shipyard during World War II. I had been invited to christen a new liberty ship, the *Booker T. Washington*. The ceremonies took place during the lunch hour, and I sang several songs. I remember that there were men on the deck of the ship, on scaffolds, and in riggings. They demanded encores, and I am afraid the program went beyond the lunch hour.

Being in the public eye has led to honors far beyond my deserts. Honorary membership in Alpha Kappa Alpha Sorority has been a valued asset. The sorority does fine work, sponsoring educational opportunities for gifted young people. When I reach a strange town it often happens that members of AKA place themselves at my disposal. They take me sightseeing or shopping and make me feel at home.

There have been awards from the governments of Sweden and Finland. The latter, through Field Marshal Mannerheim, presented me with the Order of the White Rose. I once happened to be in Caux, Switzerland, during a convention of the Moral Rearmament movement, and the Finnish delegation sent a gorgeous bouquet of white roses to my room.

There have been honorary degrees from Howard University, Temple, Smith, Carlisle, Moravian, and Dickinson. There have been such things as the Springarn Medal from the National Association for the Advancement of Colored People, which meant much to me because I have been a member of this organization for many years and have believed firmly in the importance of its work. There have been other honors, and if I do not mention them all it is not because I do not appreciate them. This is not the place to take too many bows.

The honor that I shall dwell on longest is the Bok Award, principally because it led to something in which I take special pride. The Philadelphia Award is its proper name. It was established in 1921 by Edward Bok, one of Philadelphia's first citizens, and it goes annually to a Philadelphian who has done some service that redounds to the credit of the city. To tell the truth, I scarcely knew of the existence of the Philadelphia Award in its early years. I was too busy with my small affairs. Later on I became aware of it, but it never occurred to me that I might one day be a recipient.

The first inkling that I was to be so honored came one evening when I was appearing with the Philadelphia Orchestra in Robin Hood Dell. Then I received official word, but was pledged to strictest secrecy. The date was set, and I received tickets for a box for my family and friends at the Academy of Music for the ceremonies. The family came, and if anything was suspected, no one gave any sign. When I left them in the box and went backstage I suppose they began to understand.

There was a speech, and the presentation was made. It was my turn, and I could scarcely talk. I had not prepared anything, and I am no speaker, extemporaneous or otherwise. I don't recall what I said—not all of it, I mean—but I do remember that I ended in song, with the words of the spiritual: "I open my mouth to the Lord, and I will never turn back. I will go, I shall go to see what the end will be."

The Philadelphia Award carried a sum of ten thousand dollars. I used it to set up the Marian Anderson Scholarships. Over the years I had realized how many fine young voices there are in this country, and I remembered from my own youth that many young singers need help to go on with their studies. With the advice of good and thoughtful friends we set up auditions, with qualified judges to make decisions. I do not listen to the contestants before or during these auditions. Indeed, I have not heard some of the scholarship-winners at all.

Those who wish to compete apply in the spring for the entry blanks, and then the money is paid out to the winner's teacher. In the first year there were twenty-eight contestants. Recently there were five hundred applicants, with three hundred rated as qualified to compete. The judges needed three days to hear them all. It has grown to be quite a business. We furnish the accompanist, so that the contestant will not have that additional expense.

The judges try to maintain a very high standard. Some of the winners—and some who failed to win—have made names for themselves in concert and opera. Others have had a chance to sing for experts and have learned that they needed more work. I heard of one girl who had come a long way to Philadelphia and who withdrew her name before she was called on to sing. "I have heard some of the contestants," she said, "and I can see that I am not ready to compete against them."

The amount of the scholarship is a thousand dollars. When there is a tie—and there have been ties in three different years—each winner gets seven hundred and fifty dollars. When more than one or two persons of talent appear, additional prizes are awarded by the judges. One year twenty-two hundred dollars in prizes went to competitors. The original ten thousand dollars has had to be supplemented with additional funds on several occasions.

I do not think that contests, which do not fit all people, are always the best way of finding persons with ability. No one need tell me that there are imponderables, that one youngster may be calm as a contestant and another too nervous to do himself justice. The results, however, lead me to feel that the contest has been worth while. And it has given me particular satisfaction that this competition is open to all singers, whatever their background or origins may be.

Not having met all the winners, I arranged to have a day

in the country one September several years ago for all those who had received any award or citation in the contest. It was arranged that a bus would pick up the young men and women in New York and drive them to our place in Connecticut. My sister Alyce, who has a lot to do with handling the applications for the contest and keeping a file on the winners, was in charge of assembling those who were available. It was quite a party, but no one was asked to sing, though we could have arranged a formidable program.

If some of these people have gone out and brought pleasure and satisfaction to publics of their own, and if the scholarship helped them to climb another rung on the way to their goal, I feel that the people who have listened to me over the years deserve the credit. Their faith opened the way for me to be useful to younger singers.

# CHAPTER 25

# Recordings

I HAVE no idea whether RCA Victor has a copy of the first recording I made, back in the twenties. It was the one I mentioned earlier, and it included "Deep River" and "Heaven, Heaven." There is no reason why the company should still have the master; it was made when I was unknown. I am sure that I earned little from it, for I doubt that many copies were sold, and, frankly, I don't have a copy myself. It is not my idea of an indoor pastime to sit and listen to my own recordings.

After I came under the management of the Judson office a contract was drawn up with Victor. Not too many recordings were made at that time. I recorded several spirituals, with Billy King at the piano. Whether they attracted enough interest to amount to anything I do not know, but the evidence would seem to be against it.

When I was studying in Germany a company there suggested that I make some recordings. I was not sure whether I was free to do so. After making inquiries by mail in the

United States, I found I would have to get clearance from authorities of His Master's Voice, the English company. I got in touch with His Master's Voice, which naturally had never heard of me. Permission was granted readily.

After my return to the United States in December 1935 the question of recordings came up. Victor wanted me on its regular roster, and there were some problems about clearing up the obligations to the German recording company. When this was done I began to make disks exclusively for Victor. The first, with Kosti Vehanen at the piano, was songs by Schubert and some spirituals. Eventually I also made recordings in the H. M. V. studios in England, and these were released in the United States under the Victor label.

I have made quite a few recordings, and they cover many of the things I have sung on my programs down through the years. There are Lieder by Schubert, Schumann, Brahms, and Strauss; sacred arias by Bach; some Handel and Mendelssohn; Christmas carols; old American songs; Negro spirituals; and some operatic arias.

The Hurok office felt that it would be valuable to have my recordings available in the shops of towns where I sang, and I tried to include one or two of the numbers that had been recorded on each concert program. Recordings have undoubtedly played their part in my career, and they have also produced their share of income. I have been told by the Victor people that my "Ave Maria" disk has sold seven hundred and fifty thousand copies, and, more than two hundred and fifty thousand of my albums have been purchased. The best-selling collections have been *Marian Anderson Sings Spirituals, Marian Anderson Sings*

*Beloved Schubert Songs,* and *Marian Anderson Sings Christmas Carols.*

I am constantly being urged to make recordings. Mr. Hurok recently admonished me, "We'll have to have records, we'll have to have records." He is probably right, but I find it difficult to get around to making them. I like to spend a lot of time preparing for a job, and to make records properly I need an uninterrupted stretch of time. Someone suggests that when I happen to have a three- or four-day break between concerts I ought to use the interval to make records, but I don't like to make them that way. I have done it in the past, but I was not completely pleased.

To tell the truth, I never liked the idea of singing into a microphone. I like to see faces before me. I like to sense a reaction. Singing into a microphone in a studio is like performing into dead space; there are engineers and technicians around, but even them I cannot see.

Furthermore, I find it a necessary evil to listen to playbacks of my singing. The voice does not sound at all like mine. After a while you get used to the strangeness of the voice, and you accept the fact that this is how you sound.

Some small things may be tossed off quickly in the recording studio. There are some songs that I have been doing so often that I can see the printed music, though my eyes are closed. Such songs should be recorded satisfactorily at the first try, though at the studio they want a second recording in case something should happen to the first.

The serious works, however, require more time and effort. I look through the music to fix clearly in my mind the places that may give me difficulty. I record the song, and it turns out that those places have gone well, but then new weaknesses appear. I mark the passage that has created trouble, and we record a third time. Eventually there should be a satisfactory take, but one can never tell.

I know that the engineers in recording studios, who work nowadays with magnetic tape, have become so skillful that they can take several versions and piece together the best sections so well that a perfect rendition emerges. For some singers who have as little time as I to give recordings and who always sing the same way, this is probably a desirable technique. I do not think it is right for me. I know I feel happier if a full recording is made from beginning to end. It has greater spontaneity done in one piece—at least I feel that it has.

It could be that if I recorded more often I would be more at ease in the studio, I would develop an aptitude for this type of work and be able to handle it smoothly. Since I don't record that regularly I shall have to go on thinking that it is an exacting and exhausting chore.

When I record with piano accompaniment I am much more relaxed than when I work with orchestra. I want to be in the best possible vocal form for every session, particularly with orchestra. The cost to the company of mistakes by anyone involved in the recording is formidable. If I do something that does not go well, and repeats have to be made on my account, the embarrassment is painful. Of course, if a serious error is involved I swallow my pride and insist on the retake. But if it is merely a feeling on my part that by doing a thing once more I could get just a little more depth into a passage, I am not insistent. It is a fault in me, I know. Perhaps that is one reason why I am not always happy in the recording studio.

There are occasions when the singer who records with an orchestra is not responsible for difficulties. Once we did three or four takes, and in all modesty I may say that it seemed to me that I did well each time. Each time something went wrong in the orchestra. It was a nuisance to do the piece over and over, but I did not mind much as I knew that I was not the culpable party.

Of the recordings I have made, one that I liked a great deal was Brahms's "Die Schnurr, die Perl an Perle." It was recorded about fifteen years ago and released several years later on a shellac disk. I suspect it is no longer on the market, and I am not sure how popular this song would be with the public at large. But I am fond of it and have warm memories of the recording session. It was on the second try, I think, that we got a pleasing performance. The mood was right. But even this disk was flawed for me. The next to the last note was not perfect, but I did not get around to doing the song again.

The recording that has disappointed me most, if Victor will forgive me for saying so right out in public, was the one of "He's Got the Whole World in His Hands." We did two takes in the studio. Franz Rupp said, "We don't have to do that over again. It's fine." Jofe said, "That's it!" And I agreed. When we walked out of the studio I felt happy.

An album of spirituals was released, and "He's Got the Whole World in His Hands" was part of it. I listened to it, and the performance seemed remote from what I had heard in the playback at the studio. I can tell you what was wrong in the record: it was too fast; it did not have the feeling it should have and that I like to convey; it even seemed in the wrong key.

What could have gone wrong? I could not blame myself entirely. Jofe and Franz are honest men, and they would not say a thing was good if they did not think it really was. I had thought it satisfactory too. But there it was—the weakest performance you can imagine.

The studio knows how I feel and has suggested that I make a fresh recording of the spiritual, and I shall at the earliest opportunity. I do not know whether it will be released separately or inserted into the album in place of the old recording. I should hope the latter. I would not want the beauty of this spiritual and the profundity of its message underestimated because I did not take the trouble to rerecord it properly.

I hope I am not stuffy about what I sing or record. Victor recently suggested a recording of "Zigeunerlieder," and I like the idea. I would not mind singing such songs as "The Lost Chord," which I sang as a girl in half a dozen different keys just for the sheer fun of it, and "Believe Me if All Those Endearing Young Charms." I may even get around to trying musical-comedy numbers. Good music in any genre is worthy of respect.

# CHAPTER 26

# Husband and Home

SEVERAL years before our marriage King and I decided we wanted a home in the country. We went househunting on Long Island, in New Jersey, and in Connecticut. We liked Connecticut best. We were shown some properties that were not available to us, and then we saw the one we bought. I had made up my mind that I wanted a house with high ceilings and fireplaces in all the principal rooms, and I wanted to be near a lake. Well, the farmhouse settled upon had low ceilings, one fireplace, and no lake at all. We lived there for several years. It had always been too large for us, and eventually we sold it and built a new home on the other side of the road. This one conformed to my ideas of a dream house. We dammed up a brook to make a pleasant swimming hole.

At the time of the purchase King was working in New York and could be at the farm only on week ends. In his spare time he drew up plans for the alterations we wished to make, got bids for the work, and arranged to supervise it. Whenever I had as much as twelve free hours I took a train to Brewster, New York, and he met me at the station and took me to the house. I remember walking into the front door once and seeing that the steps had been torn out; the place looked a wreck. To get to the second floor you had to climb up a ladder.

I was appalled by the mess. "You've ruined the house," I said to King. Nothing he could say by way of reassurance consoled me. I continued with my concert tour, and my heart was heavy. I just couldn't visualize what the place would look like when it was finished. Finally I returned fearfully. The work was done, and the house looked beautiful.

The business of furnishing and decorating went on for a long time. King would mail me swatches of materials for furniture covers and bits of wallpaper on which he scribbled his recommendations, and I would return them with my suggestions. When he saw furniture he liked he sent me photographs for my approval.

King and I have had some lovely times together. He is an understanding person, and without such a man our marriage could not have worked out, for I am still away from home entirely too much. He now practices his profession, architecture, using a room in our new home as an office, and stays in Connecticut the year round, save on the rare occasions when he accompanies me on one of my trips. He loves working outdoors, and he is one of the handiest men I have ever seen. He can do carpentry, masonry, electrical work—anything needed around the house or on the grounds. When he is not on an outside professional job he thinks up exciting projects for our place.

King designed and helped build our new home. He had

some really good workmen, but he did much of the labor with his own hands and is proud that most of the machinery needed on the job was available from his own workshop.

He has taught me to read a blueprint—at least he has tried. On occasion I have asked some question, and he has sat down and explained patiently, as though he were talking to a child. "I wouldn't want people to say," he remarks, "that the wife of an architect does not understand these things."

I try to be a homemaker, but I can function only on a part-time basis. I try to keep my summers clear. My tours usually end in April, and if there are no trips abroad I can remain at home until the early fall. While I am home I try to make up for the time I have been away.

We do not entertain a great deal, but we have many friends in common, and we try to see them when I am home. We do not belong to many organizations. King is a fraternity man, and a member of the volunteer fire department of our community. I wish I had time to do the things other women do, such as working with local organizations that serve such needs as schools and hospitals. Some day perhaps I shall be able to give more time to such activities.

As I have said, I like to work with my hands. I spent some of my spare time one summer trying to upholster a piece of furniture. Learning was fun, and I think I should like to undertake something more ambitious along those lines.

I also like to sew, can do a fair patching job, and can darn socks. I like to garden, and I have brought back interesting seeds from my travels and made an effort to get them

to grow in Connecticut. I am especially fond of straw-
berries, and we have a bed for plants that produce extra
large berries, but our luck is variable. For many years we
hired a man named Thurston, who had the proverbial
green thumb, and everything flourished under his care.

We have a girl who looks after the house and cooks, but
on Thursdays and every other Sunday I take over, and I
enjoy the change. When the girl is away I prepare King's
breakfast—he has been thoughtful enough to serve mine in
bed many times. However, I do not like to stay in bed of a
morning. I like to be up and stirring.

I try to arrange varied menus. Occasionally King takes
over, giving the girl instructions. He knows that I have
been looking at menus day in and day out on tour and that
I am tired of thinking of them. It becomes a luxury to sit
down to dinner without having advance knowledge of what
will be served. Since King has a cultivated taste for good
food, I can depend on him to arrange interesting meals.
When he has a hankering for something different, he says
so; it sometimes happens that on my day to cook King
proposes something extra special. I may never have made
this dish before, and I have learned to rely on good cook-
books.

One day I was in Chicago, having a bite of lunch in my
room and looking at television. A family was illustrating
the making of a certain dessert, and the demonstration
was fascinating. When they suggested that one ought to
purchase their cookbook for further advice I went right
out and bought it. I could not wait to get home and try
the dish I had seen them making.

I have had some compliments for my cooking and baking. I can make a good plain cake, and my cheese soufflé has emerged at times without turning temperamental and collapsing before reaching the table. King is game; he will try most of the things I make. I remember that once we were talking about the kind of cooks who do not lean on books but who gaily make things as if they were improvising, and as we were going to have meat loaf that day I decided to do it without consulting any guides. I had the ground beef in the freezer, and when I prepared it for the oven I followed the impulse to put in a bit of this and a bit of that without stopping to measure quantities. I served it with some trepidation, and King proclaimed it the best meat loaf he had ever eaten.

"Let's have another like it sometime," he said.

"Fine," I said happily.

When I undertook the next meat loaf I wasn't feeling the same. Perhaps the divine afflatus was not on me. It came out a mess. I don't know what happened, but King has not suggested that I make that dish again.

One day, after returning from a tour, I had a call from a British manager, Mr. Hill, who had arranged my concerts in the Carribean countries. He was in the United States, and I invited him up to the country. It was the girl's day off, and I determined to cook a fine dinner for him.

Franz Rupp was in the country with us at that time, working with me on the coming season's program. I knew that I would have to spend certain hours with him, and I tried to budget my day to make time for the cooking. I planned the menu the previous night, and early in the

[288]

morning I phoned the butcher and ordered a fillet of beef. He was not sure that he would be able to deliver it, but he said he would try.

Franz and I worked all morning. Then we went up from the studio to the house, and I threw together some lunch for King, Franz, and myself. I called the butcher, and he said he had not been able to find someone to deliver the roast. I hurried through the dishes, rushed to the studio for an hour's work with Franz, and then drove into town to pick up the meat.

I returned and addressed myself to the cookbook. I prepared the meat, preheated the oven, and placed the roast in it. I went down to the studio, where I worked with my mind half on the music and half on the roast. I doubt that this work session was very profitable, for I kept glancing at my watch, mindful of the meat in the oven. Finally I excused myself and dashed up to the house. I examined the roast, and it looked wonderful. I was delighted until it occurred to me that dinner was an hour and a half off.

Something had to be done. The roast, alas, was ready to serve, and it had to be kept hot and tender. I put a cover over it, turned down the heat in the oven, and looked after some of the other elements of the dinner.

The gentleman arrived, and we finally sat down to dinner. Thinking that the roast ought to be heated again, I had turned up the oven. When I took it out and looked at it my heart sank. The poor thing was shriveled and hard. I served it, because there was no alternative, and my husband gave me a glance. When he tried to carve, the meat was unyielding.

As for the rest of the meal, the spinach was hot but not very soft, and the potatoes, though they looked good, were hard inside. The salad, praise be, was all right.

After the meal I said to my husband, "That was not very good, was it?"

"No, darling," he replied, "it was not. It was very bad. But you get an E for effort."

The truth is that the meal was so bad it was funny, and we laughed and laughed. And gallant Mr. Hill declared, "I shall be able to tell my children and grandchildren that Marian Anderson prepared a whole meal for me."

"Please don't tell them what kind of meal," I begged.

Hope springs eternal in the human breast, and I bring back interesting, even exotic recipes from my tours and then attempt to put them into practice. I learned to make a wild-duck dish in Sweden, which I cooked with fair success at home. I picked up a sweet-and-sour shrimp recipe in France, and we found that it worked in Connecticut. A Chinese friend has given me some recipes that have proved attractive.

Occasionally I pick up spices and herbs on tour. I like to have all sorts of things available in the kitchen. I brought home something called filé, which is used in Louisiana to give gumbo a choice kind of consistency. King happens to love gumbo. One of our nephews, who is fond of cooking, brought up some hard-shell crabs, which we stowed away in the freezer. When the weather got cold I cleaned the crabs and took out the meat and added all sorts of things, and the gumbo that emerged was simply wonderful. We had a tremendous quantity of it, and we filled several pint and quart buckets and kept them in the freezer. We were able to enjoy that gumbo for weeks.

We grow an abundance of things in our garden, far more than we can consume during the season. There are also fruits and berries. We try to store supplies for the winter. If I were energetic I would do a lot of canning—I manage to do some.

I find that it is a pleasure to keep house. If I were doing it on a year-round basis I am sure that I could work out some shortcuts. I don't have trouble with cleaning, for I don't mind getting out a broom and dustcloth, and I know how to use a mop, hot water, and soap. I like the smell of things that are clean, and I like to see objects polished and shining. When I can spare a few moments from my other preoccupations I tackle jobs of this kind.

My husband and I like to spend quiet evenings at home. Occasionally we make music together. King used to sing to my accompaniments, and his "masterpiece" was "Sylvia" by Oley Speaks. He is a television fan. After dinner and a short walk he brings in one of the dogs, turns on the TV, ensconces himself in his favorite chair, and stretches out comfortably with the dog at his feet or in his lap. Presently he drops off into a light sleep. I may not be too interested in what is on the screen, and I get up to go out. The minute I stir he speaks up. "Where are you going?" I go back to my chair and continue watching.

I feel differently about baseball, particularly the Brooklyn Dodgers. When they get into the World Series I am lost to the world. In 1955, when they finally won the Series, I was so hopelessly ensnared in the drama that I actually took the phone off the hook so that I would not be interrupted during the games, and some of the upholstery I was working on had to be done over.

When we were married we made plans to have a family. But I had more concert work than ever before, and we postponed other things. We both felt that we wanted to raise our own children, not turn them over to nurses. Certainly I did not want to drag a child with me on my travels, remembering that out of seven nights in a week we might spend five or six in different beds.

When I see other people with children I wonder whether our decision was right. I know that children make a home complete, and I know that my husband would have been a good father. In the summers we have our nephews come and stay with us, and they fill the house with cheer. When Jim, my sister's son, was very small and came to visit us, I found that it was a joy to look after him, keep him clean, well fed, and happy.

We have animals, on whom we lavish much affection, but they do not take the place of children. I admire the women in my profession who manage to sustain singing careers and raise families. Perhaps I should have been more daring. But one has to be true to one's own nature, which left me no choice but to make this additional sacrifice, which King shares.

# CHAPTER 27

# At the Metropolitan

I WAS still in high school when I decided that I must see a performance of the Metropolitan Opera, which played once a week in Philadelphia during the season. I set aside what sums I could, and when I had a little less than four dollars I went off to the Presser Building to buy a ticket. They told me that they had only five- and six-dollar tickets left, and I was under the impression that they thought I wanted to buy a pair for that kind of money.

Some time later I did get to a Metropolitan Opera performance in Philadelphia. It was *Madama Butterfly*. I don't remember who the singers were; I was much too involved in the injustice of the story. I had no book at home about the operas, and, although I might have gone to the library, I didn't; I suppose I was lazy or busy. But I was briefed in advance by my companion and was able to follow what happened. The authors, it seemed to me, could have arranged things to end differently, and I wondered why they wanted it to be so tragic. I was thrilled by the music, and I determined to see more opera. How wonderful, I thought, to sing in opera.

I liked the songs I was studying at that time, and soon I was launched on my tours. There was joy in this work, and I did not cast too many envious glances in the direction of opera. There was—there still is, I believe—a company founded and maintained by Mary Cardwell Dawson, a Negro woman who devoted her time to giving her own people a chance to perform in opera. She wrote to me a long time ago, inviting me to take part in some performances, but I happened to be quite occupied with concerts. I was sorry; I would have liked to do it. Some talented people have appeared with this company, including Robert McFerrin, the baritone, who became a member of the Metropolitan Opera the season I did.

As the years rolled by there seemed less and less likelihood that I would ever appear in opera. I had let the opportunity to prepare Carmen with Stanislavski slip away. I had not shown much interest when a feeler was sent out from a European opera house or two. I must say that I was not losing any sleep over the prospect of having an operaless career. One day three years ago Mr. Hurok mentioned the possibility of singing at the Metropolitan. He said that a certain role had been discussed, and he wanted to know what I thought. I did not know this role or think any of this serious, and I did not bother my head with it. "I'll do what you suggest," I told him. Nothing happened in the ensuing weeks, and I assumed I had been right not to pay the subject much mind.

In September 1954 Mr. Hurok brought the Old Vic

production of *Midsummer Night's Dream* to America from England, and he was thoughtful enough—he is unbelievably thoughtful about such things—to invite my husband and me to the New York opening at the Metropolitan Opera House, where the show played. Following the opening there was to be one of those fabulous parties that Mr. Hurok knows so well how to give, and we were invited to that also. The party was for the entire company, and I knew that there would be many, many guests and that Mr. Hurok would be so busy he would not miss us if we did not go.

"It was grand of Mr. Hurok to invite us," I told my husband outside the theater, "but he'll have plenty of guests to take care of. Let's go home."

We have a little apartment uptown because there are many evenings when I must perform in and around New York and it becomes difficult to travel to the country. My husband agreed to my suggestion.

"I'll telephone Mr. Hurok from the apartment," I said, trying to assure myself that this was the right thing to do, "and make our apologies."

My husband turned the car north. "If that's what you want, all right," he said amiably.

We rode some distance, and I said, "I have a strange feeling that we should go to the party and say hello. Then we can leave immediately. I'm sure that's best."

"I don't see why we have to leave right away," he said as he turned the car around.

We got to the party, met some people we knew, and soon were having a good time. Presently I saw Mr. Rudolf

Bing, general manager of the Metropolitan Opera, coming toward me. He did not stand on ceremony but drew me aside and came to the point immediately.

"Would you be interested in singing with the Metropolitan?" he asked.

I looked at him with some surprise. I could not be sure that he was serious.

"Would you be interested?" he repeated. He was not urgent. Indeed, his tone was casual.

"I think I would," I said, trying also to be casual.

"Do you really think you would?"

"Yes, I would."

"Would you call me tomorrow morning?" Mr. Bing asked.

"Yes, I will."

"Oh, just a moment," he said. "Here comes Max Rudolf." And he introduced me to his artistic administrator.

"Didn't Mr. Hurok say anything to you about this?" Mr. Rudolf wanted to know.

"He mentioned it, but I thought it was all very vague."

"We spoke to Mr. Hurok a year ago," said Mr. Bing.

Mr. Rudolf mentioned the part they had in mind— Ulrica, the old sorceress in Verdi's *Un Ballo in Maschera* (*The Masked Ball*).

"Do you know it?" he asked.

"No," I said, and I surely did not. I could have answered in the same way about any other opera. I did not know any role from beginning to end. I had never had a pressing need to learn operatic roles.

We stayed at the party quite a long time. We had supper,

and Mr. Bing sat and chatted with me. I spoke briefly to Mr. Hurok and Mae Frohman at the party so that they would be informed of what was happening.

The next morning the Metropolitan Opera phoned the Hurok office. There was a question of whether my concert schedule could be rearranged to make time available for rehearsals and appearances at the Opera, and the Hurok office thought that it could be done. The Metropolitan then sent over a score of *The Masked Ball,* and the Hurok office got it up to my apartment immediately.

I glanced through the part of Ulrica. My first impression was that it lay too high for my voice, and I felt like saying no at once. But by this time I had agreed to spend some time working on the part. The understanding was that after I had studied it a bit I would have an audition with Dimitri Mitropoulos, who was to be the conductor, and then we would give our opinions as to whether I would do the role.

Jofe was excited when he heard the news. Opera is the thing he cares about most. I daresay that he spends more of his free time in New York at the Metropolitan than anywhere else. He knows most of the singers, and as for the operas, I would not be surprised if he could sing them all by heart. He was, of course, ready with advice about a coach. He suggested Paul Meyer, a very sensitive person who knows every role in the opera and could probably sing them all in several languages.

Jofe took me to the first session with Mr. Meyer, and he came to all the other rehearsals and did not hesitate to make suggestions and criticisms.

The time came for the audition with Mr. Mitropoulos.

Although I knew his work as principal conductor of the New York Philharmonic-Symphony Orchestra, I had not worked with him for many years. I had sung with him in Monte Carlo when I had appeared there with orchestra in the course of my first visit to the Riviera.

"This role is too high for me," I told Mr. Mitropoulos before we began.

"Please sing it through, and we'll see," he said.

I sang, and Paul Meyer played the piano while Mr. Mitropoulos followed the score.

There is a high A in Ulrica's aria, and I must confess that I was not too happy about it. By then I was no longer going out of my way to sing high notes above the staff. Furthermore, it was morning, and I don't like reaching for top tones that early. I got to the A and squeezed it out. As I sang it I glanced at Mr. Mitropoulos. His head remained bent over the score, and he gave no sign, which was wonderful of him.

When I had finished going through the entire part Mr. Mitropoulos spoke calmly. "You haven't worked on it enough yet and you don't know it thoroughly," he said. "When you know it, it will go."

"Well," I said, not convinced, "I'd like to have another week or ten days. Then I'd like to come back."

"All right," he said.

We parted, and I returned to my apartment, assuming that the final decision would wait for the next session with Mr. Mitropoulos.

I took the long way uptown. When I opened the door of our apartment the phone was ringing insistently. I picked it up, and Franz Rupp spoke.

"Where have you been?" he asked.

"On my way home."

"Mr. Hurok has been trying to get you like mad, and he thought you were with me. It's important, he says."

"What is it?" I asked.

"I don't know. He didn't tell me."

I called Mr. Hurok, and his first word was "Congratulations!"

"Beg pardon?"

"Congratulations."

"What for?"

"We meet at the Metropolitan this afternoon at four to sign the contract. We'll meet here at the office and go over together."

I hung up and sat down. I was flabbergasted. Mr. Mitropoulos had not told me that he intended to report that I could manage the part. But he had called Mr. Bing as soon as I had left him, and Mr. Bing had called Mr. Hurok and had fixed terms. All of this had been accomplished within the three-quarters of an hour it took me to get home.

The excitement was too much. I telephoned Mother in Philadelphia. She knew that I had been offered this role. I fear I must have been incoherent; I seemed to think that I must not be specific on the phone, as though somebody might overhear my great secret. I told her that I was going to a certain place to sign a contract. I telephoned my husband and gave him the news. I telephoned the Rupps because I wanted them to hear the news first from me rather than through the radio or a newspaper, for I had gone over portions of the role in their studio too.

Once the contract was signed, work had to resume in earnest. I continued studying with Paul Meyer, and I also did some coaching with Mrs. Rupp, with whom I wanted to study the part from the vocal point of view. When I worked with her, Franz served as our pianist.

The time came to begin working at the Opera House. It was suggested that a member of its conducting staff, Victor Trucco, should work with me. I remember that when I told Jofe about the arrangement to study with Mr. Trucco he said, "Do you want me to go with you?" I said "Of course," and I called Mr. Trucco to see whether he would mind. He said he would not.

Mr. Trucco made sure that I knew not only the tempi and phrasing as the Metropolitan would want them but also the meaning of the words I was to sing. He encouraged me to interline my score with the English translation of the Italian text. It was not his function to worry over the acting, but he sought to give me little hints that would relax me and help me to get into the character of Ulrica by understanding the story.

There was a gesture we were working on—the arm held high with the hand and fingers at an angle. Jofe, watching everything like an expert, came over and took my hand and slapped my fingers.

"They're too stiff," he said.

Gradually I began to meet other people involved in the performance. Herbert Graf, the stage director, took over at intervals. He did not attempt to turn me into an actress overnight. He made suggestions, but always advised, "Do the thing that seems natural to you."

Each day brought a new step in the collective enterprise that is opera. We had sessions with piano in which singing and acting were fused. Then came the rehearsals of the duet with the soprano, Zinka Milanov, who was doing the principal female role. Next the tenor, Richard Tucker, joined us for the trio. The entire act was assembled, and then I met the chorus and later the orchestra.

The rehearsals moved up to the roof stage, and the ever-present Jofe's excitement, it seemed to me, equaled mine. Hearing those magnificent voices and working on a fixed schedule in a theater that could afford no other way of operation were unbelievably stimulating. Some people know how to order their lives so that they do things on schedule. I do not have that gift, but I had to adapt myself to the way the Metropolitan did things. I had become so saturated with my concert life that I found I scarcely had time for anything but getting my work done. At the Metropolitan I had to stretch my hours to crowd more activity into them, and somehow all this caused the blood to race through me with new meaning. I felt incredibly alive, able to do any amount of extra tasks. I even managed to get some of my letters answered, and that's really something.

There was a wonderful family feeling in all the preparations. I was not wholly unfamiliar with the Metropolitan Opera stage, for I had sung concerts from it on a number of Easter Sundays. And yet it looked entirely different when the sets were up and we were assembled for the dress rehearsal. I kept thinking of the words a member of the administrative staff had spoken to me when I had arrived that afternoon in October for the signing of the contract. "Welcome home," he had said simply. And home it had become, thanks to the good will of every one connected with the company.

The night of the performance arrived—January 7, 1955. My husband drove me down early in the afternoon, and when I arrived at the theater Jofe and the people from the Hurok office were waiting for me. My family had come up from Philadelphia and were put up at our apartment; they were in their box at the Met early. The leading members of the cast came to my dressing room to wish me well in various languages. Jofe was backstage, dashing about madly. He knew the wardrobe mistress and the make-up man, and he fussed over them as if this were his Metropolitan Opera debut. As soon as I had put on my costume he returned to make sure that I had an opportunity to warm up the voice. I could hear other singers doing their warm-up exercises, and for once I did not feel hesitant about doing mine. Jofe left to take his seat in the auditorium. Then there was a tap on the door, and a voice said, "We're beginning now. Your call will come in twenty minutes. Good luck."

The curtain rose on the second scene, in which Ulrica appears, and I was there on the stage, mixing the witch's brew. I trembled, and when the audience applauded and applauded before I could sing a note I felt myself tightening into a knot. I had always assured people that I was not nervous about singing, but at that moment I was as nervous as a kitten. I was terribly anxious that this of all things should go well, but there were things that happened to my voice that should not have happened. With all the experience I had behind me, I should have been firm and secure, but my emotions were too strong. I suppose it is well not to be so blasé that nothing will effect you. I know I tried too hard; I know I overdid. I was not pleased with the first performance; I know it was not the best I could do.

The audience was unbelievably sympathetic. So were my colleagues. I was given a little push at curtain-call time so that I would be on the stage a moment by myself, although this is against Metropolitan policy. And Miss Milanov embraced me on the stage in full view of the audience.

Jofe, I think, was in the dressing room before I reached it. He was beaming, and he acted like a combined receptionist and traffic cop, making sure that people could get in and out. Mother arrived, and she threw her arms around me and whispered in my ear, "We thank the Lord." Her only words before the performance had been, "Mother is praying for you," and after it she just stood there, and though she is not outwardly demonstrative I could see that there was a light around her face. She did not know much about opera, but she knew the significance of what was going on that night and she was profoundly moved by it. If she had said more she would have said, "My cup runneth over."

As Jofe said, there was electricity in the air that night, and there was more of the same the next week when the company brought *The Masked Ball* to Philadelphia and I sang as a member of the Metropolitan in my native city. For me there was a lift in seeing the big sign, MET OPERA, in Penn Station at the entrance to the special train. For the others in the troupe it was perhaps a matter of routine; to me every aspect of the trip was exciting.

The Philadelphia performance, for me, went better. I felt happier about it, and securer. It was good that this was so. I wanted to do well for this audience that included people who had helped to raise money to pay for my early training.

I was gratified to hear that the Metropolitan wanted me back the next season. When the Hurok office was asked about free time it had been a little surprised. "You didn't think," the Metropolitan representative said, "that we were doing this as a stunt, did you?"

It was my idea, too, to continue with the part of Ulrica for a second season. After my agreement to do Ulrica for my Metropolitan debut, I received a letter berating me for accepting so small a part. "Couldn't you have insisted on a bigger role?" the writer demanded. I could have, I suppose, but Ulrica was enough for a beginner in opera to learn, considering the full schedule of concert dates I had. My objective for the second year was simply to do a better Ulrica.

The chance to be a member of the Metropolitan has been a highlight of my life. It has meant much to me and to my people. If I have been privileged to serve as a symbol, to be the first Negro to sing as a regular member of the company, I take greater pride from knowing that it has encouraged other singers of my group to realize that the doors everywhere may open increasingly to those who have prepared themselves well. There are young singers of exceptional talent, such as, to name a few, Camilla Williams, Lawrence Winters, Leontyne Price, Leonore Lafayette, and Mattiwilda Dobbs, who have sung with important opera companies in our country and abroad. There will be others. One does not expect them to be accepted because they are Negroes; one hopes that they will be welcomed only for their worth. I am grateful to the Metropolitan for the tactful way in which the entire thing was managed, and I will never forget the whole-hearted responsiveness of the public. I may have dreamed of such things, but I had not foreseen that I would play a part in the reality.

# CHAPTER 28

# Looking Forward

LOOKING back, I see stretching out behind me year upon year of singing, traveling, packing, unpacking, rehearsing, and studying. Some periods have contracted and form small corners in my memory, while others have moved to the forefront. The edges of good times and bad have become fuzzy. What once seemed a hard choice has become amusing in retrospect.

Sacrifices? Yes, but not too great. And there have been wonderful compensations. Some time ago I was in Atlantic City, where a division of the Elks conferred an honor on me. There was no singing for me to do; I just had an award to receive. There were in the gathering people from Philadelphia—some who had known me in childhood and had gone to grammar school with me. It was fine to know that they felt the same friendship and took a certain pride in coming up and saying hello.

These little things are among the big things that have made it all worth while. They help to give me the courage to go on. I have been asked, I suppose because I

have been singing in public so long, whether I have fixed
a time limit on public appearances, whether I am beginning to think of retiring. No, I have no time limit and
no immediate plans for quitting. I like to feel that there
is still time to do some worth-while things.

Oh, I have all sorts of projects. There are several roles
that would tempt me to go on with opera if I had the
time. I have many things in mind for the concert hall,
and, if not there, for my personal pleasure in the studio. I
would like to work on my pianissimo. I would like to do
several Bach cantatas that I am fond of. I would like to
wrestle with Mozart's "Alleluia," not for public performance but for development of agility. I once did it in concert, and a singer I know took me aside and said, "That
is not for you." She was right. I should not sing it in
public. But I would like to learn it well enough to prove
to myself that I can do it.

I would like to prepare all twenty-four songs of Schubert's cycle *Die Winterreise*. I have browsed through these
beautiful songs in the studio and have sung about five
in public. It would be a privilege to devote myself for a
time to the entire cycle, and it would be a challenge to
give a concert in which it would be the entire program.
I would not expect to sing it in a large hall, and I would
not be unhappy if the audience were modest in size.

There are foreign journeys that beckon enticingly. I
have promised to go back to Scandinavia soon, and I
should, for I owe a special debt to those countries. I would
like to return to Vienna and immerse myself in the spirit
of the city that produced my beloved Schubert and his
songs. I have drawn so much strength from Schubert, and

I feel that I could now find new strength in his city, for when one is maturer one can see more deeply into things one glanced at superficially a long time ago.

I have been fortunate in many, many ways. Best of all, I have lived in a time of change, and the end is not yet. It has been good to see these changes taking place in our America, good for all of us.

It was awkward and painful for me personally to have to decide in 1935 that I would continue with my European accompanist instead of resuming with the one I had had in this country. The decision, as I have said before, was based entirely on musical grounds. To some of my people, however, it looked for a time as if I were turning my back on my own. I was not. I would not. A few thought that I had been coerced into this decision by my new manager, and this too was an utterly unfounded suspicion. Mr. Hurok did not intervene, and would not—and certainly not for an ignoble reason.

I mention this issue again because it leads to an important point. My people were right to expect that if an opportunity were open one of our own should not be by-passed. But the facts must be faced, and they have two aspects. A Negro must qualify on musical grounds and must be equal to the best competition if he is to find a place. On the other hand, there is no incentive for him to qualify if he knows that there will be no place open for him. There were a few very well-known accompanists, and the ones I knew were already engaged. But most young Negro musicians could be excused if they did not think that there was much reason to work hard at learning to be first-class accompanists. Where could they take their talent and experience?

Happily, the picture has been changing. I know of a young Negro in Chicago who is a very able accompanist. He works in the studio of a voice teacher and is learning his business thoroughly. Given the proper opportunity, he will make an enviable place for himself.

There is hope for America. Our country and people have every reason to be generous and good. If we could only spread out the Christmas spirit to encompass the entire twelve months, or remember our behavior in a national emergency or a trouble like a crippling snowstorm (schools closed, traffic halted, business curtailed) when those stout-hearted enough to brave the elements see only that there is another soul needing help—and it has no color. When incidents occur in our land that show a disregard for brotherhood among races our America belittles herself, and her prestige is injured. For he in the highest place can be no greater and no more effective than the least of his followers. He must answer for all.

It hurts me when these things happen through thoughtlessness, neglect, lack of understanding, or acts of calculated humiliation. The United States could set a shining example and could reap rewards far beyond any expectations. All the changes may not come in my time; they may even be left for another world. But I have seen enough changes to believe that they will occur in this one.

The war gave powerful impetus to change. America became interested in the welfare of far-off peoples, and perforce the focus turned on what was going on here at home. It had to be that way. You cannot give thought to what is good for one group without thinking of what is good for all. During the war all young Americans were asked to serve, and they did. Though the doors did not open wide to all men in uniform, they opened a little more to those who in the past had been barred. And this happened even in the South—in a small, halting start.

Some years ago I was invited to Atlantic City, and the mayor handed me a large key in a plush box, and he made a grand speech. I had the key to the city, but could not get a reservation there in a hotel near the auditorium. Recently I was in Atlantic City; I did not need to stay overnight, but a reservation had been made for me. Some of my people stayed at the hotel and reported that the service was excellent.

Progress has touched some concert halls. In Baltimore's Lyric Theatre, Roland Hayes had once appeared, but then there was a time when Negroes could not appear in it. Several years ago that changed. And when a little girl charmed the nation with her spelling and personality on a television program, her home city of Baltimore made special provisions to have that program fed into a local station so that the community as a whole might see her and take pride in her achievement.

It would not be truthful to say that everything in every way has progressed, but there are more people who are convinced of the necessity and rightness of change. Others may continue to resist. When you take something away from people you must give them something in its place. An ideal may not seem at first a good enough substitute to some people. However, time and education and good will could establish the higher value of the ideal. If a man believes that a thing is right and has to struggle with himself to do it, he will get astonishing strength and peace of mind when the act is accomplished.

We have seen Negro ballplayers, starting with Jackie Robinson, accepted in the major leagues. I know that in the South there are flourishing businesses owned and run by Negroes. I have seen several pages in Negro magazines devoted to pictures of Negroes who now hold and skillfully fill jobs that were once open only to white persons. I have a young friend in Philadelphia who is acting as a flight announcer. The *Philadelphia Inquirer* ran her picture and a story reporting that she was the first Negro to occupy such a post, and that, in the City of Brotherly Love, is a step forward. I have seen a television play in which the problem of a Negro family, played by Negroes, was honestly dramatized, a story about a father and his son. The son wanted to study for a profession that the father had dreamed of entering but had found closed to him. The father felt that it was his duty to discourage the son, for he did not wish him to be disappointed and disillusioned, but there was nothing else the son wanted to do. The agonized father was like many other devoted parents.

In the mass-entertainment fields many talented Negroes have had opportunities—singers, dancers, bands, a few actors and actresses—and there are hordes who get no breaks at all. Those who succeeded did so because of their special gifts, and that is all to the good. But one rarely encounters on television a Negro woman talking about homemaking, a Negro husband-and-wife team, a Negro announcer selling some manufacturer's wares. It must not be forgotten that there are millions of Negro consumers of most of the products advertised, and it would be just if they were represented.

If we are distressed by some of the things that are happening in South Africa—I have had first-hand accounts from people in that country, and I know that the situation is bad—our influence can be greater as we ourselves improve the situation of all people.

There are many persons ready to do what is right because in their hearts they know it is right. But they hesitate, waiting for the other fellow to make the first move—and he, in turn, waits for you. The minute a person whose word means a great deal dares to take the open-hearted and courageous way, many others follow. Not everyone can be turned aside from meanness and hatred, but the great majority of Americans is heading in that direction. I have a great belief in the future of my people and my country.

# Index

Abyssinian Baptist Church, 28
Academy of Music, Philadelphia,
    110
Aeolian Hall, 102
Aldrich, Amanda Ira, 127
Alpha Kappa Alpha sorority, 273
Anderson, Alyce (sister), 4, 5, 6,
    18, 93, 277
Anderson, Annie (mother), 4;
    character, 89–90, 92, 95–98;
    church affiliation, 93; employ-
    ment, 18–20, 89–91; European
    trip, 94–95; homemaker, 4–6;
    mother-in-law's home, 16; own
    home, 77–78; retirement, 91;
    spiritual life, 96–99
Anderson, Ethel (sister), 4, 5,
    6, 93
Anderson, John (father): death,
    14–15; Easter bonnets for fam-
    ily, 7; employment, 4; physical
    description, 3; pride in Marian,
    8; Union Baptist Church
    officer, 7

Anderson, Marian: accompanists
    (see King, William [Billy];
    Raucheisen, Michael; Rupp,
    Franz; Vehanen, Kosti); admi-
    ration of mother, 89–99;
    awards (see Bok Award [Phila-
    delphia Award]; Spingarn
    Medal); boyfriends, 79–83;
    broken ankle, 162–66; Camp
    Fire Girls, 26; card player, 237–
    38; children, 292; church
    choir tours, 28; church sing-
    ing, 7–8, 13–14, 23–24, 27 (see
    also Union Baptist Church);
    confidence in career, 71; con-
    tests (see Contests); cooking,
    287–91; correspondent, 270;
    courtship of "King," 80–83;
    difficult songs, 201–3, 204; dis-
    illusionment with singing, 75–
    76; early schooling, 9; early
    singing engagements, 31–34;
    earnings, 11, 145, 150; emo-
    tion in singing, 203–4; Euro-

Only a Miner: Studies in Recorded Coal-Mining Songs
*Archie Green*

Great Day Coming: Folk Music and the American Left
*R. Serge Denisoff*

John Philip Sousa: A Descriptive Catalog of His Works
*Paul E. Bierley*

The Hell-Bound Train: A Cowboy Songbook   *Glenn Ohrlin*

Oh, Didn't He Ramble: The Life Story of Lee Collins, as Told
to Mary Collins   *Edited by Frank J. Gillis and John W. Miner*

American Labor Songs of the Nineteenth Century
*Philip S. Foner*

Stars of Country Music: Uncle Dave Macon to Johnny
Rodriguez   *Edited by Bill C. Malone and Judith McCulloh*

Git Along, Little Dogies: Songs and Songmakers of the American West   *John I. White*

A Texas-Mexican Cancionero: Folksongs of the Lower Border
*Américo Paredes*

San Antonio Rose: The Life and Music of Bob Wills
*Charles R. Townsend*

Early Downhome Blues: A Musical and Cultural Analysis
*Jeff Todd Titon*

An Ives Celebration: Papers and Panels of the Charles Ives Centennial Festival-Conference   *Edited by H. Wiley Hitchcock and
Vivian Perlis*

Sinful Tunes and Spirituals: Black Folk Music to the Civil War
*Dena J. Epstein*

Joe Scott, the Woodsman-Songmaker   *Edward D. Ives*

Jimmie Rodgers: The Life and Times of America's Blue
Yodeler   *Nolan Porterfield*

Early American Music Engraving and Printing: A History of
Music Publishing in America from 1787 to 1825, with Commentary on Earlier and Later Practices   *Richard J. Wolfe*

Sing a Sad Song: The Life of Hank Williams   *Roger M. Williams*

Long Steel Rail: The Railroad in American Folksong
*Norm Cohen*

The University of Illinois Press
is a founding member of the
Association of American University Presses.

---

University of Illinois Press
1325 South Oak Street
Champaign, IL 61820–6903
www.press.uillinois.edu